CW00662202

J
£12-50
FL

The  Motorcycle

Alfred Angas Scott with his own sidecar outfit, near the Mornington Works. Circa 1913

The  Motorcycle

The Yowling Two-stroke

Jeff Clew

© J. R. Clew 2004

First published December 1974 to mark the centenary of Alfred Scott's birth
Reprinted April 1977, January 1979
Reprinted with revised dust jacket March 1990
Re-issued with minor text and jacket amendments July 2004

Published by
Haynes Publishing, Sparkford, Yeovil, Somerset BA22 7JJ, UK

ISBN 0 85429 164 4

Library of congress catalogue card no. 2004104373

Haynes North America Inc.
861 Lawrence Drive, Newbury Park, California 91320, USA

G. T. Foulis Limited is an imprint of
Haynes Publishing, Sparkford, Yeovil, Somerset BA22 7JJ, UK.
Tel: 01963 442030   Fax: 01963 440001
Int. tel: +44 1963 442030   Int. fax: +44 1963 440001
E-mail: sales@haynes.co.uk
Web site: www.haynes.co.uk

Printed in England by J. H. Haynes and Co. Ltd.

DEDICATION

To Eric and Edgar Gill, who started me on the slippery slope of becoming a Scott enthusiast

Rules Illustrated.

AN AMATEUR IS ONE WHOSE MACHINE ENTERED AND RIDDEN IN THIS TRIAL IS HIS OWN PERSONAL PROPERTY

One of a number of amusing illustrations taken from the 1925 Scott Trial souvenir programme

CONTENTS

PUBLISHER'S FOREWORD

A SCOTT motorcycle is very special. Special enough for the publishers of this history to have two forewords. The first is by Allan Jefferies, whose name will for ever be linked with the Scott motorcycle. Appropriately, his motorcycle business was located in Shipley, where it still exists today, even though Allan and the Scott motorcycle are no longer with us. The second is by Harold Scott, nephew of the inventor, but never involved with his business. Without Harold's enthusiasm and assistance this book could never have been written. The first President of the Scott Owners' Club, sadly, he too is no longer with us.

BEING asked to write the foreword of any book must I suppose be regarded as an honour. That I have not read the book in question reveals the common denominator of the author and me — The Charisma of the Scott.

For thousands of motorcyclists during 65 years there has been a kind of Love-Hatred for this unique marque. Sprouts Elder the famous American Speedway Ace once told me that if the crowd were not cheering him he hoped they would be booing. The Scott machine exemplified this, one moment you could be gliding along in transcendental bliss and in a flash the 2 speeder's high gear chain would snap. You then knew that the timing of your forward progress relied a lot on Dame Fortune, especially if it was more often than not a dark and lonely night. I say forward motion as if perchance you had been careless with the ignition timing it was not uncommon to bang into gear and hurry backwards.

Although I rode all the later models I have particularly mentioned the 2 speed as even in its last year of manufacture it retained most of the originalities born of Alfred Angas Scott's amazing genius.

Born and brought up within the sound of the Scott engine test bed I had no chance. Daily I heard in my imagination the start from the T.T. Grandstand with the glorious sound dying away on the approach to Quarter Bridge and a short time later to catch the cadences of the speeding Trumpet Voluntary negotiating Braddan Bridge and Union Mills. From the T T wins of 1912 and 1913 until the final rites of the creditors meeting in 1951 I worshipped at the Scott shrine.

Oh my Tim and Clarrie Wood, oh my Harry Langman long ago

Allan Jefferies

Allan Jefferies
Shipley
Yorkshire
July 1974

FOREWORD

IN THE days of pioneer and veteran motorcyclists, there was a great creative effort, and a splendid spirit to excel. Competitions were soon started: friendly rivalries between the makes encouraged; there were early hill-climbs; two-stroke versus four-stroke controversy and resulting handicaps; long endurance tests as from Land's End to John o' Groats; the Isle of Man T.T. Races; Six Days Trials; advertising stunts such as 100 ascents of the notorious Sutton Bank in one day; and a tough moorland trial started 60 years ago and still going strong. All these and more, began an era of sheer sportsmanship hard to equal.

It was not unusual to see a stranded rider at the roadside, trying to put things right, and most fellow motorcyclists would stop to help. This friendly camaraderie caught on, and our hobby is noted for this fellowship to this day, even though modern machines are so reliable.

We are only young in heart once, and this sense of fun, freedom, adventure — and achievement — yes, and determination and disappointment too — is so well captured by Jeff Clew, in his fascinating book, *The Scott Motorcycle — The Yowling Two-Stroke.*

The history of other great names since those early days in the motorcycle world, like Norton, Triumph, Douglas, Velocette, etc, already has been well covered.

It is therefore with the utmost pleasure that I respond to the author's invitation, to write this Foreword and commend his illustrated history of the Scott — a thoroughbred, reared over the moors of Yorkshire and Scotland, and a marque with a unique reputation, having special appeal to those inclined to good engineering.

Harold Scott

Harold Scott (Nephew)
Leamington Spa
Warwicks
July 1974

ACKNOWLEDGEMENTS

FIRST published in December 1974, and reprinted in 1977, 1979 and 1990, this is still the only comprehensive history of the Scott motorcycle. With second-hand copies realising £30-£35 each at autojumbles, it seemed appropriate to consider a further limited reprint and I am grateful to the original publisher for agreeing to this.

When I started work on the history of the Scott motorcycle, I was aware that I would be faced with at least two major problems. Firstly, so much has been published in the form of magazine articles that the comparatively small number of early photographs available have been used to such an extent that they have become over-familiar to the Scott enthusiast. Secondly, those who had played an active role in the story have been approached to recount their story on more than one occasion and were not too happy about going over the same ground yet again. Fortunately, I received such a magnificent response when the seriousness of my intent was known that it has not been too difficult to select some of the lesser-used photographs and to include a few that may not have been published before. As far as personal contacts were concerned, most have been only too willing to talk to me at length so that I have their part of the story first-hand. And so the book became a reality and, hopefully, a serious attempt to record the most enthralling of all one-make histories that has so long escaped comprehensive documentation in continuous form.

My chief source of encouragement came from Harold Scott, nephew of the inventor, who could not have been more helpful. Many of the photographs reproduced are from his personal collection. Andrew Marfell, Secretary of the Scott Owners' Club, went to infinite trouble to copy some of the less accessible material and include a number of photographs which he had taken himself. Dave Bushell, the Club Librarian, provided an excellent bibliography of Scott data, which saved many hours of fruitless searching. Others who helped supply material included Don Lafford and Neil Smith, the latter from far-away Rhodesia.

A letter to the Dalesman brought forth a remarkable response from readers, all of whom were anxious to help. Amongst the 50 or so replies received was a letter from a Mrs N. Milnes (nee Suddard) of New Zealand, whose father helped Alfred Scott manufacture motor cycles under the latter's name. She kindly provided a resume of the early days of the company and a few rare photographs – typical of the response from all those who wrote to me. Mrs Ethel Oliver, of Australia, sent some photographs too, whilst Tom Chapman wrote from Colorado, offering help. So many kindly Yorkshirefolk responded that it is not possible to mention them all. Dr Stephen Craven researched into Alfred Scott's potholing activities and reported on same, whilst John Fenton, Brian Stephenson, G. E. Young, J. A. R. Horsley, and E. Gower all presented various facts about the Scott. Nearer home, Dennis Howard responded instantly whenever confirmation was needed about some obscure item or when photographs were mentioned. Brian and Shirley Cumming, of the Humberside Section of the Scott Owners Club, loaned me their unique photograph collection.

I was able to visit Harold Wood, Allan Jefferies and Noel Mavrogordato, all of whom need no further introduction to the Scott enthusiast. Such a fund of memories and recollections resulted that I hope I have been able to do them justice. Rory Sinclair supplied some elusive data about the Cyc-Auto, whilst Derek Cox commented on the guncars and the 'Sociable' era. I was fortunate in contacting George Halliday, one time personal assistant to Alfred Scott, who had some interesting stories to tell. Alan Crouch of the Newark Air Museum revived memories of the ill-fated 'Flying Flea' and George Silk described how his Silk Special came into being, to open up a new dimension.

Perhaps the most arduous task of all is reading through the completed manuscript, with all the hand-made annotations and other corrections. My special thanks are due in this respect to Harold Scott, Robert Rawlins, Jack Dodds and John Underhill, all of whom did a wonderful job whilst working against a tight deadline. It is unusual to use four referees, but I am aware of the Scott enthusiast's quest for complete accuracy. I make no excuse for the fact that so few catalogue illustrations have been included. To my mind they are of doubtful value in a work of this nature, especially since they are often little more than artists impressions. It has been said on numerous occasions (no doubt with some truth!) that no two Scotts are made exactly alike and if catalogue illustrations are needed, they are best obtained through the Scott Owners Club, as part of the Club service. They may otherwise have excluded photographs more pertinent to the continuing history of the marque.

Some of the photographs have been reproduced from albums and in several cases it has not been possible to identify the photographer. I offer my sincere thanks to whoever may be concerned. Finally, my tribute goes to George Stevens and to the late Philip Smith, both of whom have written so much about the Scott. It was this more than anything else that aroused my interest in these wonderful machines.

Jeff Clew
Queen Camel
Somerset
July 2004

The earliest surviving example of one of Alfred Scott's many drawings. Dated 1890

CHAPTER ONE

From Snowden Street to Grosvenor Road

ALFRED Angas Scott was born on 5th October, 1874, at Oakleigh, 23 Oak Avenue, Manningham, Bradford. His birthplace was a sizeable Victorian detached house which is a small private hotel today. His father, Walter, was a merchant of Bradford; his mother Jesse had the maiden name Forbes and was of Scottish descent. She had spent her early life in Paisley, near Glasgow. In those days, large families were by no means uncommon and the Scott family was no exception. Alfred was the tenth son and a twin, in a family of twelve children.

Alfred was educated at a school near Melrose, Selkirk in Scotland, and then at Abbotsholme, the public school near Uttoxeter, Staffordshire, for his final year's schooling. It was during his schooldays that he developed a high degree of self-reliance, a feature that underlined his individual and often unorthodox approach to problems. As later events will show, he insisted on utter originality and would not profit from the knowledge or mistakes of others, even though he was possessed of many talents. He went his own way, gaining experience and profiting from his own mistakes as he progressed.

When he left Abbotsholme, Alfred trained as an engineer, serving his apprenticeship first with Douglas and Grant, of Kirkcaldy and then with W. Sisson and Co. Ltd. of Gloucester. During this period he became well acquainted with steam engines used for marine work and it is interesting to record that some of the features embodied in these engines impressed him sufficiently to apply them to engines of his own design at a later date. For example, the Corliss two-cylinder steam engine had a central flywheel with overhung cranks and the Sisson high-speed steam engine had the cylinder axes brought very close together in order to eliminate the rocking couple that is inherent with this design of engine.

About the turn of the century, Alfred Scott returned to his birthplace, where there is a record of him acting as a consulting engineer. Some of the projects he undertook were in conjunction with H. S. Smith of the Bowling Dye Works, Bradford, as some patent applications show. He took lodgings in Bradford, first at 2 Park View Road and then at 6 Spring Gardens Road, Heaton. He rented premises in Snowden Street, which he used as his experimental workshop.

Alfred's interest in the two-stroke engine commenced soon after his return, no doubt heightened by the assistance he gave to one of his elder brothers, Arthur Forbes Scott, in the construction and testing of a single cylinder two-stroke gas engine his brother had designed. This engine was later used to drive some of the machinery in the Snowden Street workshop. Alfred had already shown interest in the bicycle as a means of transport by designing a unique cross-frame two wheeler in which wires under tension formed the brace between the rear wheel spindle, bottom bracket and steering head. In 1897 he applied for his first patent, British Patent 1626, which related to a design of caliper brake that acted on the rear wheel of a bicycle.

During 1897 or 1898, Scott commenced work on a 2 hp twin cylinder two-stroke engine which, for convenience, he attached to the frame of his Premier bicycle. He mounted the completed engine in the same position as that adopted by the designer of the Werner motorcycle in 1897, immediately in front of the steering head, above the front wheel. Drive was transmitted direct to the front tyre by means of the central flywheel in a manner not unlike the roller drive to the rear wheel that was adopted by manufacturers of cycle motor attachments made after the last war. It was good in the dry but hopeless in the wet. The engine differed in a great many respects from the designs that were to follow, even though the general principles were the same. Frank Philipp, a cousin by marriage, rode the machine soon after its completion, and little realised that he was destined to become much more involved with the Scott motorcycle in later years.

The engine had two vertical cylinders that were completely independent of one another and each with a separate crankcase although they shared the common crankcase casting. Each cylinder comprised a steel tube of 1 7/8 inch diameter, with aluminium radiator flanges shrunk over the outside. Plain phosphor bronze bearings were fitted initially, but they were later replaced by metallic bearings with a floating gland joint. An overhung crank arrangement was employed with an exposed, centrally disposed flywheel. Ignition was by means of the then customary trembler coil and a surface carburettor was used to supply the mixture. Both components were contained within a rectangular box suspended from the crossbar whilst the fuel was drawn from a cylindrical tank mounted transversely on a carrier above the rear mudguard. Although there is no mention of lubrication, this was almost certainly by drip feed. The main problem related to the use of steel for the cylinder bores, which proved to be a bad choice. Even when copiously lubricated they scored badly and would not polish.

Various theories have been expounded about the originator of the vertical twin engine and it is not unexpected that Alfred Scott is considered to have prior claim with regard to the vertical twin two-stroke. The Hildebrand and Wolffmuller of 1894 can be regarded as the first practical twin cylinder motorcycle, but the engine was of the four stroke type and had cylinders mounted in the horizontal plane. It was water cooled and featured long, exposed connecting rods that coupled direct with cranks attached to the live rear wheel spindle.

16

Sir Dugal Clark anticipated the two-stroke cycle in 1881, when he designed an engine that had a separate chamber for gas. Ten years later, Joseph Day designed and patented a gas engine that utilised crankcase compression. Alfred Scott undoubtedly perceived the significance of Day's crankcase compression principle and employed it in his own twin cylinder design, thereby substantiating the claim that his 2 hp engine of 1901 was the first really practical vertical twin two-stroke.

Development work continued and in 1902 a modified version of the original engine emerged having cast iron cylinders of 2¼ inch bore. Still using the same Premier bicycle as the test bed, the new engine was located immediately behind the steering head, at approximately the same height as the original version. Changes in the transmission layout dispensed with the direct drive to the front tyre. In its place, the boss of the central flywheel was grooved on the left hand side to accept a twisted leather belt. The belt was arranged to drive a much larger drum positioned to the rear of the seat tube, adjacent to the bottom bracket. This drum transmitted the drive to the rear wheel by frictional contact with the tyre tread. No doubt a lesson had been learnt from the way in which the engine had been located in the original design. Although the 1897 Werner represented a significant advance in motorcycle design at that time, it had its own inherent disadvantage. The high centre of gravity and the concentration of weight over the front wheel made the machine treacherous to handle in the wet — side slip was by no means uncommon. Alfred achieved better weight distribution by moving his engine back into the frame diamond, even if it was left to others to pioneer the much more satisfactory bottom bracket location that was soon to follow.

In 1903 the motorised bicycle underwent further modifications. The friction drive arrangement was abandoned and in its place a countershaft was substituted, which could be arranged to give either a free or fixed pulley.

The 1903 version of the Scott Premier, showing the countershaft drive and Bradford registration number

THE SCOTT MOTORCYCLE

The pulley, which was mounted within the left hand chainstays of the bicycle, was driven by the same section belt from the groove in the central flywheel of the engine. Drive from the opposite end of the countershaft to which the pulley was attached was by means of a chain, to a sprocket fixed to the rear wheel. In December 1903 the machine was allocated the registration number AK 166, in preparation for the forthcoming legislation that would make it necessary to register a machine with the local licencing authority before it could be used on the public highways. The need for such a requirement soon became apparent. By the midsummer of 1904, no less than 21,974 motorcycles had been registered in the UK, a convincing indication of the growing popularity of the motorcycle.

As if to pay allegiance to his Scottish ancestry, Alfred used to spend his holidays on the river Clyde, at Tighnabruaich, near Rothesay, in the lovely Kyles of Bute, where he had the use of a rowing boat fitted with an old MMC four-stroke engine of about 3 hp — the type fitted to some of the early motor tricycles. An old photograph shows Arthur Forbes Scott, Herbert Scott and a boatman named McKeller seated in the stern of *Petrel I,* with the MMC engine in the foreground. A two-gallon petrol can served as the fuel

Arthur Forbes Scott, McKeller the boatman and Herbert Scott aboard *Petrel I* on the river Clyde. Note the old MMC engine with the trembler coil mounted in a cigar box. The dish on the right holds the sponge used for water cooling!

container; ignition was provided by a trembler coil mounted in an open cigar box. The engine was air cooled, but when necessary, additional cooling was arranged by the simple expedient of wringing out a sponge full of water, held above it! In due course the MMC engine was pensioned off and the Scott engine substituted, after temporary removal from the Premier bicycle frame. Much of Alfred Scott's experimental work at this time related to the development of two-stroke marine engines, for he found he could learn much by running them for long periods at full power on a water brake.

By now the development of the twin cylinder two-stroke engine had reached the stage where Scott could apply for patent rights. Accordingly he filed his application and after the customary examination of his claims, British Patent 3367 was granted on February 11th, 1904. Study of the patent shows that it related primarily to a twin cylinder two-stroke engine with the cylinders in parallel but included mention of some of the ancillary components such as the design of the silencer, carburettor and piston deflector profile, the latter at 90° to those used in subsequent designs.

Making full use of Joseph Day's crankcase compression principle, the cylinders were attached to a common casting that had a number of chambers that served to distribute the mixture to the cylinders, via their separate crankcases. The crankcases were two separate castings bolted to the distribution box and were recessed so that a dished flywheel and pulley could be fitted between them in order to keep the cylinder axes as close together as possible. The patent emphasised the two-stroke principle of operation and the position of the inlet, transfer and exhaust ports. There was also a full description of the crankcase construction, the upper part of which was described as the distribution box. The distribution box casting contained four separate chambers, two of which fulfilled the role of side transfer ports. The remaining two chambers were employed to connect the exhaust ports of both cylinders and to provide a so-called suction chamber to exercise control over the incoming charge. Each chamber was made quite independent of the other by inserting the cylinder skirts through the distribution box. The cylinders (with integral heads) were secured by large ring nuts that engaged with their threaded ends.

The inlet and the exhaust ports of each cylinder were located opposite each other, necessitating the use of pistons fitted with a deflector. A thin section connecting rod coupled each piston to the crankpins, which had plain bearing big ends. The crankshaft was supported on ball bearings located behind each triangular shaped crank arm, the latter arranged to carry the cranks at 180°. As mentioned earlier, the flywheel and pulley was fixed to the crankshaft and the crankcases were recessed to keep the cylinder axes close together. In consequence, the rim of the flywheel passed as close to the connecting rods as safety would permit. Access to each crankcase and overhung crank assembly was by means of a circular cover that screwed into each side of the main casting. The cylinders carried horizontal finning that extended to the top but there were no fins on the cylinder head.

Both pistons were machined all over and were very light in weight. The gudgeon pins were retained by a somewhat unorthodox method. Each had a flat milled in each end that abutted against ledges within the piston skirt, to prevent them from rotating. They were secured by a bolt in the centre of each pin, that passed through a nut immediately behind each piston crown, and through the eye of the connecting rod and small end bush which were cut away to give the required clearance. A curious feature was an extension above each bolt that resembled a thick, circular disc resting on the top of each piston crown. A perpendicular rod attached to each disc projected upwards to form the sparking electrode when it was in close proximity to a special type of sparking plug mounted in the centre of each totally unfinned cylinder head. This arrangement provided a simple and convenient means of spark distribution for the single trembler coil used. Unfortunately it had its limitations too, since the ignition was fixed and could not be advanced or retarded. Later a plain coil with a mechanical make and break was substituted and then a rotary contact breaker actuated from a pin located in a hole drilled in the solid integral crankpin. This enabled the points to follow closely the engine movements and not suffer from the inertia lag of an oscillating wipe contact. The patent specification also embraced a design of silencer in which a chamber received the gases from a pipe connected to both exhaust ports. Tubes passed through the chamber from end to end and were slotted near their exit so that the exhaust gases could enter and mingle with the air drawn through the open end. Small deflectors close to each slot caused the gases to exert an injector effect on the air within the tubes that accelerated the rate of flow and produced a cooling effect that cooled the exhaust gases and reduced their volume.

When describing the operating cycle of the engine, Scott went to great lengths to explain that when the exhaust port opened the gases escaped to the exhaust chamber and then to the silencer, before the transfer ports were uncovered to admit the new charge. At this time it was not generally recognised that the exhaust gases were expelled by their own pressure and not by the action of the incoming charge displacing them.

Carburation was effected by a fixed jet carburettor of Scott's own design, fitted with a rotating barrel with port openings that controlled both the induction suction from the engine and the atmospheric air intake. It was of the fixed jet type and the mode of operation can be likened to that of the iris of a camera insofar as the administration of the mixture to the engine was concerned. This instrument too was covered by the 1904 patent.

Development work continued, including that of a 4 inch bore marine engine that was kept on test for the greater part of a year. Operating on the two-stroke cycle, this large capacity engine developed 10 hp at 800 rpm and had a high mechanical efficiency. The project was financed by the Tighnabruaich Syndicate, a group of boating enthusiasts composed of Alfred, Herbert and Norman Scott and two others. Alfred proposed the formation of the syndicate during April 1905, to construct an 8 hp (1570 cc) twin cylinder engine for a motor boat to be known as the *Petrel II*. It was his proud boast that *Petrel II* was one of the first motor boats on the Clyde. It had a particularly sonorous exhaust note that is remembered up and down the lochs, caused by the so-called silencer under the stern. An unusual feature was a pawl and ratchet starter that was to be applied to the Scott motorcycle and become the subject of a patent application in the form of a kickstarter. Here it is interesting to note that Herbert Scott was an inventor in his own right too. He had taken out several patents relating to the design of an electric clock, which was eventually taken up by the Ever Ready Battery Company.

Petrel IV at Tighnabruaich, Kyles of Bute

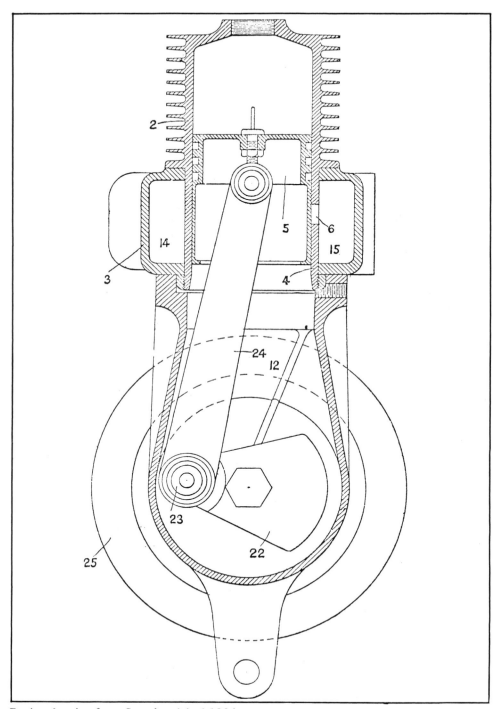

Engine drawing from Scott's original 1904 patent

During 1906, another inventor of similar name and initials produced a design for a spring frame motorcycle, to win a competition initiated by *Motor Cycle*. The situation was rendered all the more confusing by the fact that the other Alfred Scott was based in nearby Leeds. Although Scott's namesake employed four stroke engines in his designs, this confliction of name and address has led to much confusion and there are instances where THE Alfred Scott has been wrongly associated with designs that were vastly different in concept from his familiar vertical twin two-stroke. Even *Motor Cycling* fell into the trap when comment was made in their 8th October 1953 issue about an 1896 design that had originated from Alfred Scott and Co of Leeds. Seemingly they were unaware of the existence of the two Alfred Scotts.

The ratchet starter was not the only invention that originated from Scott's fertile brain at this period, which is perhaps just as well because the patent was loosely worded and easily circumvented by others. In total, he was responsible for over 60 British patents, covering aspects ranging from frame design to the famous two-speed gear and 'telescopic' forks. The patent application relating to the two-speed gear was the subject of much controversy because Joah Phelon of Phelon and Moore Limited, the other Yorkshire motorcycle manufacturer of distinction, claimed it was based on his own design. Subsequent investigation showed that both parties had probably infringed much earlier patents dating back to the time of Lawson and the Motor Manufacturing Company.

The other Scott patent of note during 1908 was British Patent 16564, which related to the triangulated frame layout that was to remain virtually unaltered until 1930. Scott had a hatred of cranked rear frame members, particularly those designed to afford clearance for the belt drive transmission of the era. His faith in the triangulated layout, using completely straight tubes, was upheld. His frame design became as much his trade mark as that of his engines and it was certainly one of the more endearing features of the Scott motorcycle that gave the machine its legendary handling characteristics.

1908 was a memorable year as far as the Scott motorcycle was concerned in more than one respect. A new patent application relating to engine design was made at this time (Application Number 1033) which was subsequently abandoned for reasons unknown. It would seem probable that the application related to a greatly improved engine, a design that can best be described as the true forerunner of the Scott engine as we know it today. The engine had bore and stroke dimensions of 58 mm x 63.5 mm, giving a cubic capacity of 333 cc. As in the previous design, the cylinder barrels were air cooled, but the integral cylinder heads now had a water jacket retained by a simple stud and nut arrangement, with the outside surfaces finned to aid cooling. Water circulated through the jacket by thermo-syphon and was cooled by a small radiator.

The system of distribution chambers had been abandoned, although the cylinders still retained long spigots at their joint with the main crankcase casting. Cut into each spigot was a semi-circle of inlet ports that communicated with an encircling 'suction' chamber to which the carburettor was connected at the rear. Part of the transfer passageway was also included in the rear of the main casting, with a detachable cover bolted to each cylinder that conveyed the gases from the crankcase to the cylinders, via an extension of this passageway. These detachable transfer port covers had faced joints and were fitted with a gauze, to act as a flame trap. Both cylinders were now inclined forwards.

The piston crowns had fully-shaped deflectors and dispensed with the upward projecting electrode that formed part of the original ignition system. Conventional sparking plugs were positioned at right angles to each cylinder bore, at the rear of the cylinder block — where they were in a more favourable position. Whilst the overhung crank arrangement was retained, the mode of construction was entirely different. Each shaft was now tapered and inserted into the boss of the centrally-disposed flywheel, which now carried a sprocket on each side of the boss. The two cranks were drawn together by a long bolt inserted through the hollow left hand crank that threaded into the crank on the right. A nut screwed on to the end of the bolt that projected through the right hand crank, to provide an effective locking device by utilising a left hand thread. Roller bearings were specified for the uncaged bearings behind both cranks and the crankcases were now reduced in volume by a significant amount through the use of slim section connecting rods. The crankpins used for the roller bearing big ends were fitted with right and left hand screws, threaded to countermand the direction of rotation of the engine. The circular crankcase doors were retained for purposes of access; a strap and wing nut made access easier, in place of the original threaded fitting. At the top end of the engine, the centre bolt method of retaining the gudgeon pins was continued.

Coil ignition was employed initially, but a magneto was soon substituted due to the heavy drain on the battery and the rapid rate of wear of the platinum contact breaker points.

It will be observed from this brief description that the Scott engine of 1908 was similar in many respects to the designs that were to follow in later years, even though the cubic capacity was much reduced. More important, it was now incorporated in a complete Scott motorcycle, a design that included such revolutionary features as a two-speed foot operated gear and all chain drive. The final planning of the design represented the culmination of some ten years development and was completed whilst Alfred Scott lay in bed, recovering from a broken leg caused by a fall from a motorcycle. Even this temporary setback was not permitted to impede his progress.

The two-speed gear is worthy of special mention, for it is simple in the extreme, yet amazingly efficient in practice. Each gear has its own separate chain drive from the engine, by means of the sprockets on either side of the flywheel boss. Gear changing is effected by expanding a split ring with a thrust lever so that the ring expands in diameter and engages with the inner surface of either the low gear drum or the high gear drum, depending on the direction in which the gear change pedal is pressed. Because the mode of operation can be likened to that of a pair of brake shoes within an internally-expanding hub brake when the brake is applied, it can be seen that gradual movement of the pedal will cause the drive to take up slowly, as the friction between the expander ring and the gear drum increases. In consequence, the need for a separate clutch is obviated. No gear pinions are required; the main essential is an adequate drip feed of oil for lubrication purposes, since the gear is not enclosed within a casing like the conventional gearbox. Reference to the early Scott catalogues shows the principles of the two-speed gear in the form of well-executed drawings, yet another of Scott's talents.

Having evolved what seemed to be a very promising prototype design, Scott decided to commence manufacture of machines that would bear his name. Having no capital, financial backing or manufacturing facilities, he came to an arrangement with two Bradford motor engineers, William and Benjamin Jowett. They already had experience of engine erection and were busily engaged in developing a flat twin engine of their own design that was to power a cycle car. A contract was drawn up in which it was agreed that the Jowett brothers would manufacture motorcycles to Scott's design, for a royalty of £3 10s per machine.

Only six Scotts were built by the Jowett brothers during 1908, before they decided to relinquish the contract so that they could concentrate on the

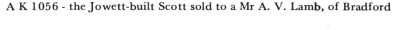

A K 1056 - the Jowett-built Scott sold to a Mr A. V. Lamb, of Bradford

development of their light car, a design that was showing great promise. A highly skilled precision engineer by the name of James Charles Suddards was responsible for the production and erection of these machines, one of which he ultimately purchased. When the break came and the formation of the car company was imminent, Charles Suddards was asked to join Willie and Ben Jowett, but he declined. Already enamoured by the high standard of engineering applied in the Scott design, he elected instead to join Alfred Scott, who was about to form his own production company. Regrettably, none of the original Jowett Scotts has survived the passage of time. It is known that a Mr A. V. Lamb of Bradford purchased another of the six prototypes during May 1908, which was allocated the registration number AK 1056. Like Charles Suddards, he was also a Jowett employee.

Little is known about the Jowett Scotts, although Frank Philipp later claimed that it is best to draw a veil over them. They gave much trouble and tended to give the later models such a bad name that they were bought back by the Company as and when the opportunity arose. Not the least of the troubles was the carburettor, which was placed down amongst the chains, making it almost completely inaccessible. Air to the intake was drawn through a hole in the cheek of the crankcase. The transfer port gauzes also gave trouble. They would blow without warning and necessitate a roadside stop to make replacements.

During 1908, Alfred Scott decided to enter one of his machines in a competition event, even though he had no outstanding ability as a rider. Although a hard proving ground, success in competition events brings its own rewards. The value of the publicity gained from an outright win has helped establish many of the early pioneers, who had great faith in their designs and were willing to stake all in the supreme test. But in most cases they employed skilled and accomplished riders to ride their machines in these events and rarely put in an appearance themselves.

Scott's first public appearance with a machine bearing his name was at the Bradford M.C.C's Wass Bank Hill Climb, on 29th July, 1908. He won the Dyson Shield and a Gold Medal. Three weeks later, he followed up this very impressive debut by winning no less than three Gold Medals at the Coventry M.C.C's Newnham Hill Climb on August 15th, an annual event held near Daventry that attracted both the trade and the press. The fact that the purple and silver Scott took the Open, Twin Cylinder and Variable Gear classes did not pass unnoticed and by the end of the day there were many who protested that the machine should be handicapped in future competition events. After all, did it not fire at more frequent intervals than its four-stroke counterparts? Shamefully, this view became accepted and in their wisdom the Auto-Cycle Union, who organised most motorcycle events, pronounced that for all future competition events an air cooled two-stroke should have the engine capacity multiplied by a factor of 1.25. In the case of a water-cooled model, this factor was increased to 1.32!

Two of Alfred Scott's Gold Medals. Left - The medal won at the Coventry Motor Club's Newnham Hill Climb during August 1908. Right - The Medal won for best performance in Class 4 at the Amulree Hill Climb, Perth during October 1909

Undoubtedly Scott created a great amount of interest at Newnham, whether or not the machine was accepted by other competitors. On more than one occasion it has been stated that one of the more endearing features was the ease with which the machine could be started by means of a kickstarter, a device hitherto unseen on a motorcycle. However, a photograph of Scott's machine, taken at the time of the event, and subsequently published by *Motor Cycle* shows no evidence of a kickstarter. Indeed, it was not included in the Jowett Scott specification, according to drawings made at that period. The *Motor Cycle* photograph shows, however, what appears to be two deviations from standard. A header tank for the cooling system can be seen suspended from the top down tube of the open frame, whilst an empty battery carrier, clamped to the offside chainstays in the position that would have been occupied by Scott's kickstarter, shows evidence of some earlier experiments with ignition systems.

When the Jowett brothers relinquished the contract for the manufacture of Scott motorcycles, Alfred Scott had to seek some alternative means of production, even though he was still handicapped by lack of capital. His solution was to form a company in conjunction with his cousin by marriage, Frank Philipp, and Eric Myers, a close friend. His brother Charles provided the capital and the Scott Engineering Company Limited was formed with a share capital of £4,000. Charles was a solicitor in Bradford, a partner of Scott, Eames and Mossman. The original subscribers were Alfred and Charles Scott, Adolphous Philipp (Frank Philipp's father), Eric Myers, a Bradford wool magnate named Walker and a Mr Ormerod. Frank Philipp agreed to accept the position of Company Secretary and Eric Myers to become

Commercial Superintendent, with a salary of £600 per annum. Myers also purchased shares in the Company to the value of £500. Alfred Scott held 1,600 shares in recognition of his patent rights and for the use of his machine tools and the lease of his workshop in Snowden Street. A small two-storey factory known as Mornington Works was rented in Grosvenor Street, Manningham, Bradford and the production of Scott motorcycles recommenced, this time under the direct control of the inventor. Some work was contracted out, mainly the manufacture of the frames and forks, which was entrusted to Royal Enfield with instructions for them to be made to Scott's design.

Initially, Alfred Scott and Eric Myers were designated joint Managing Directors, a decision Scott disliked intensely because he believed it restricted his mechanical prowess. Ultimately Eric Myers withdrew and the situation resolved itself without giving rise to further problems. Charles Suddards was appointed Works Manager when he joined the newly formed company, a job to which he was ideally suited. He had served the long and rigorous apprenticeship that was customary at that period and had become an engineer for whom a piece of precision machinery or a machine tool had beauty. He was on the short side, with a pleasant face and dark curly hair. He was respected and liked by those who worked with or for him. A high degree of mutual respect existed between Charles Suddards and Alfred Scott, even though there was the occasional disagreement between them when the inventor's eternal search for design perfection irrespective of cost had to be balanced against the works manager's need to standardise tools for increased production and reduced costs. On one such occasion, Scott grudgingly admitted that he valued Suddard's many fine qualities very highly, but that nevertheless, he was a stubborn Yorkshireman! Others who joined the company in the early days included the young Tim Wood and his brother Clarrie, Bentley Rigg, a young apprentice who became Repair Shop Foreman, Walter Clough, Walter Smith and Harry Dewhurst.

It was decided to commence manufacture with a target of one hundred machines in mind, embodying many improved features that were considered to represent an advance when compared with some of the frailties of the original Jowett Scott design. These included a radiator of Scott's own design that resembled a smaller version of the traditional serpentine household radiator, made in sheet metal. Across the top was positioned a cylindrical header tank, of the type that is common today. One particularly unusual feature of the engine was the exhaust stub, that was arranged to vent into a small chamber cast in the front of the main crankcase casting before the exhaust gases passed into the larger, external, expansion box. The objective was to provide a preliminary expansion chamber, but in practice it was found that this arrangement caused unnecessary heating of the crankcase and it was soon discarded.

One hundred sets of castings and forgings were produced, a move that proved to be a most unwise decision. When the parts concerned had been machined to size and shape, it was found that a great many no longer fitted, due to modifications that had been made to the previously untried parts when they had failed for one reason or another. The design changes that followed meant the ready-machined parts had either to be scrapped or modified by brazing and filing so that they could be reclaimed and re-used. Even components such as pistons gave trouble, because the foundries at that time had not perfected a method of locating cores in a mould so that the results were reproduceable. In consequence, piston heads were either too thick or too thin in section and were prone to seize as the result of their uneven expansion. Other problems that occurred were frame and fork breakages, which were wrongly attributed to Royal Enfield, their manufacturer. In point of fact it was Scott's own specifications that were at fault, for he had underestimated the strength of these parts in his design calculations.

Big end bearings were also prone to premature failure. The big end rollers were made on the premises because Scott was experimenting with the use of this type of bearing in motorcycles. Troubles occurred when the shouldered pins that connected the inner and outer races caused the occasional roller to break in two. The remedy, promptly applied, was to dispense with the shouldered pins and let the roller plates run free. Scott's own design of kickstarter was not free from troubles either, mainly because it had been designed on the weak side and was easily damaged if the engine kicked back. The design was improved by adopting the crown ratchet principle, and yet another problem was eliminated.

In the improved design, the kickstarter remained in its original location, close to the rear wheel spindle, on the offside lower chainstay. When at rest, it lay parallel with the lower chainstay tube. A bell crank was attached to the other end of the short spindle that formed the kickstarter pivot, after it had passed through the frame end lug. To the end of this bell crank was attached a rod that terminated in a yoke end, that in turn was attached to a length of chain wrapped around a sprocket that had a ratchet face and formed part of the two-speed gear drum. The other half of the ratchet carried a clock-type return spring within its centre. When the kickstarter was depressed in a forward direction, it pulled on the chain wrapped around the sprocket and this in turn caused the engine to revolve, via the two-speed gear.

Frank Philipp road tested the first few machines off the production line and it is fortunate that the late Tom Ward, the doyen of all Scott enthusiasts, joined the Company during April 1909. He witnessed first hand the many problems that arise when any new product goes into manufacture, problems that could not have been predicted during the design stage. He progressed from assembling kickstarters and rear brakes to the two-speed gear and then to dealing with customer complaints.

The very first Scott to leave the Mornington Works was purchased by a Mr C. W. Lupton, who was at that time Chief Engineer at the West End Mills, Bradford. Later, he purchased another, to which he added several of his own refinements such as detachable mud shields to protect the otherwise exposed chains and gears. He also perfected a design of honeycomb radiator, which was duly taken up by Alfred Scott and fitted to the 1911 models.

Outwardly, the 1909 models differed little in appearance from their Jowett-made predecessors, apart from the addition of the kickstarter already mentioned, a valanced front mudguard, a different crankcase that had an angular profile at the rear and a smaller expansion box for the exhaust system. A separate bolt-on rear carrier was now fitted. The wheelbase had been lengthened slightly and it was no longer necessary to recess the lower end of the petrol tank to provide clearance for the horseshoe magnet of the open Bosch magneto, driven by chain from the two-speed gear. Because the original engines were underpowered, the bore and stroke measurements of the 1909 engine were increased to 66.7 mm x 63.5 mm, giving a cubic capacity of 450 cc.

The first advertisement to originate from the newly-formed Company was published in the March 10th 1909 issue of *Motor Cycle*. It was simple in the extreme and took the form of the word Scott in bold, surrounded by a heavy oblong border with rounded corners. Small oblongs within the border carried the legends two-stroke, two-speed, two-cylinder and two years ahead, anticipating the 'catalogue' registration number AK 222 that Scott was to apply to illustrations of his machines.

As mentioned earlier, the colour purple figured prominently in his catalogues and on the cylindrical petrol tanks that surrounded the saddle tube of all his machines. Purple was the colour of his sister-in-law Alice's favourite dress, the same person who suggested that the addition of two silver bands around the petrol tank would be symbolic of two-stroke.

A decision was made to enter one of the production models in the 1909 TT, with Eric Myers as the rider. Such was the haste to prepare the machine that it was fitted with unsprung front forks. The machine was allocated Scott's personal registration number AK 775, a number already well-known in competition events because it was the number of the machine that made the successful appearance at the Newnham Hill Climb the year previous.

The 1909 TT was run over the old 15¾ mile course that started at St John's, ran to Ballacraine, then turned sharp left along part of the present course as far as Kirk Michael, before it turned left again to Peel, before it returned to St John's. Unlike the present event, the early TT races were staged during late September. The 1908 event had been overshadowed by a petrol consumption allowance, which decreed that the single cylinder machines must average 100 mpg and the twins 80 mpg, a regulation that turned the event into little more than a glorified petrol consumption test. For 1909, the Auto-Cycle Union had seen fit to dispense with this stipulation, but in its place they substituted a capacity limit of 500 cc for the singles and 750 cc for the twins. Twin cylinder machines were considered to be inefficient from their past showings and it had been overlooked completely that the Scott, about which there had been such an outcry under a year ago, was regarded as a super-efficient machine and had to be handicapped accordingly! Fortunately, even when the factor of 1.32 was applied, the falsified engine capacity was well below the twin cylinder class limit.

The two other two-stroke entries in the event did not fare so well, according to contemporary reports. The Rex Manufacturing Company had entered an air-cooled single of about 470 cc capacity, which when multiplied by the air-cooled two-stroke factor of 1.25 brought the capacity well above the class limit. They had to withdraw in consequence, and substitute a four-stroke single. The other two-stroke, a Premo made by the Premier Motor Company, was fitted with a water-cooled engine and although there is no record of the engine capacity, it would seem that the 'equalising factor' of 1.32 placed it way above the 750 cc class limit. In this case the manufacturer resolved the problem by fitting a smaller cylinder barrel and piston, in order to qualify.

The Premo and the Scott presented themselves for the practice sessions that preceded the race, but for some unaccountable reason, the Premo rider, J. Leno, collided with another rider when he decided to ride round the course in the opposite direction! This brought about his immediate disqualification and eliminated the Premo altogether. Thus of the original trio, Eric Myers and his Scott faced the starter's flag alone, making the Scott the first two-stroke ever to participate in a TT race. Quite unwittingly, the Scott motorcycle had scored a distinctive first in the motorcycle world, before the event commenced.

When Myers kickstarted his machine into life, he drew loud cheers from the spectators, since no one had previously witnessed this unusual method of starting in a race. Sad to say, Myers' luck was out. The machine was not exceptionally fast and on the seventh lap he had the misfortune to take a toss, loosening the footrests and the magneto and, according to some reports, breaking a piston. Despite his enforced retirement, the machine could not have been too badly damaged, for he was able to effect the necessary repairs and stay on until the Friday after the race so that he could compete in a local hill climb.

One evening, when he was resting at the Villiers Hotel, Douglas, where he stayed whilst he was in the Isle of Man, a young man spotted his machine outside and ventured into the hotel to see whether he could have a word with Myers. Much to his embarrassment, the barmaid called up the stairs, "Mr Myers, there is a young gent called to see you!", whereupon Myers appeared and was only too pleased to enter into conversation with the caller. The young man introduced himself as Jesse Baker, a motorcycling enthusiast on holiday from Wigan to see the races. He had been very impressed by the Scott and commiserated with Myers about the latter's unfortunate retirement. He enquired about the possibility of purchasing a Scott and was delighted when Myers suggested that he should contact him soon after he returned to the mainland so that he could visit the Bradford Works and meet Alfred Scott. The offer was accepted with alacrity, for offers such as this are few and far between.

THE SCOTT MOTORCYCLE

The hill climb in which Myers competed before he left the Isle of Man was held at Crogga, a steep hill close to Port Soderick. During the afternoon, riders had to attempt a climb of Snaefell, the mountain that towers some 2,000 feet above the lowest part of the TT course. Myers returned home satisfied, having finished in third place on overall performance. To an extent, this made up for his disappointing debut with the Scott in the TT that had dashed the hopes and aspirations of all at the Mornington Works.

Soon after Myers return he was contacted by Jesse Baker, who set off for Bradford with some other Wigan enthusiasts to fulfill the appointment for the visit. The visitors were received most graciously by Alfred Scott and his fellow directors, who placed three of the current models at their disposal. After a short ride up Lister Lane, one of the back streets of Manningham, Jesse and one of his companions placed a firm order for a Scott each, even though it was unlikely that delivery could be effected until early in the new year. Neither Scott nor Myers could have perceived that this was the early beginning of a partnership of man and machine that was to establish Jesse Baker as one of the more promising trials riders of that era and enhance the name of the Scott motorcycle even further.

During October, Alfred Scott decided to contest another open hill climb, this time in far away Amulree, near Perth. The event was organised by the Edinburgh M C C and he obviously had good faith in his chance of success. He came away with another Gold Medal, for winning the Class 4 category.

Although many of the earlier engine troubles had been eliminated, the Scott carburettor now came in for its fair share of criticism because it proved difficult to obtain the correct mixture strength without having to juggle constantly with the settings. Frank Philipp was well aware of this defect and approached Scott on more than one occasion in the hope that he could persuade him to change to the proprietary Binks design.

By the end of the year less than forty machines had been manufactured and sold, under half that of the original production target. In a bid to improve sales, space had been taken to exhibit the 3½ hp model at the Stanley Show, held during late November.

Jesse Baker took delivery of his new Scott early in 1910, after travelling to the Works from Wigan to collect it and then ride it home. Although much impressed by the quiet purr of the engine and the way in which the machine handled, he was plagued by constantly oiling plugs and was convinced he had not adjusted the oiling correctly. In desperation he telephoned Alfred Scott direct and was given the necessary advice, which confirmed that his adjustments were correct. Oiling troubles continued and in due course he returned to the Works with the machine for further advice. Fortunately, by then Scott had obtained a batch of American-made Reliance sparking plugs, which would tolerate an excess of oil more readily. It is interesting to observe that this type of sparking plug is fitted to the sectioned engine in the Science Museum, South Kensington, which would seem to indicate their popularity amongst owners of early Scott motorcycles.

32

A frank exposition of Jesse Baker's troubles with his first Scott is given in the paragraphs that follow because these are probably typical of those encountered by other Scott riders of that period. It should be remembered that the development of the motorcycle was still not so far removed from the earlier experimental stage at this time, a factor that has to be taken into consideration when looking objectively at the problems of the early motorcyclists.

Although the Reliance plugs overcame the oiling problem, the bottom end of the engine still showed signs of imbalance. Despite the fact that early riders were instructed to keep a haze of blue smoke in the exhaust as a rough guide to the effectiveness of the lubrication system, Baker's engine had one crankcase that was over-oiled whilst the other tended to run dry. Somehow he managed to escape engine seizures, although he averred this was due more to good luck than good judgment.

Postcard from a Scott enthusiast in Moscow dated February 1910

A few weeks later the fork stem fractured within the steering head, fortunately at a time when Baker was riding slowly. This defect was duly repaired and the machine went back into service. The other component that gave constant trouble was Scott's own design of carburettor which seemed to have little control over the mixture strength. When the throttle was closed it was not unknown for the machine to accelerate swiftly, whilst opening the throttle again had little effect on the situation. No wonder Frank Philipp had suggested a change to a Binks carburettor would be advisable! It was primarily this carburettor failing that led Jesse to develop his 'everything forward and trust in the Lord' riding technique, which landed him in dire trouble on more than one occasion!

Although the 1910 models were similar in most respects to those of the year preceding, some design changes were made as are evident from the few examples that still exist. The earlier method of retaining the gudgeon pins had been dispensed with and in its place a quite different arrangement was substituted in which a threaded insert that screwed into the base of each piston carried a raised ring within the threaded boss, that projected upwards. The gudgeon pins had a groove cut near each end and when the threaded insert was fully home, the projecting ring engaged with these grooves and locked the gudgeon pin in position. To prevent the threaded inserts from working free whilst the engine was in motion, a brass locking screw passed through the piston into the threaded insert retaining the gudgeon pin. It was filed flush with the piston skirt and in consequence had no head. This is a feature that has foiled renovators who wish to remove the pistons and has no doubt led to a great many broken pistons in its time. Even so, the arrangement must have proved relatively successful, for it was continued until 1912.

The central flywheel now featured a lead-filled rim and had four curved spokes. The triangular cranks that fitted into the flywheel boss were made in one piece, with no detachable big end or main bearing bushes. This led to engine troubles because the hardened $3/8$ inch diameter uncaged rollers of the big end assembly bore directly on the case hardened 'eye' of each connecting rod. The depth of hardening extended for some forty thousandths of an inch and sooner or later the rollers chipped their way into the surface and destroyed it. This underlined the need to fit replaceable hardened nickel chrome steel bushings into the connecting rod bearing surface and over the crankpins, to alleviate the rate of wear and to permit the renewal of the bearing surfaces without need for expensive replacements. The appropriate modifications were made for the following reason.

When the regulations for the 1910 TT races were published by the Auto-Cycle Union, Scott decided to enter two machines that would be prepared specially. Although it was apparent from the 1909 results that the twin-cylinder machines were now beginning to gain the upper hand, the Auto-Cycle Union refused to accept that the regulations were more favourably inclined towards this latter category of machine. But as a gesture, they lowered the capacity limit in the twin cylinder class to 670 cc. This caused the Scott entries no undue handicap since even if the true engine capacity was multiplied by the 1.32 factor, the falsified capacity of 640 cc was still below the capacity limit. Two riders were entered, Eric Myers and Frank Philipp, both riding machines fitted with the Scott telescopic forks and cylinders with generous finning. Frank Philipp finished 9th at an average speed in the region of 40 mph. Although his machine was capable of much higher speeds, it showed a marked reluctance to go fast for any length of time and progressed in a series of spasms that were quite uncontrollable. It was not until after the race that the cause of the trouble was located, a thin section of solder about the size of a penny that periodically blocked the petrol outlet and starved the carburettor of petrol. Eric Myers was less fortunate. After a spate of punctures and endless plug troubles, he completed the race in 24th position.

As had happened during the year previous, Myers rode in the Snaefell Hill Climb, but without any success on this occasion. Frank Philipp came along to watch and was able to witness the splendid performance put up by a newcomer, J. Hoffman, on a standard 4 hp model. Hoffman secured a very creditable 4th place in the results that merited special mention in the motorcycling press.

It was during early autumn that Jesse Baker had the top frame tube of his machine fracture near the steering head. He telephoned Alfred Scott and was told to strip the bike and bring the frame to Bradford during early closing day in Wigan, so that the frame could be repaired on the spot. As events turned out, the frame was replaced without question and Scott enquired whether the machine would be reassembled and running for use during the weekend. A provisional meeting was arranged for the following Sunday at the Black Bull, Skipton, for 1.00 pm and Jesse saw to it that the appointment was kept. He joined Scott and Philipp for lunch and then the trio set off for Kettlewell and Whernside so that Jesse could try his hand at Park Rash, a fearsome hill covered with loose boulders that has figured in innumerable early long distance trials. After taking a close look at the first bend, which was on a very rough gradient up to 1 in 4½, he made a masterly climb at the very first attempt, just grazing one of his hands on a stone wall. All three returned to the Red Lion at Burnsall for an evening meal and plans were laid for a further meeting the following weekend if Jesse would care to spend the weekend in Bradford as Alfred Scott's guest. The offer was accepted and during the Saturday afternoon that followed, Scott and Baker were again joined by Philipp, to embark on a journey to Sutton Bank, Whitby and Robin Hood Bay. During the run, Scott and Philipp devised all manner of tests so that Baker could show his ability as a rider. At the end of the day, Baker was offered an official works support in all future reliability trials, plus one of the new 1911 models as soon as they were available. Jesse Baker now joined the ranks of the 'Shamateurs', a name applied to all those so-called private owners who received unofficial help from the manufacturer of the machine they rode. J. Baker, 3¾ hp Scott was to become a familiar entry in the results sheets issued at the conclusion of each event. It was not often that an award was not appended to this entry.

For the 1911 season, further design changes were considered necessary, including an increase in engine capacity to 486 cc, achieved by increasing the bore size to 69.8 mm. The stroke dimension was maintained at 63.5 mm, the familiar 2½ inch stroke that is characteristic of all engines designed by Alfred Scott.

The new engine featured water-cooled cylinder barrels that were used in conjunction with an improved design of water-cooled cylinder head that took the form of an unfinned polished aluminium alloy cover above the cylinder block, retained by two bolts. Improved cooling necessitated a more efficient radiator and the honeycomb design pioneered by Mr Lupton was adopted. These radiators were made by the Pendleton Radiator Company Limited of Pendleton, Manchester. Other improvements included a redesigned crankcase top that had an annular ring around the inlet ports and an exhaust duct that joined both exhaust ports and led to a central stub that projected into an expansion box.

Having received his 1911 model, Jesse Baker, in company with Frank Philipp and L. S. Parker, contested the A-CU Six Days Trial that was based on Harrogate. The Scott Team were out of the running for the Team Prize, but Baker won a Gold Medal in due recognition of his brilliant riding throughout the event.

Meanwhile, attention was being given to the Scott entry for the 1911 TT which, for the first time, was to be run over the 37½ mile mountain course that took competitors up the long climb from Ramsey towards the summit of Snaefell, some 2,000 feet above sea level. Although the 'new' course broadly followed the route that is so well known today, it turned right at Cronk-ny-Mona, and continued past Edges Corner, with a left turn at Willaston and then to Parkfield Corner before rejoining the present course at the top of Bray Hill. In effect, part of the later Clypse Circuit was used in reverse, cutting out Governors Bridge and Glencrutchery Road, where today's grandstands and pits are erected. Prior to 1914, the start and finish was at Woodlands, just beyond the bottom of Bray Hill. In 1914, the start was resited close to St Ninians Church, but after the war a final change was made in favour of the course and facilities still in current use. These facts are not generally known and account for the difficulty in relating some of the background found in early photographs taken at the start and finish of the Mountain Course races. For some time Scott had perceived the need for a form of mechanical device to control the induction cycle more accurately and had designed a rotary valve attached to the rear of the cylinder block in place of the transfer port covers that would administer the incoming charge at exactly the correct time. The design formed the subject of British Patent 5895, which was granted on March 9th, 1911. Three special machines were built, each having a chain driven rotary valve of the type specified.

Despite the kitting out of each of the three riders in a set of purple-coloured leathers, Frank Philipp, Eric Myers and Frank Applebee, the Scott bid to achieve success in the 1911 Senior race failed as the result of an unforeseen mechanical problem. The rotary valve had a tapered shaft, to which was attached a sprocket that was chain-driven from two brass pinions which transmitted the drive from the crankshaft. No provision had been made for locating the sprocket by means of a keyway or pin and as the race progressed, the sprocket began to slip on the taper and throw the timing of the rotary valve completely out of phase. Of the three riders, only Frank Applebee — a newcomer to the team from Godfrey and Applebee of London — managed to complete the course and finish in last position. This was a particularly valiant effort, for Applebee was forced to stop at regular intervals in order to re-adjust the constantly slipping rotary valve timing. Myers retired early on with the same trouble, which also put Philipp out of action, but not before he had set a record lap for the new mountain circuit at 50.11 mph. The exhaust note of the Scotts as they commenced the long climb up the mountain left an indelible impression on those fortunate enough to witness the 1911 races. Harry Bashall, who rode a BAT into 7th position in the same event still has vivid recollections of the noise during practice, which was unlike anything he had ever heard before. It was not by coincidence that some later Scott advertisements used the slogan "The bus with a roar like a plane". Ironically, the Senior event was won by O. C. Godfrey riding a 3¾ hp Indian. He was Applebee's business partner!

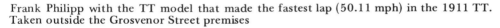

Frank Philipp with the TT model that made the fastest lap (50.11 mph) in the 1911 TT. Taken outside the Grosvenor Street premises

THE SCOTT MOTORCYCLE

At the post mortem held after the race it was obvious that the rotary valve drive was defective in a number of respects. Apart from the need to locate the chain sprocket in a more positive manner the taper was too small and it was also questionable whether the exposed brass pinions of extremely thin section were robust enough to transmit the drive from the crankshaft. There could be no question of retaining the drive in its present form.

An event that somewhat clouded the year was a road accident that befell Mr Ormerod, one of the Company's principal shareholders. He was riding a new Scott near the Devonshire Arms Hotel, Bolton Abbey, when he came into collision with a car and sustained injuries from which he died. He was out for a run with Frank Philipp who, at that particular moment, was following about a half mile behind on a similar model. The outcome of this sad accident was the withdrawal of Ormerod's capital, a situation that caused slight financial embarrassment until other arrangements could be made.

Achievements of note during the year included W. D. Smith's win in the Colmore Cup Trial and the award of the P and M Cup to him for the best sidecar performance in the Bradford—Dunbar—Bradford 24 hour trial. The latter award was rather ironic, in view of the earlier opposition to the Scott two-speed gear patent by Joah Phelon.

By way of a publicity stunt, Frank Philipp made 100 successive climbs of Sutton Bank, a notorious Yorkshire hill with a gradient of 1 in 4 at its steepest point. The climbs were completed in 7½ hours on May 28th, without need to add water to the radiator, a time that included an 18 minute stop to mend a puncture.

Frank Philipp during one of his successful 100 ascents of Sutton Bank during 1911

Towards the end of November, the 1911 Motor Cycle Show at Olympia provided the occasion for the release of information about the new models for the 1912 season. The specification included an improved two-speed gear which ran entirely on ball bearings and the elimination of drag when the gear was in the neutral position by arranging the expanding bands to clear the gear drums all the way round. The front number plate formed part of a combined mudguard extension with side valences that was the subject of British Patent 22695 of October 14th, 1911 — another of Scott's innovations. All frame clips were eliminated and the various lugs and stops for the Bowden cables were either brazed to the frame or incorporated in the crankcase casting.

Engine improvements included increasing the bore sizes to 73 mm, to give the now familiar cubic capacity of 532 cc. The inlet and exhaust ports were cut in the form of slots rather than circles as previously and a new and improved type of carburettor was fitted, which had the controlling slides in the walls of the vaporising chamber. The practice of fitting spring footboards was continued, with a C spring replacing the earlier coil springs that showed a tendency to jam. The footboards were made instantly detachable by means of a special rear clip, rubber covering being an optional extra.

A distinguishing feature from earlier models was the use of smooth cylinder jackets, without waists, for the cylinder bolt nuts. Quick release cotters facilitated this change, which gave the model a much improved appearance. A small but also noticeable improvement was the re-arrangement of the crankcase door straps, so that they were in line with the cylinder axes.

The new carburettor was based on Scott's original 1904 design and represented the final development, since the design was discontinued after 1914. Basically, the carburettor comprised two units, the mixing chamber and the automatic air valve. Two contra-rotating sleeves were arranged to operate within the mixing chamber, actuated by the throttle lever, via a crank. This gave an iris opening effect similar to that of a camera lens, directly in line with the main jet. It was also possible to achieve the necessary right angled turn within the carburettor, demanded by the engine layout. A curious feature was the provision of a spring-loaded float needle, held against the needle valve seating. The needle was lifted by the weight of the float acting on a rocking lever, the more weight required to counteract the spring pressure, the lower the petrol level. Thus if a richer mixture was required, a weaker spring had to be fitted. Unlike other carburettors, this unusual mode of construction necessitated raising the needle to flood the carburettor.

A swivelling jet cover on the mixing chamber provided access to the main jet, which was released with the aid of a special tool, at one time made under contract by Tom Ward.

When closed, the automatic air valve sealed the front face of the mixing chamber and air entered the carburettor via a slot in the air valve body through cuts in the seating to raise the spring-loaded dashpot air valve. When open, the seating moved away from the front face of the mixing chamber via the air control screw, thereby permitting the incoming air to by-pass the dashpot valve. As may be expected, the carburettor was not particularly easy to manufacture and the cost of the carburettor as a separate unit was reflected in the purchase price which was approximately 1/8 of the cost of a complete engine.

The Scott advertisement in the Show Issue of *Motor Cycling* was simple in the extreme. It stated cryptically, with an absolute minimum of words,

Olympia, Scott, Stand 125. Price £65, still two years ahead.

CHAPTER TWO
Island Successes

AS SO many motorcycle manufacturers found during their early struggles to gain recognition, an outstanding competition success, with all the accompanying publicity, provides the much needed breakthrough and the means of expanding business at a hitherto unforeseen rate. Unfortunately there is no means of predicting when, or even if, this breakthrough will occur, for even with the very best of endeavours so many unforeseen factors can influence the outcome. When success seems assured, many hopes and aspirations have been dashed at the last moment, when some vital component has failed or an unpredictable incident has occurred. Yet it is imperative that support be given to competitive events, if only to gain practical experience by testing machines under arduous conditions and thereby ensuring a much better product reaches the purchaser. The bonus, if and when it eventually comes, hopefully more than offsets the development expenditure over the years and may also pacify even the most vociferous of shareholders who is inclined to question the rate of expenditure on these ventures. Yet on the other hand, repeated failure to achieve success, no matter what ill fortune has occurred, may have quite the reverse effect. It is very much a gamble and a matter over which the manufacturer can exercise but little control.

Like most other manufacturers, Alfred Scott was well aware of the value of a TT win, even though he believed the races should live up to their original designation and encourage the development of true road-going machines rather than monsters engineered for the sole purpose of winning the race. He continued to give his support and entered two machines for the 1912 Senior event with a somewhat similar specification to the 1911 TT machines which made the fastest lap at 50.11 mph. Success had been almost in his grasp when the rotary valve drive let him down. The background to the 1912 races was, however, rather involved with regard to both the attitude of the Manx authorities and that of the manufacturers and riders. Some explanation is therefore necessary, in order to set the scene.

Although the 1911 races were considered to be a success by all concerned, especially in view of the decision to use the new and much longer Mountain course, for some inexplicable reason the Manx authorities decided that the 1912 races should revert to the original St Johns — Ballacraine — Kirkmichael course, that silencers should be fitted to every machine taking part and that more control should be exercised over the competitors who, they claimed, were inclined to annoy Manx residents by their somewhat boisterous behaviour when they were relaxing. Not unexpectedly this brought forth a storm of protest, which in turn, placed the Auto-Cycle Union in a somewhat delicate position, as the organisers of an event on Manx soil. Some twenty or so leading manufacturers signed an agreement whereby they withdrew their support from the event, claiming the TT races were leading to the development of machines somewhat remote from the original concept. They also objected to the cubic capacity advantage still enjoyed by the twin cylinder machines, to accessory manufacturers who persuaded riders to fit equipment that would invalidate the contracts between the manufacturer and the rider, and to the inference that the horse play referred to by the Manx authorities was associated only with the Isle of Man. There was even the hint that the races were unfair to the private owner, who had riders with full works support pitted against him! This last point was, however, little more than a clever ruse to cover up the fact that most manufacturers had full order books and saw no necessity in incurring further development expenditure if the event was restricted to private owners who would race existing designs.

A cutting from the *Old Abbotsholmian* referring to the success of one of the school's former pupils

By the courtesy of Alfred A. Scott we are able to give a picture of the celebrated " Scott " Motor Bicycle, now the best in the market; and we are very proud of the fact that an Old Abbotsholme Boy has been the successful inventor. We hoped to have given a description of *The " Scott " Ideals*; but,

on looking through the prospectus that has been sent us, we feel we cannot do better than refer our readers to the pamphlet: " *Scott* " *Two Stroke, 1912*, published by The Scott Engineering Company, Limited, Mornington Works, Bradford. We hope that all Abbotsholmians, past and present, will make a point of using the " Scott " Motor Cycle and no other.

Clearly the A-CU were in an unhappy position and matters were not helped by the resignation of Mr F. Straight during March 1912, who had held the post of Secretary for the past six years. Fortunately, a Mr T.W. Loughborough was appointed as successor, a man destined to play a leading role in the growth and status of the A-CU in the years to follow. After a series of quite fruitful negotiations with the Manx authorities at House of Keys level, the 1912 event went ahead as originally planned, without need to use Brooklands or any of the continental speed venues recommended as a substitute by the Manufacturers' Union. Although the races suffered from the lack of trade entries, many professional riders pledged their support and saved the day. They were entered by some of the larger agents who marketed the brand of machine their riders elected to ride. In a few instances, even manufacturers who had signed the ban relented to some extent. They agreed to prepare the machines before they were passed over to the rider concerned, thereby partially nullifying the effect of the ban. Fortunately, Alfred Scott was not one of the manufacturers who had signed, despite his obvious sympathies with some of the claims. He was therefore able to proceed with his preparations unhindered, encouraged by the announcement that the A-CU had decided to abandon completely the handicap factor applied to all air and water-cooled two-strokes. The Senior event was described as a five lap race over the Mountain circuit for single cylinder machines of up to 500 cc capacity and multi-cylinder machines with a capacity limit of 585 cc. This move was made primarily to encourage the development of variable speed gears and more efficient small capacity engines. Scott set about the manufacture of two 486 cc models, with a gear driven rotary valve and slightly higher compression ratio. No riders were nominated initially; the entry was made under the Company title.

An interior shot of the old Mornington Works, Grosvenor Street, Bradford

THE SCOTT MOTORCYCLE

Meanwhile, Scott motorcycles were appearing in all manner of other events. Frank Applebee took a Scott and sidecar across to one of the French hill climbs organised by *Motor Cycling* with Billy Wells of Indian fame as his sidecar passenger. The event took place during February and although Applebee did not compete, he used the opportunity to gain much useful experience of the Scott as a sidecar machine. At this time, Scott himself had given much attention to sidecar chassis design, utilising his famous triangulated tubes principle. His patent relating to a sidecar chassis made of completely straight tubes (British Patent 1387) was granted on January 17th 1912. Alfred Scott asked Charles Suddards to try out one of the prototypes, which took the form of a wickerwork body in classic bath chair outline, attached to the chassis by sofa-like coil springs. Since the Suddards were about to set off on holiday, they decided to use the sidecar, which was hurriedly attached to Charles' own Scott. They set off down the east coast for their destination in Kent, mother seated regally in the sidecar and daughter Nellie astride the pillion, which took the form of a cushion attached to the luggage grid. All went well initially, despite a tendency for the sidecar to lean outwards and lift the front wheel on some corners. Gaining confidence, Charles entered a sharp bend in a winding Lincolnshire lane just a shade too fast, whereupon the sidecar developed a rhythmic swing from side to side. Mother was catapulted head first into a bed of stinging nettles, and Nellie over the hedge into a field, whilst Charles wrestled with the outfit to prevent it from doing a wall of death act along the hedge! Although somewhat shaken, mother stoically refused to complete the journey by train, and the remainder of the trip was completed as intended. It later transpired that other employees had similar experiences; the trouble was ultimately eliminated by spring adjustments.

Only a few weeks later, Applebee won the Members Gold Medal when contesting Aston Hill with a Scott and sidecar at the Essex M.C's open event. Obviously he had learned much from his continental visit. Jesse Baker, on the other hand, was much less fortunate. He was riding his 1912 Scott (EK 247) flat out at a local hill climb cum speed trial when one of the HT leads detached itself and lodged against his ankle. The violent electric shock caused him to lose control, writing off the complete front end of the machine. He broke his right arm and was unconscious for a week, such was the severity of the ensuing crash.

It was not until publication of the pre-race programme that the names of the two Scott riders in the 1912 Senior TT were disclosed, Frank Applebee and Frank Philipp. When the machines appeared for practice, it was immediately obvious that they differed in several respects from the models entered the year previous. Although the rotary valve had been retained, it was now driven by a train of gears, protected by a detachable aluminium alloy cover. The cylinders were of an entirely new design, with only the cylinder walls water-cooled. The heads were left plain and unfinned. Each cylinder had two plugs, inclined at an angle above the rotary valve. A

44

push-on connector from the magneto enabled a change of plug to be made very rapidly. The carburettor was positioned at the left hand side of the crank chamber, to allow the larger inlet pipe to accommodate the rotary valve. Because the water-cooled surfaces of the engine were reduced in area, a smaller and lighter radiator was fitted. The petrol tank had an exceptionally large filler cap some four inches in diameter, an innovation that had its advantages as events later showed.

From the practice sessions that preceded the race, it was obvious that both Applebee and Philipp stood more than a good chance of winning the Senior event. Applebee had a narrow escape before practice commenced, when he hit a wall whilst riding from Douglas to Ramsey. Philipp had his problems too, when he collected a large bird in his front wheel during one of the practices. Fortunately both riders escaped injury and neither machine was too badly damaged.

Conference outside the Prince of Wales, Ramsey, probably after one of the 1912 practice sessions in the Isle of Man. Alfred Scott (centre) chats with Frank Applebee (left) and Frank Philipp (right)

THE SCOTT MOTORCYCLE

The Senior race was held on Monday, July 1st, over a rutted and greasy course made damp by early morning rain. The Junior event, held the previous Friday, was characterised by bad weather, which had also plagued competitors during most of the practice sessions. Conditions around the course were so bad that at Ramsey, competitors were diverted onto the footpath, in order to miss out some of the worst road sections! Jack Haswell set the pace on his single cylinder Triumph, but he was soon overhauled by both Applebee and Philipp who had the advantage of better acceleration. At the end of the first lap, Applebee and Philipp were lying first and second respectively, a position they maintained for the next couple of laps despite a strong challenge by Haswell. But on lap four, tragedy struck. At Ballaugh Bridge, Philipp's rear tyre blew off the rim and he was forced to stop and make repairs, a setback that relegated him to an eventual 11th place at the finish. Applebee continued unabated, unaware of his partner's fate, and finished first, at an average speed of 48.69 mph. It was a double first in another respect, for this was the first TT win by a two-stroke and the first occasion on which the winner had led from start to finish.

Frank Applebee astride the machine on which he won the 1912 Senior TT

Some of the more exciting scenes occurred at the Ramsey depot, where competitors took on fuel. Applebee stopped on the second lap and completed his fill in the amazingly short time of fifteen seconds, due to some remarkably good pit work. A two gallon petrol can was inverted over the large filler orifice whilst the tang of a file was used to pierce the bottom of the can to increase the rate of flow. An oil gun was used to replenish the oil in the oil tank. On this occasion, Applebee's pit attendant was none other than O. C. Godfrey, his business partner and winner of the 1911 Senior event on an Indian, who was one of those who had signed the ban. A repeat fill-up later on was accomplished in fourteen seconds, proving the original performance was no fluke.

Frantic pit stop! Frank Applebee grabs the petrol can whilst his pit attendant, O. C. Godfrey, squirts in oil. On his way to victory in the 1912 Senior TT

TT winner Frank Applebee with his family after the 1912 Senior TT. Frank's wife is seated on his left and his father and mother on his right

In an interview after the race, Applebee claimed his only problem had been a loose rear stand that had fallen twice, although on each occasion he had managed to kick it back into position. He also experienced trouble with a loose brake block in the rear rim brake. Throughout the race his machine had averaged between 40 — 50 mpg and was in generally good condition when the engine was stripped for measuring. It is interesting to note that Reliance plugs were included in the machine's specification.

As may be expected, the Scott Works were elated with the news. Orders for machines of their manufacture came flooding in and it was soon apparent that production would have to be increased to help keep pace with the ever increasing demand. Some dealers in the south with a single agency were placing firm orders for six machines weekly. It became obvious that the Mornington Works could never hope to meet the increased production rate necessary to fulfil these orders and so it was agreed to raise additional capital so that new premises could be acquired. The principal subscribers were A. G. G. Walker of the Bradford wool trade and George Douglas, then Managing Director of the Bradford Dyers Association. Adolphous Philipp and Eric Myers sold their shares and as a result of the reconstruction, the Scott Engineering Company went public, with a share capital of £100,000. A large plot of land was acquired at Hirstwood, Shipley, for the erection of the buildings that would constitute the new factory.

Meanwhile, attention was being devoted to the three Scott entries in the A-CU Six Days Trial, an important annual event that was to be held this year in the Taunton area towards the middle of August. The three riders were Frank Philipp, J. Norman 'Fluffy' Longfield and Jesse Baker, all on 3¾ hp solos. The latter two were officially classified as private owners and it is fortunate that Baker had recovered from his accident sufficiently well to take part. The event was notorious for the severity of the route and for the inclement weather that made conditions even worse. The climb of Porlock Hill in the wet, on the final day of the event, was a typical example. Jesse Baker won Dr Iles's prize for the best performance on the slow hill climbs, which represented a departure from his normal 'flat out' approach as mentioned in the preceding Chapter. He also won a Gold Medal. Frank Philipp did even better, with the award of a Gold Medal plus fifty bonus marks, whilst Norman Longfield was also awarded a Gold Medal, thus completing the success of the Scott trio. The Team Prize, however, went to their local rivals, P and M of Cleckheaton, near Bradford, who had a better aggregate of marks.

It was during October that a small and somewhat amusing incident occurred. It applies to Harry Langman, who's name was later destined to become synonymous with the name Scott. As a young lad, mad keen on motorcycles, he had joined the Company earlier in the year as an assistant to Alex Dovener, the Company Secretary. Although engaged in general office duties, none brought him into close contact with the actual machines and it was whilst he was searching for such an opportunity that he became aware that the labourer who was employed to push the completed machines from the Works to Bradford Forster Square station was very partial to a drop of ale! One afternoon, he took advantage of the labourer's weakness and offered to buy him a drink which he could consume whilst he (Langman) pushed the bike to the station. The offer was accepted with alacrity and no sooner had Langman moved out of sight of the Works than he pushed down a side street, removed all the wrappings and filled up with petrol and oil for a crafty ride, planning to re-wrap and deliver the Scott at the conclusion of his illicit run. Unhappily his plans went awry. He had the misfortune to hit a wall, damaging the Scott and breaking his collarbone. The dreadful truth became known and Harry's father had to find £14 to meet the repair bill, a quite considerable amount of money at that time. Harry faced an interview with the Directors and was severely admonished by Alfred Scott, who secretly was highly amused by the whole episode! Langman's enthusiasm did not pass undetected and he was allowed to clean Scott's personal machine on Saturdays. Later, he entered the works as an apprentice and commenced an association with the Scott that was to continue throughout his whole riding career.

Details of the 1913 models were announced just prior to the 1912 Show at Olympia, held towards the end of November. Detail improvements included the abolition of the water cooled cylinder head since Scott was convinced the area around the sparking plug was over-cooled. In place of the shapely aluminium alloy head, the water jacket cavities were sealed off by means of two circular plates which were clamped down by two threaded lock rings. The tops of the cylinders were threaded to receive these rings. The oil filler cap was repositioned under the nose of the XL-All saddle, oil now being contained in the seat tube, and as a result of the new rexine covering for the centre section of the petrol tank, the two silver 'Two-Stroke' lines were eliminated. The tail pipe from the exhaust expansion chamber terminated in a short, squat silencer. As in 1912, the 3¾ hp model was priced at 65 guineas.

A curious exhibit on the stand was a solo 3¾ hp model fitted with a Laird-Menteyne machine gun. John Bryan's cartoon in *Motor Cycling* dated 3rd December 1912 suggested the Scott management had overlooked the opportunity to attract even more attention to their exhibits by not arranging the machine gun to take pot shots at the Indian brave's head effigy on the nearby Indian stand. The cartoon depicts the Scott petrol tank with a slot in the top to act as the receiver for a penny a shot, money back if a direct hit is recorded! The machine to which the gun was fitted differed from the other models on display in having water-cooled cylinder heads.

The machine gun project was the outcome of an attempt to interest the War Department in an armed motorcycle, following a series of tests carried out at Brooklands earlier in the year. Although the Army were slow in realising the potential of the motorcycle under active service conditions, the

The solo Scott fitted with a Laird Menteyne machine gun that was exhibited at the 1912 Olympia Show

gathering of war clouds in Europe had instilled the need to mobilise those who would offer the services of both themselves and their machines, should the occasion arise. Appeals for volunteers were made during the year and several trial mobilisations were staged, to check the general effectiveness of the scheme. Apart from this approach, the Army staged its own demonstrations with several manufacturers and appointed observers at many of the principle motorcycle events. Two observers were present at the 1912 TT and it would seem probable that Harry Bashall's win in the Junior event influenced the decision to purchase a vast number of Douglas motorcycles for use by dispatch riders during the Great War.

The Laird-Menteyne machine gun had a long magazine that projected downwards and only a machine with an open frame such as the Scott would permit full lock traverse without the magazine encountering a frame tube. In action, a special front stand lifted the front wheel clear of the ground and permitted the gun to be swung through the full handlebar lock, after it had been released from the lug on the steering head that locked it rigidly, barrel downwards. The gun itself weighed only 16 lbs, was air cooled and would fire at a rate of 220 rounds per minute. It was manufactured by the Coventry Ordnance (Cammell Laird) who had selected a Scott as the most suitable carrier as a result of its measure of success in the nearby Newnham Hill Climbs.

The other exhibit of note was a sidecar chassis that weighed only 38 lbs, the design briefly mentioned by Alfred Scott when he was interviewed during May at a Bradford hill climb by a *Motor Cycling* staffman. It was catalogued as the 'Myers' model and although displayed on the Scott stand, it was marketed by Eric Myers of Bradford, who had left the Company to establish his own Scott agency. This was the chassis design covered by British Patent 1387 granted to Alfred Scott at the beginning of the year, as mentioned earlier in this Chapter.

By the end of the year, almost 550 machines had been produced at the Mornington Works, an increase of some 250 machines over the 1911 production accentuated mainly by the 1912 Senior TT win.

Early in 1913, the Company moved to their new single storey factory at Hirstwood, Saltaire, a site close to Shipley alongside the then Midland Railway and with Baildon moor as the backdrop. The total work force was just under sixty.

Although the 1912 TT races had gone well, despite the manufacturers' ban and the initial objections raised by the Manx authorities, the Tynwald Court again made reference to the noisy behaviour of the visitors and the desecration of the Sabbath. After a lengthy debate, it was agreed that the roads would again be closed for racing. More stringent regulations were drafted to ensure no motor vehicles would use the roads on the Sunday preceding the races, that no motorcycling would be allowed on the promenades at Douglas, Peel and Ramsey, and that no passengers were to be carried in the towns. Furthermore, it was made compulsory for all motorcyclists to register on landing and to give the name of their club. They had also to ensure their machine was fitted with an efficient silencer. And so, it seemed, the whole future of the Isle of Man TT was in the balance.

This year, an innovation by the Auto-Cycle Union changed the whole pattern of both the Junior and Senior races. In order to subject the competing machines to an even more exhaustive test, it was decided to increase the total number of laps to six and seven respectively. It was appreciated that this would make even heavier demands on the physical endurance of the riders and no doubt as a result of a race fatality that had occurred during 1912, the two races were to be spread over two days. Competitors would cover three laps on the first day before they were flagged off and their machines stored under A-CU observation until each race was re-started two days later, in order of finishing. No repair work or even refuelling was permitted until the rider re-started at his allocated time.

The list of entries, published at the end of April, showed that Scott had submitted four entries, with only two named riders, Frank Applebee and Percy Butler, the latter of whom had previously been associated with the Triumph marque. Frank Philipp was not able to take part because he was still recuperating from an accident. J. Norman Longfield was nominated in his place, in view of his already considerable experience as a Scott works rider. It was largely through Longfield that H. O. 'Tim' Wood was selected as the fourth rider — a very wise choice as it subsequently transpired. But the names of these latter two riders were not officially disclosed until practice commenced.

Tim Wood was employed in the capacity of Foreman Tester at the Scott works and had achieved an enviable reputation for his riding ability. Longfield was quick to perceive his potential to the team and made the recommendation to Alfred Scott. In typical fashion, Scott took Tim Wood for a weekend's trial at speed on the Yorkshire roads, whereupon Wood's exceptional riding ability was only too apparent, especially on the more twisty sections. Scott was impressed and after further tests, Wood was appointed fourth member of the Scott team. As a matter of interest, his nickname was given at Bradford Technical College, where he was educated, to distinguish him from his brother 'Splinters'. Hence the abbreviation to Tim, by shortening 'Timber'!

Basically, the machines were similar to those entered the year previous. An improved rotary valve was fitted and a new type of throttle, according to comments in the motor cycling press. Gear ratios were 3 : 1 and 4½ : 1. Although the cylinder heads were again air cooled, the single sparking plugs that projected from the rear were encased in a water jacket. Externally, the 1913 TT models were not far removed in appearance from the standard production models, a move much in keeping with Scott's principles.

Practice passed without any serious mishaps, although Longfield had the misfortune to drop his machine at Kirk Braddan, damaging it rather badly. Wood scared the spectators at Quarter Bridge when he approached too fast on one occasion and seemed as though he would ride right through them! On the last day of practice, Longfield turned out in a sidecar outfit, in order to 'learn the course'. He had injured his arm in the previous day's incident.

Senior race day on Wednesday, June 4th, was hot and sunny. The riders provided a colourful sight as they lined up for the start at Woodlands; in addition to the numbers on each machine, the Senior event riders wore red waistbands and carried their numbers on their back. Some riders, notably those of the Rover and Triumph teams, wore coloured leathers, a striking contrast to the brown or black colours that were used predominantly in the past. The Scott riders were clad in purple leathers.

Sharp at 12.30, Frank Applebee set off on his Scott. As last year's winner, he was permitted to start first in the Senior event. For once the weather was on the riders' side, with brilliant sunshine encouraging high speeds. Yet at the end of the first lap, not one of the four Scott entries was on the leader board. Fortunately, the situation improved dramatically by the time the second lap was completed. Some very spirited riding by Tim Wood carried him into second place, only a matter of some four seconds behind Manxman Tom Sheard on his Rudge. On the next and final lap of the first day, Wood established a new lap record of 52.12 mph, which put him in the lead by the slender margin of 4 seconds. Such was the pace that Sheard dropped back into seventh place. The challenge now came from F. Bateman, a young rider who was one of the Rudge works team. No mention was made in the race reports of the fate of either Longfield or Butler, both of whom were experiencing plug troubles. Glowing reports of Wood's riding ability flowed in from all round the course. His ability to corner at seemingly impossible speeds and with such confidence was the talking point of the day.

When the second day's racing was resumed on the Friday, weather conditions had deteriorated and mist hung low on the mountains as Wood started in number one position at 10.00 am. But all was not well. At Ballacraine, Bateman had passed Wood and was back in the lead. Wood had been forced to stop at the Ramsey depot to take on water and to mend a broken petrol pipe. Later he was forced to stop yet again and bandage a water pipe with insulating tape. A flying stone had cut the water pipe, which accounted for the earlier water shortage. These delays dropped Wood back to fourth place. At the end of lap two, Wood had climbed into third place,

An historic photograph. The start of the second day of the 1913 Senior TT. Nearest the camera is Aubrey Bashall (Douglas) F. Bateman (Rudge) who was killed at the finish, Hugh Mason (N.U.T.) and Tim Wood (Scott) in his purple leathers

A. BASHALL.   F. BATEMAN.   H. MASON.   TIM WOOD.
DOUGLAS   RUDGE   NUT-JAP   SCOTT.

1913 T.T. RACES.

when Alfie Alexander (Indian) dropped back. At the end of the third lap he was first once again, although it was questionable whether he could hold this position. Another Rudge rider, A. R. Abbott, was now presenting a serious challenge and some calculations showed that on the corrected time over the two days, Abbott would retain the advantage if he could finish one minute and forty seconds in front of Wood. And so all eyes were turned towards the two race leaders, who were battling it out to the finish. The first man to appear at the top of Bray Hill was Tim Wood, who finished first on corrected time a mere five seconds ahead of Abbott. Never before had the Senior race been won by such a slender margin. Poor Abbott had the misfortune to let his foot slip off the brake pedal as be braked for Parkfield corner at the top of Bray Hill. The delay before he could turn round and re-start cost him the race. Alfie Alexander finished third, on his Indian, nearly four minutes later. Regrettably, none of the other Scott riders completed the course.

In the post-race interview, Wood seemed to regard his remarkable performance as nothing exceptional. Like the rest of the Scott riders, he had experienced plug troubles and was disappointed that the special twin spark Bosch magnetos ordered for the team had not arrived in time. Alfred Scott had calculated they would add some 5 mph to the maximum speed of the race machines. When in the Island, an attempt had been made to compensate for the missing magnetos by increasing the crankcase compression, enlarging the inlet ports and lapping the cylinder bores out by hand, because the pistons had shown an inclination to seize. The pistons themselves were lighter in weight than those used the year preceding. Perhaps the most surprising statement was that the 1913 TT was the very first competitive event Wood had entered!

This year the meeting ended on a sad note. Poor Bateman crashed at Keppel Gate on the last lap when the deplorable road conditions caused the rear tyre to be wrenched from the wheel rim. He died in Douglas hospital on the Saturday evening, as the result of his injuries.

The Scott advertisement that followed the TT win depicted Tim Wood cornering in typical style with one foot on the road. Two huge wings were attached to the rear of his machine and the simply-worded text read, "Still two years ahead. Wins the Senior Tourist Trophy Race the second year in succession. Also makes fastest lap third year in succession and record for the course".

The next event in which a Scott motorcycle team participated was destined to be another that made history, although for a quite different reason. The event, the 1913 A-CU Six Days Trial, proved to be the most remarkable of the series so far held. The extraordinary road conditions and the severity of the route, to say nothing of the weather, caused the event to end in what amounted to little more than a farce. Many asked whether the event was intended to test the durability of the machines the competitors elected to ride, or the sheer physical endurance of the competitors themselves.

Tim Wood on his way to victory in
the 1913 Senior TT. Note the
appalling condition of the road
surface

The return of the TT winner to
Ramsey. Tim Wood can be picked
out by his riding number; Alfred
Scott is the person wearing a cap,
beside the car

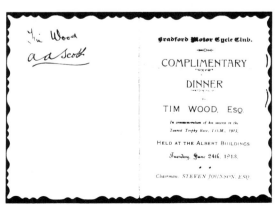

The Menu cover for Tim Wood's
Celebration Dinner given by the
Bradford Motor Cycle Club. Note
the signatures of Tim Wood and
Alfred Scott on the back

THE SCOTT MOTORCYCLE

The Scott team once again comprised Frank Applebee, Jesse Baker and Norman Longfield. Frank Philipp accompanied the trio as a spectator, having not completely recovered from his accident. The event was based on Carlisle and it was not long before competitors became well acquainted with the precipitous declines, walls of rock and mile upon mile of appalling tracks across open country. On the second day Longfield encountered chain troubles, whilst Baker suffered from a number of punctures. In an attempt to make up time, Baker had several spills and was seen riding without either footboard. By now, most competitors were tired and weary, with their machines literally falling apart. There was even talk of a strike when one of the more notorious sections was encountered. Somehow Applebee continued unchecked, to finish in second place and win a Gold Medal — well earned under the conditions that prevailed. Baker and Longfield managed to struggle along to the finish and each qualified for a Bronze Medal. Baker afterwards claimed that his machine, which he collected from the works only a few days before the event, had unhardened gears and a crankcase that was porous with blow holes!

A beautifully restored 1912 model, rebuilt by Stan Greenway of Leamington

At the 1913 Olympia Show, further design improvements were again evident, all of which were incorporated in the models for the 1914 season. They comprised a drip feed lubricator, to obviate the tendency to over-oil as a result of the inability to control the previously used oil pump within fine limits, improved caps to prevent water leakage from the cylinder heads and an oil cup mounted on the right hand side of the rear mudguard to facilitate the lubrication of the two-speed gear. A neat centre stand that pivoted on the front portion of the crankcase casting permitted the front wheel to be lifted clear of the ground, when extended. Heavier gauge forks were specified, with a straight taper and additional rollers to withstand the additional side stresses that originated when a sidecar was attached. A stronger seat pillar tube passed through the rexine-covered petrol tank and a handlebar cross brace was fitted, the handlebars now having a black, celluloid covering. As a legacy from the TT races, the size of the filler caps was increased to three inches in diameter. To help improve rider comfort, the XL-All saddle completed the ensemble. Still priced at 65 guineas, the Scott represented a very sophisticated if somewhat expensive design, more likely to appeal to the rider who considered himself a connoisseur.

Frank Philipp poses for an illustration used in the 1913 catalogue. The registration number embodies the 2 cylinder, 2 stroke, 2 speed slogan

A view of the new Hirstwood factory, Shipley, taken during 1913. Baildon Moor is in the background

It was during January 1914 that a quite casual conversation amongst three Scott employees sparked off the idea for an annual event that was destined to become almost as famous as the Scott motorcycle itself. It occurred when Walter Smith, a native of Birmingham, recounted details of his recent venture into the Yorkshire Dales and the many and varied hazards he encountered when he attempted to reach some of the more remote parts. His two colleagues, Alex Doverner and Charles Suddards, were both Yorkshiremen by birth. Not unexpectedly, Smith's account of his escapades aroused much friendly but ribald comment and when Alfred Scott happened to enter the room, he was soon drawn into the conversation. Unlike most other folk, Scott had an encyclopaedic knowledge of the dales and it was claimed that he had only to follow a route once for it to become engraved indelibly in his memory. He was also aware that very few others were similarly gifted with this ability and that most would be lost immediately they strayed from the main road. He voiced his opinions, which evoked fierce protestations from Smith himself. Scott's retort was that he would organise a cross country event in the same area that would lose the whole entry! And so the Scott Trial was born, an event so well described in the late Philip H. Smith's book *The Greatest of all Trials* that it is pointless to elaborate further. Suffice it to say that the very first event was held on March 15th, covering a ninety mile course that included crossing the river Nidd at Angram and the inevitable climb of Park Rash. Invitations went to all Scott employees and those of Eric Myers' establishment in Bradford. Fourteen employees took part, including Walter Smith. Frank Philipp emerged the winner and the event gained a reputation as being the toughest of all competition events — an event that placed almost unbelievable demands on both man and machine alike.

Frank Philipp crosses the River Nidd like a motor boat during the first Scott Trial held during 1914

Having won two Senior TT races in succession, it was only to be expected that the Scott riders would try for the hat trick. Once again, four entries were made in the 1914 Senior race, Tim Wood, Frank Applebee, Roy Lovegrove and H. V. Prescott, the latter two being new additions to the team. K. J. Bowman, an amateur rider, had also entered on a Scott. It is alleged his mount was Frank Applebee's 1913 TT model, which he had purchased for £10!

When the regulations for the 1914 event were published, it was apparent that further changes in both structure and organisation had again taken place. The Junior and Senior events were to be run as separate events, on the Tuesday and Thursday respectively of the third week in May. Furthermore, the race distance was shortened to five laps for the Junior event and six for the Senior. One of the objections lodged by riders at the conclusion of the 1913 event was that the two-day time schedule prevented them from competing in both events. Furthermore, there was now doubt expressed as to whether much was accomplished from extending the total mileage covered. Most machines had reached the stage where they had the ability to withstand high speeds over comparatively long distances and there was little point in extending the rider fatigue factor, especially in view of the previous year's fatalities. With the occurrences of the previous event in mind, the Auto-Cycle Union decided to make the wearing of some form of protective headwear compulsory. Most of the course was heavily rutted and not unlike a cart track in appearance. Passing was impossible in places and hazardous in others, whilst there was every prospect of encountering wandering sheep on some of the more remote parts of the course! Even worse, if the weather deteriorated, the dust clouds raised by every competitor vanished, to be replaced by another hazard — that of a gradually deteriorating road surface

59

that turned the event into little more than a high speed time trial. Some form of protective riding wear for the competitor was clearly overdue, especially in terms of headwear. In this respect, the A-CU took the initiative, for which they were duly commended.

When entries closed, the A-CU found themselves in a predicament, for they had not been able to find any protective helmet on the market that would match up to their requirements. There was only one answer — to have some helmets made to their own specification and to sell them to those who entered for the 1914 races. And so a helmet priced at just under £1 qualified as being the first in a long series of A-CU approved headwear. Meanwhile, whilst the safety factors were receiving attention that was long overdue, speculation grew in another respect. It had not passed unnoticed that the previously scorned twin cylinder machines were now beginning to demonstrate their advantages, even when they competed on level terms with their four-stroke counterparts. It was anticipated that the 1914 Senior event in particular would prove little short of a needle match, especially since the Rudge singles had suffered such a narrow defeat at the hands of Tim Wood's Scott when their race leader had the misfortune to overshoot on virtually the last corner of the race.

It would, of course, have been easy for Alfred Scott to rest on his laurels and merely make detail improvements to the rotary valve two-strokes that had already proved their superiority with three record laps and two outright wins to their credit. But this was not in his character. Always striving for advancement, he designed and built four entirely new machines that were so revolutionary in concept they merit further detailed description. Some of the features formed the basis of Patent Specifications granted to him during the year.

The machines bore little resemblance to their predecessors in outward appearance. The open frame, always an outstanding feature of the design, was now filled by a two-gallon petrol tank of triangular shape that had slab sides and a horizontal top. A leather tool box was mounted on the top, immediately to the rear of the filler cap. The saddle was mounted on a leaf spring that extended along the machine and pivoted from one of the rear mudguard stays. The front of the spring terminated at a plunger, fitted in the position normally occupied by the saddle pillar. A half-gallon oil tank nestled between the rear mudguard and the petrol tank; a foot operated pump delivered oil to the engine.

The engine was of 486 cc capacity (bore 2¾ inches, stroke 2½ inches) and was constructed along familiar lines, having the customary central flywheel and overhung cranks with their separate crank chambers. But there the similarities ended. Each cylinder was now deeply spigoted into the crankcase and fitted with a detachable, air-cooled head, retained by three studs. Each cylinder had two sparking plugs, one facing forwards and one facing rearwards, in the horizontal plane. They were used in conjunction with the special Bosch magneto that had failed to arrive in time for the

George C. Stewart, of Pocklington, Yorkshire, displays his riding uniform. He was another of the Work's testers

Dick Stansfield, one of the Work's Testers, photographed on Ramsey promenade during 1914

previous year's event. Induction and transfer was controlled by an adaption of the Corliss valve, the valve used on the large steam engines made at the Gloucester factory where Scott had served his apprenticeship. A pivot bearing halfway up the connecting rod formed the elliptical locus for a short connecting link that coupled with the valve, the valve being located in the position normally occupied by the transfer port covers. The connecting link imparted a twisting or oscillating movement to the valve, in an attempt to more closely control the breathing of the engine. By incorporating a rotatable port sleeve, the carburettor was left to run on full throttle, using the sleeve to control engine speed by varying the port timing. A changed piston deflector, now almost symmetrical on both sides, gave a useful increase in compression ratio. The carburettor of Scott's own design was extensively modified and had a conventional throttle slide and housing. It extended rearwards behind the petrol tank, the induction manifold forming part of the frame. A Brown and Barlow float chamber completed the ensemble.

Another departure from standard was the gearbox, built in unit with the engine. Provision was made for either two or three gears, the third being engaged by a handlebar trigger lever which overrode the foot pedal used to select the first two gears. As far as can be ascertained, only a two-speed gear was used in the 1914 Senior TT, giving ratios of 4.7 and 3.3 : 1. The whole gear assembly was eccentrically mounted on plates, which could be rotated within the main engine casting to facilitate chain adjustment. The final drive sprocket was exposed, on the extreme right hand side of the machine. This necessitated mounting the gear change pedal on the left. It is understood that it was Alfred Scott's intention to develop the design as a sidecar model for the 1915 production range, which would explain why the machine was arranged with all adjusting points on the right hand side.

The original design specified twin pannier petrol tanks mounted below hub level, to help keep the centre of gravity of the machine as low as possible. This necessitated pressurising the tanks so that petrol could be fed to the carburettor. In typical fashion, Scott utilised the movement of his leaf spring saddle to good effect. The plunger at the front mounting, mentioned previously, formed part of a pump so that every time the machine hit a bump, the plunger was actuated and pressure built up in the tanks. Eventually this unique system was abandoned in favour of the single, triangular tank with gravity feed, for reasons unknown.

Some of the more notable design features formed the subject of British Patent applications made by Scott. On April 21st 1914, patent rights were duly granted for the use of a frame tube as an induction manifold (British Patent 9877), for his leaf spring saddle (British Patent 9878) and for his oscillating valve (British Patent 9880). The missing number — 9879 — relates to an engine design patent that was subsequently abandoned. Several experimental engines were constructed during this period, some of which had two separate crankcases vertically separated on the centre line and bolted together. Two of these still exist.

Tim Wood pushes off at the start of the 1914 Senior TT

The first week's practice was severely handicapped by bad weather that curtailed high speeds and made the roads treacherous. Fortunately, the weather improved during the second week, leaving riders to contend with the usual clouds of dust. Tim Wood had a bad week, mainly due to dust clogging the oscillating valve mechanism. Somehow he managed to qualify, mainly by swapping number plates with other Scott riders who had somehow managed to keep their machines running. He had one consolation. Since he was due to start first, in recognition of his winning ride of the previous year, he was less likely to encounter the dust thrown up by others.

Displaying his riding number 51, Tim Wood was first man away at 9.30 am on the Thursday morning. The weather was dull, with mist swirling around the mountain, but there was a strong wind and every prospect of the weather improving as the race progressed. Living up to his reputation, Wood completed his first lap at an average speed of 53.3 mph, an absolute record for the course and from a standing start too! His nearest challenger was

John Adamson, one of the Rudge Team who was some two minutes in arrears. As had been expected, the Rudge challenge had been made right from the start and was a foretaste of what was to follow. On the second lap, Wood pulled away still further, giving rise to comments from all round the course about his lurid cornering. Adamson dropped out with a puncture and Harry Collier took up the challenge with his Matchless twin. But Wood maintained his lead whilst Roy Lovegrove pulled up into eighth position.

Disaster struck on lap three, when Wood was forced to make an involuntary stop at Willaston Corner to change a plug. This let Harry Collier into the lead, but not for long. The Matchless developed a misfire on one cylinder too and by the end of the fourth lap, Wood was back in the lead, with almost a minute and a half's advantage over Collier. But for once fate was not on the side of the Scott rider, or for that matter on the side of the Matchless rider either. Wood came to a permanent halt at Union Mills with an oil drenched magneto. Despite the use of two armatures, four slip rings, four pick-up brushes and the ability to provide two sparks per engine revolution, his special Bosch magneto was out of action. Not even the change-over switch on the handlebars could help provide the necessary spark for his Scott to continue. Harry Collier took over the hard fought lead, which ended abruptly a short while afterwards on the same lap when his frame broke at Sulby and cast him off. Lovegrove moved up into sixth position, but he too had his problems and eventually finished eighteenth, just outside Gold Medal time. Frank Applebee took 25th place; Prescott had faded out on lap three for unspecified reasons. At last a member of the Rudge team took the honours, the winner being Cyril Pullin, a young lad of 21 who had finished last in the 1913 Junior event on a Veloce.

After the race, Alfred Scott permitted one of the *Motor Cycling* staffmen to try the new racer on which so many hopes had been pinned. The rider was clearly impressed by the high standard of roadholding and the ease of operating the gears and the foot-controlled oil pump. On paper the Scott should have won, but any race is subject to all manner of unforeseen factors, many of which can never be taken into account, let alone foreseen. By way of consolation, a Scott had once again scored the fastest lap speed for the fourth year in succession, even if the hat trick of three consecutive wins had not been achieved. As the Scott advertisement concluded in the TT Report issue of *Motor Cycling*, "There's nothing to touch a Scott for speed".

It is especially fortunate that parts of one of the actual 1914 TT models have survived and that one enthusiast has been keen enough to construct a replica using these parts, working from some of the original drawings and having many patterns and castings made. This highly commendable project will ensure that one of Scott's more interesting designs is not lost with the passage of time and, more important, some first-hand experience can be gained of the machine's capabilities and general handling characteristics.

The remains of one of the 1914
TT models, as discovered during
1938

Close-up of the remains of one of
the 1914 TT engines. The eccen-
trically-mounted gearbox is clearly
visible as is the housing for the
rotary valve

The next event of any consequence was the A-CU's Six Days Trial, this
year centred on Sheffield. After the debacle of the previous year, it was to be
expected that the event would be less severe, with provision for route
modification if the weather proved particularly uninviting. As luck would
have it, nothing was further from the truth and the event was unparalled in
its severity. Rain fell almost incessantly throughout the entire event and the
climax occurred when close on one hundred and thirty wet and bedraggled
competitors arrived in a downpour to attempt a climb of Litton Slack. In a
very short time, the ascent was strewn with those who had failed, yet to the
amazement of the watching pressmen, Jesse Baker decided to try his luck.
The result was one of the few clean climbs of the day and although the section
was eventually deleted from the results sheet, the incredible performance of
Baker and his Scott did not pass unnoticed. Although the Scott team were
not in the running for the Team Award, Baker won a well deserved Gold
Medal.

THE SCOTT MOTORCYCLE

Fierce controversy followed the publication of the results of the Trial, which in some cases were directed at the way in which the Officials had handled the event. Litton Slack had been deleted from the results sheet because the dispirited competitors had eventually decided to strike. The resultant delay, whilst matters were sorted out, caused nearly everyone to be heavily penalised for lateness at the following check points. In consequence, the hastily amended results stopped little short of a farce. But before the whole future of the Trial was threatened, another event cut short all arguments. On August 4th, Britain declared war on Germany and matters of greater importance assumed precedence.

It may be expected that with the outbreak of war, the production of all motorcycles destined for the civilian market closed. Surprisingly this was not so, for it was not until November 3rd 1916 that the Ministry of Munitions terminated production for the duration. Although Scott soon became involved with the development of military vehicles, he continued working on a very advanced design of machine that embodied features such as an in-line twin cylinder engine, with shaft drive to the rear wheel and the engine unit enclosed completely within a form of bonnet. British Patent 1294 relating to this design was granted on January 26th 1915 and it is particularly unfortunate that the war coupled with Scott's ever increasing interest in military vehicles, curtailed any further developments along these novel and highly unorthodox lines. The existing 3¾ hp model was continued for the 1915 season with only minor modifications that included substitution of an American made magneto for the now unobtainable Bosch design, more deeply valenced mudguards and bushed forks to replace the existing roller type. The retail price escalated to 95 guineas, a sharp increase no doubt resulting from the limited production as the result of other commitments. One report suggested the immediate shortage of magnetos was temporarily overcome by an appeal, in the motor cycling press, for patriotic Scott owners to send the Company magnetos from their own machines which would be replaced as soon as the first deliveries of American (or British) magnetos became available. This ruse enabled the manufacture of military motorcycles to continue unabated whilst several of the larger manufacturers engaged on government contract work had temporarily to call a halt whilst supplies of magnetos were arranged from other sources. Until the outbreak of war, the British motorcycle industry had been almost wholly dependent on the German-made Bosch magneto for the ignition system. It was extremely reliable and gave an intense spark, even at low rotational speeds. The war provided the necessary impetus for British electrical manufacturers to produce their own magnetos and in due course a variety of different makes were available, including the Fellows which became an acceptable substitute for the Bosch magneto previously fitted to the Scott range. In order to bridge the gap, magnetos were imported direct from the USA, and both the Splitdorf and the Dixie were used as the initial substitute, the choice depending on whichever make was available at the time when the need arose.

Another superb restoration of an early model. Derek Cox's 1914 model at one of the Evesham rallies

The Dixie had the distinction of employing a rotating magnet armature, with fixed stator coils, representing a considerable advance in the design of rotating electrical generators that is much in accord with today's theory.

By the end of the year, Scott production had risen to a grand total of some 650 machines, a third of which were destined for military purposes. Production continued at Saltaire, although as subsequent events will show, the continuing rise in production was soon to decline when the manufacture of civilian machines was terminated by the Ministry of Munitions. If the war was to be won, every facet of manufacturing industry had to be deployed in the production of munitions or in other work of national importance.

Consulting Engineer to
The Scott Engineering Co. Ltd

Inventor and Patentee

SCOTT TWO-STROKE

— Motor bicycles.
— Sidecars and Guncarriers.

telephone N° 3957

Alfred A. Scott.

Mechanical Engineer.

DRILL PARADE BELLEVUE,

October 8th 15   BRADFORD.

Dear Charlie

I hope all is going on all right with you. I hear occasionally from Madge about you and others at the front. It looks as though we shall be a long time in getting through with the war and I think some form of conscription will be put in force before the end of the year. I have completed the two machines for the Company and am sending enclosed some photos of N°2 in the unpainted state. N°1 I have here making various alterations to the gun fittings etc. It of course looks quite different to N°2 owing to the arrangements for carrying the gun in both forward & rearward firing positions. I intend to take some photos of it later on. The Company have had it tested with overload for 1000 miles. & altogether it has done 10'000 miles on the road. Lieut Colonel Bradley has had it with his training camp for a week. & the suggestion now is to send it for an extended trial to one of the batteries at the

A letter from Alfred Scott to his brother Charles who was then under active service in France. Note the reference in the letterhead to his capacity as Consulting Engineer to the Scott Engineering Co. Ltd

CHAPTER THREE
Machine gun carriers and gun cars

ALTHOUGH Alfred Scott had exhibited a solo motorcycle fitted with a machine gun at the 1912 Olympia Show, it appeared just a little too early to arouse any deep rooted interest from the War Office. Admittedly the Army had decided to investigate the potential of the motorcycle in future military operations and had appointed two 'official' observers, who were present at the 1912 TT amongst other events. But the Army's involvement with the motorcycle industry was still minimal and not likely to develop until several months later when the first of a series of tests were initiated. It was not until the outbreak of the 1914–18 war that any substantial orders were placed for the acquisition of suitable machines.

Even so, the exercise with the Laird-Menteyne gun had not been in vain. Immediately war was declared, Sir Arthur Dawson, Superintendent of Vickers Ordnance, approached Alfred Scott about the possibility of supplying sidecar outfits that would carry a machine gun and ammunition. The challenge was accepted instantly and in the remarkably short period of three weeks, the first patent for such a machine was granted. The patentees were Scott, Sir Arthur Dawson and a Vickers engineer named Thomas Buckham. The patent, British Patent 19,175, related to an open frame Scott motorcycle, to which a fully triangulated sidecar chassis was attached. Unlike the earlier design, the sidecar chassis formed the machine gun tripod and was constructed to withstand the recoil of the gun, a Vickers machine gun capable of firing 300 rounds a minute. In consequence, the gun was permanently in the firing position, without need to erect a tripod or undertake other preliminaries. A prototype was constructed and taken to London, where it was inspected by none other than Winston Churchill, then First Lord of the Admiralty. He approved, and a contract was placed for 300 Scott outfits, to be divided between the Admiralty and the War Office. The actual requirement was for 200 machine gun carriers and 100 solo machines, for use by dispatch riders.

A second patent, British Patent 20,874, was granted to the same three patentees on October 12th. This related to a machine gun carrier in which the machine gun was controlled by a gunner seated on the 'sidecar' chassis. This arrangement permitted the gun to be operated whilst the outfit was in motion, but only in a forward direction. It was not possible to mount the

Vickers gun so that it would also fire to the rear. On October 19th, British Patent 21,195 was granted, the third and final patent granted to the trio. This patent related specifically to an ammunition carrier. In addition to the rider and passenger (a mechanic and gunner respectively), the outfit was designed to carry 2,250 rounds of ammunition, spare tyres and tubes, four gallons of petrol and one gallon of oil. Provision was also made for the inclusion of tins of calcium carbide for lighting sets, water for the cooling system and a complete set of spare parts for the Scott motorcycle, thereby adding to the already considerable weight of the fully laden outfit. During October, Alfred Scott advertised in the motor cycling press for Scott riders who were willing to enlist in the army. Applicants were requested to write to him direct, giving the relevant personal details. This provided an effective way of selecting riders for some of the military machines he manufactured, whilst at the same time aiding the recruiting drive.

During November three of the first production machine gun carriers were inspected in the grounds of Buckingham Palace by King George V, in company with representatives from the Governments of Britain's allies. The riders on this occasion were Frank Applebee, Norman Longfield and Alfred Scott. Scott was indeed proud of his contribution to the war effort and permitted his own photograph, along with those of the other two riders, to be used in the 1915 Scott catalogue, an unusual departure by the otherwise publicity-shy bachelor. It is alleged that during the demonstration at the Palace, Alfred Scott cornered his own outfit a little too exuberantly and modified one of the Royal flower beds!

Production of the machine gun carriers was well in hand during November. The Motor Machine Gun Service was formed on November 12th 1914, with the objective of adding one battery to every infantry division, the Royal Horse Artillery and the Royal Field Artillery. Each battery was to be composed of 64 men, with six machine gun teams, each team having three motorcycle outfits, one with a gun, one with gun mountings only, and one in the form of a supplies carrier. Six solo riders and six mechanics were to be allocated to each battery, together with nine cars and their drivers.

Training was carried out on War Department land at Bisley, each complete course lasting about a month. It was during these courses and the autumn trials that had preceded them that some of the deficiencies of the machine gun carriers became apparent. Despite the lower gearing employed, no doubt as the result of experience gained by Alex Doverner when he rode a Scott sidecar outfit in the 1914 Scott Trial, the full load had a very adverse effect on performance. Furthermore, as mentioned earlier, the Vickers machine gun could be fired in a forward direction only; if it was desired to fire upwards, such as in action against enemy aircraft, one of the armoured shields had to be removed first in order to gain the necessary traverse. This, in turn, afforded the rider and gunner less protection. The machine itself was vulnerable too, with no protection for the radiator, itself a delicate component.

The three different types of sidecar outfit supplied for military service. The OHMS registration mark is unusual

A Scott Motor Machine Gun Unit passing along a road in France during 1915

THE SCOTT MOTORCYCLE

One of the Motor Machine Gun outfits in action with the gun shield partly removed

Low temperatures presented an additional hazard. There is record of one instance where about forty outfits were left overnight in a marquee, without the cooling system being drained. There was a hard frost that night and in the morning all the outfits were rendered immobile by cracked blocks. As yet, none of the outfits had encountered the dreadful Flanders mud, which would stop almost any vehicle. Even wet pave would promote the most awful skids.

The reasons why the machine gun carriers had fallen short of their expectations in several respects were only too apparent to Alfred Scott. He withdrew completely from the problems of the day, in order to pursue an entirely new line of approach, commencing on a project that was to pre-occupy him to such an extent that it marked the turning point in his career and in his association with motorcycle design. Although production of the machine gun carriers continued as planned, Scott now dissociated himself entirely from this activity, with the result that the design became standardised. He also abandoned work on the civilian models and on the novel 'in line' model that never progressed beyond the patent stage. Instead, he devoted his energies to another method of solving the machine gun carrying problem, this time based on a highly unorthodox three wheel vehicle that had the wheel configuration of the conventional sidecar outfit. His basic objective was to design a much more robust vehicle that had better suspension and was therefore better able to negotiate rough terrain. Good manoeuvrability, more power and the need for an absolute minimum of maintenance formed an awesome combination of attributes that could not be met satisfactorily by what was virtually a heavily laden motorcycle and sidecar. In other words, he realised that it was necessary to design a vehicle expressly for the purpose of carrying a machine gun and ammunition and that it was not good enough to adapt an existing vehicle with the risk of inheriting some of the existing shortcomings that may not be too apparent in the early stages. Once again he sat down at his drawing board, working late into the evenings originating his own drawings.

Scott's reasons for reverting to a three wheel cycle car design were quoted in detail some two years later, at the time when he decided to market a civilian version of the gun car. Having already pioneered the triangulated mode of frame construction, in which the tubes are subjected to only direct compression or tension, it was only to be expected that he would apply the same principle in three wheel design, to which this mode of construction lends itself extremely well. The Scott motorcycle frame and that of his sidecar chassis comprised a series of triangles and it is an acknowledged fact that a triangle is much stronger than any other design, weight for weight. No amount of overloading will cause the tubes to buckle; only when the stress imposed is sufficient to compress a tube endwise or tear it in two, is the breaking point reached.

To the uninitiated, it may seem that tricycle construction, with two wheels at the rear and one wheel at the front, arranged in the form of a triangle, offers the best prospects, especially in terms of stability. But in practice this is not so. A vehicle having this type of wheel layout is difficult to balance and steer at high speeds, and presents problems with regard to weight distribution when the power unit is added. Furthermore, it is necessary to adopt the transmission layout of a conventional four-wheeler. On the other hand, the virtues of the sidecar outfit have been extolled many times, for it is an inescapable fact that when the steering wheel is more or less in line with the driving wheel, the full castor wheel advantage of motorcycle steering can be used to maximum effect. In consequence, if the wheel configuration of the sidecar outfit is applied to a three wheel design, such as in Scott's gun car, the manoeuvrability of the sidecar outfit is retained despite the somewhat odd looking appearance of the vehicle. The gun car would, in fact, turn in a circle without the 'sidecar' wheel moving, an important advantage in the case of a military vehicle.

Weight was no problem either. The chassis framework of the gun car weighed less than the framework of a Scott sidecar outfit, whilst the engine and gearbox complete with accessories such as the magneto and radiator etc weighed some 20 lbs less than a 6 hp four-stroke engine, similarly equipped. It could not even be argued that the single driving wheel placed the gun car at a disadvantage when compared with the two wheel drive of a car. Apart from the significant saving in production costs, the fully loaded gun car had an overall weight far below that of a corresponding four-wheeler, probably nearer one half. As a result, the driving wheel had less work to do and carried less weight.

As work progressed, Scott became a frequent and often unpopular visitor on the shop floor, where he caused problems by interfering with the production line in order to get parts made for his prototype design. It was difficult to refuse a request from the boss, especially when he was regarded with affection by all his employees. Nonetheless, there was a war to be won and the Company had to meet its production deadlines. Something had to give and the situation was often tense. Eventually Scott took the hint and on his own initiative acquired some premises at the rear of Eric Myers' Bradford premises. Early in the new year, he moved out of the Saltaire factory, to set up his own experimental workshop. Although in some respects the move seemed of little consequence, in view of his preoccupation with the gun car project, it marked the severance of his career as a motorcycle manufacturer. Possibly even Scott himself was not fully aware of the significance of this diversion at the time when it occurred. In characteristic manner he was so deeply absorbed in the gun car project that he devoted all his energies to it, excluding almost everything else.

His first gun car patent was applied for on December 14th 1914, convincing proof of the pace at which he worked. Seven more patents were granted during 1915 and only one was abandoned. It is alleged the gun car was designed down to the smallest detail in a period of less than eight weeks, during which time the construction of the prototype neared completion! Unhappily, not a single photograph or drawing of the original prototype appears to have survived. In consequence, it is necessary to refer to the original Patent Specification and drawing of 1914 (British Patent 24,045) to obtain a full description.

The general appearance of the chassis, as exemplified by the drawings that accompany the patent specification, confirm the whole design concept is indeed unorthodox, although highly ingenious. Designed as a built-in-one three wheeler, the wheel arrangement was virtually that of the conventional sidecar outfit, with two wheels at the rear and the front wheel in line with the rear offside wheel. This gave the vehicle an unmistakable lopsided appearance, not unlike a four-wheeler with the front nearside wheel missing. The chassis was low slung and had the engine and gearbox mounted in line with the two offside wheels, forming an integral part of the construction. The chassis was constructed from a number of steel tubes fitted with eyelet ends, arranged in a series of triangulated structures. The tubes bolted together and in accord with Scott's reasoning were subjected to only compressive or tensional stresses. The wheels were dished heavily and were supported on stub axles. They were fully enclosed by discs and could be interchanged at will. The problem of steering was resolved by attaching a pin at the same angle as a steering head, at the apex of the forward projecting triangulated structure. The front wheel rotated on a long horizontal spindle attached to the pin at right angles, which was actuated by a conventional steering box, bell crank and drag link arrangement. Suspension was provided by coil springs throughout, arranged in pairs so that one pair would act as shock absorbers for the others. This permitted each rear wheel some 4 - 5 inches of vertical movement. The front wheel retained the castor effect of the conventional sidecar outfit by having the coil springs arranged in a form to replace what would otherwise have been regarded as the forks. Shackle pins attached to the rear axle restrained all sideways movement. Lateral rigidity was achieved by forming a three point attachment with three separate radius rods. One was the propeller shaft casing, between the bevel box and the engine. Shaft drive was employed for transmitting the power to the rear wheel, an advantage bestowed by the in-line engine arrangement. Driver and passenger were seated between the two rear wheels, in a form of canvas or leather link 'hammock' attached to the upper and lower horizontal cross tubes.

The design of the engine unit, a twin cylinder two-stroke that embodied many of Scott's already well-proven features, represented a further step forward in the development of this type of engine. Although similar in many respects to the motorcycle engines, there were nevertheless some differences that were readily apparent. Most obvious was the use of separate cylinders, to facilitate ease of removal without having to break numerous joints. The crankcase top formed a manifold chamber in respect of both the transfer and exhaust functions. No induction passages were required because rotary inlet valves were used, one on each crankcase cover. Water cooling passages to the lower part of the block were, however, included. A total of five patents relating to the gun car were applied for on January 26th 1915. Two of these (British Patents 1290 and 1292) related to engine design, the induction valve and the quickly detachable cylinder barrel respectively. The other three (British Patents 1291, 1293 and 1294) covered the friction band clutch, the countershaft three-speed gearbox and the general engine and chassis layout. An earlier patent (British Patent 1019) was abandoned. This almost certainly related to the lever-type hand starter that was operated by pulling from within the car.

Viewed in some detail, the rotary valve patent (1290) related to a rotating sleeve design, integral with the crankcase cover. The rotating sleeve was mounted on the outside of a fixed sleeve and had a disc formed on one end, adjacent to the crankcheek in order to reduce the crankchamber volume. This disc was slotted to engage with a head on the crankpin end, to impart a rotary motion. Ports were cut in both the fixed and rotating sleeves, which coincided when they faced upwards, towards the underside of the piston. The outer edge of the inner sleeve had a flange that formed a joint with the crankcase cover, its inner periphery at that end having a spherical seating. This seating mated with a similar seating formed on the end of the induction pipe. Held by a simple, single bolt fixing, this arrangement obviated the need for accurate alignment of the long induction pipe, whilst at the same time preserving the essential gastight joint. The horizontal portion of the induction pipe connected both valves to the single carburettor. It should be mentioned, however, that although the single bolt fixing provided easy access to the working parts, it left no margin for error in the case of the ham-fisted owner, who could so easily overtighten it.

Each cylinder had bore and stroke dimensions of 76.2 x 63.5 mm (3 in x 2.5 in) giving the engine a capacity of 578 cc. Unlike the motorcycle engine that had the same bore size but a stroke that was 1/8 inch less, double row ball journal bearings supported the overhung cranks on either side of the flywheel and were used also for the big ends. Originally, it had been planned to use an adjustable drip feed for lubricating the engine and this was the system applied to the first gun car made. It was soon found that petroil lubrication was more effective, however, especially with regard to the lubrication of the rotary valves. A 1 in 32 mixture was used for the lubrication of the two gun cars that followed, another move towards the desired objective of simplicity in design and operation. Ignition was provided by twin sparking plugs arranged vertically in each cylinder head. Each pair of plugs was connected in series, an arrangement made necessary because one of the pair had both electrodes insulated. This made possible the use of a conventional twin cylinder magneto; obviously Scott had learned much about twin spark systems from his earlier experiences with his TT motorcycles. Because it was impracticable to employ a kickstarter, a lever-type handle starter was mounted in unit with the crankcase. A quadrant gear actuated by the lever engaged with a skew cut pinion on an auxiliary shaft, a shaft which also drove the water circulation pump and the magneto.

One of the 1915 prototype Guncars with the engine cover removed

A particularly unusual feature was the braking system. Initially the brakes on the rear wheels were interconnected, but it was soon found that when the throttle was closed the engine exercised an additional braking effect on the rear wheel alone, which was particularly noticeable on the overrun, when descending long hills. In consequence, the gun car showed a disconcerting tendency to drift to the right. Later versions of the original gun car had a modified braking system in which the rear driving wheel brake was operated independently, the 'sidecar' wheel having a footbrake and the rear driving wheel a handbrake. Anyone driving a gun car for the first time very soon learned that sudden application of the footbrake alone provoked an unforgettable experience, which was unlikely to be repeated again!

The original gun car had no bodywork and presented a curious sight when it was driven in and around Bradford. Comments by the local citizens were both forthright and ribald. One of the gun car testers was Tim Wood, recalled from army service on account of his mechanical skills. Whilst he subjected the original gun car to rigorous testing over some of the more rugged and remote parts of the county, two further models were constructed. They differed in some respects from the prototype. For example, a more positive method of wheel attachment was adopted after Wood had experienced the loss of a wheel whilst on test! Outwardly, the most noticeable difference was the adoption of metal panels to protect the occupants, and the fitting of what was virtually a form of chain mail seating, the subject of another of Scott's patents (British Patent 4146, applied for on March 16th 1915). It related to the use of interlaced rings, made of either leather or fabric. Other modifications related to the mountings for the machine gun, which would permit firing to the front and rear, and a reversible seat for the gunner.

The second and third gun cars to be constructed were submitted to the War Office for testing. Meanwhile, Scott was finding his small experimental workshop had outlived its usefulness and had not the capacity for the quantity production of gun cars, should the much hoped-for contract be awarded. Towards the end of the year he found a three-storey building, originally a Victorian school house, just off Manningham Lane. In many respects this was an ideal location, so he purchased the building and acquired some new machine tools to supplement those transported from the experimental workshop. He also brought with him the small but highly skilled band of craftsmen who had helped him produce the first three gun cars. He named the premises Springfield Works, after the passageway that connected the premises with Springfield Place, in Manningham Lane.

At the end of the year, production of Scott motorcycles had reached the all-time record of 804. This was quite apart from the other contributions made to the war effort since the Saltaire factory were also manufacturing munitions and precision tools such as limit gauges.

Alas, the anticipated War Office contract for gun cars never materialised. It was withheld, it is alleged, because the officials empowered to award the contract realised that production would be costly, complicated and slow —

Two of the prototype Guncars under test by the Army

not the best of attributes by any means. Even Scott's newly acquired premises had insufficient space for the manufacture of gun cars in numbers of any significance. His luck had run out, for the time being at any rate.

The failure to secure a War Office contract for the gun cars enabled Alfred Scott to release details of his novel design to the press, albeit in the form of a civilian version. Many already knew the true identity of the unmarked gun cars because Tim Wood had been observed at the wheel on a number of occasions and there could be no doubt as to whom he showed allegiance! Others, less kindly, ventured that no one other than Scott could have perpetrated such an unconventional and curious looking design.

As mentioned earlier in this Chapter, the first full description of the new three wheeler was published in *Motor Cycle* dated July 28th 1916. The week following, Scott gave his reasons for adopting certain design features in an article entitled *Why Three Wheels?* Although there was no hope of producing a civilian version of the gun car until after hostilities had ceased, he had little doubt about its potential when the war with Germany was over. He had already modified one of the gun cars by attaching civilian bodywork and had given the vehicle the name Sociable. After all, what could be more sociable than the driver and passenger sitting close to each other, side by side, in direct contrast to the sidecar passenger, who was separated from the driver of the outfit both physically and conversation-wise.

As may be expected, the initial announcement about the Sociable produced a considerable volume of enquiries. Some wished to place a firm order for a Sociable as soon as the first production models became available, no matter how long they waited. One person even offered to visit the Bradford Works and purchase a machine on the spot, to drive home. However, not all the letters brought forth praise. A private motorist of some ten years experience described the Sociable as horrible, when he referred to the external appearance. Scott himself once referred to the Sociable as 'The Mouth Expander', based on his observations of the facial expressions of innocent bystanders who saw one of these three wheelers approaching. Initially, a look of complete surprise appeared on the person's face, which would slowly change until the corners of the mouth turned up into a grin! Like everyone else, Scott was only too well aware that such a highly unconventional layout does not lend itself readily to aesthetic appearance.

Interest in the Sociable design was by no means confined to the UK. The November 1916 issue of *Scientific American* had a front cover drawing of two Sociables with a typical English thatched cottage in the background. It carried the caption 'A Motor Car for the Multitude — a recent development of the Motor Cycle'. The article within highlighted the principle advantages of Scott's unique design and even dismissed unfavourable comments about its appearance by claiming that many a novel creation has been slow to gain recognition until folk have become accustomed to its appearance. The analogy between the appearance of the horse drawn vehicles of some twenty years previous and that of the 'modern' motor car was quoted as an example.

R. Norman Scott in a Bean car alongside a Scott Sociable on the Scottish moors

THE SCOTT MOTORCYCLE

On November 3rd 1916, the Ministry of Munitions terminated the production of civilian vehicles for the duration. The war was dragging on and had reached a state of stalemate, whilst the valiant British Expeditionary Force had already taken a beating. From now on, munitions production was to have full priority and the Scott factory was no exception. Soon the machine shop at the Scott Engineering Company was running at full capacity. Only some 20 motorcycles were made during the year because the Admiralty and the Army contracts had been completed and were not renewed. Apart from munitions, the Company also manufactured limit gauges for Vickers Limited. This is the instrument that forms a background to the familiar Scott insignia, a constant reminder of the Company's war effort and of the precision with which the Scott motorcycle is constructed. The failure to secure the anticipated gun car contract and the death of his elder brother Charles, a Lieutenant Colonel in the 6th Yorkshire Regiment who had an interest in the Scott works, made 1916 a bad year for Alfred Scott. His brother was mortally wounded in action at Camiers and died during the month of July, one of a vast number who sacrificed their lives in the mud and desolation of the French battlefields.

Another Government contract accounted for the production of a further 80 Scott motorcycles during 1917 — the total motorcycle production for that year. Munitions work now took complete priority; there was no question of manufacturing machines other than under Government contract.

During the year, Alfred Scott started work on a number of design projects at his new premises off Manningham Lane. The most ambitious was a four cylinder uniflow scavenge engine that was intended for use in light aircraft and it is fortunate that the drawings have survived, for few of these wartime projects reached fruition. We are particularly indebted to the late Philip H. Smith, who described this engine in detail in his book *The High Speed Two-Stroke Petrol Engine*, first published by G. T. Foulis in 1965.

Basically, the engine took the form of a compact four cylinder water cooled two-stroke, with rocking beam crankshaft drive, that was capable of producing 15 bhp at 2,000 rpm. In essence, it resembled a box having a vertical cylinder at each corner. The crankshaft was set across the top of the box, driven by two connecting rods actuated by what is best described as rocking beams joined at each pair of pistons by short links. Each rocking beam had forked ends and was integral with a sleeve, the other end of which was attached to what may be likened to a half rocker arm, also with a forked end. The forked ends of the rocking beam contained the bearing that formed the link between each pair of pistons and the forked end of the rocker arm contained the bearing that joined with the small end of one of the two connecting rods. The beam and rocker assembly was duplicated, both assemblies running on a common shaft that ran along the base of the box. A two-throw crankshaft was arranged so that when the pistons attached to one rocking beam were at mid-stroke, the other pair were at the top and bottom of their stroke, respectively. This arrangement permitted the engine to fire every 90° of crankshaft rotation. Each cylinder was isolated at its base and the rocking beam was sealed at its fulcrum, thereby providing a pumping chamber below each piston. The piston itself contained a filler, to further reduce the volume of the pumping chamber. The reason for the pumping chamber will be apparent later on. An air receiver, isolated from the centre section of the box, was located between adjacent cylinders. A rotary inlet valve on each side controlled the air flow between the centre of the box and the air receiver, the main air intake being located at the top of the centre section and following a somewhat complicated route that had been planned to initiate centrifugal action.

The rotary inlet valves ensured that air was drawn under each piston on the upstroke and pumped into the adjacent cylinder on the downstroke, an arrangement that caused the air receiver to be charged twice per revolution and pressurised to a maximum of approximately 7 psi. Two additional rotary valves, mounted adjacent to the pairs of cylinder heads, communicated with the inlet valves immediately above. When an inlet valve opened to transfer air under pressure to the valve immediately above, a portion of the air was routed via separate ducts in the valve rotor to a fuel vapouriser, which charged it with the correct fuel/air ratio. The exhaust gases were discharged by means of a ring of exhaust ports that encircled each cylinder at the bottom of the stroke. The basic objective of the design was to utilise a scavenge air flow to separate the exhaust and inlet charges. After the exhaust gases had been expelled, a charge of air only to scavenge the cylinder, followed in turn by the fuel/air mixture. Two versions of the engine were planned, one of 650 cc and the other 800 cc. The design progressed to the stage where several parts were made for the construction of a prototype engine, such as the crankcase, main box casting, rocking beams and cylinder liners. Unfortunately it would appear that the Sociable engine then claimed priority and the project never progressed to the stage where it would have received the greater acclaim it undoubtedly merited.

No motorcycles at all were produced during 1918 and it was with deep relief that at last the war ended during November when Germany surrendered. But it was not until January 1919 that the Ministry of Munitions gave the motorcycle industry permission to resume production of civilian machines, opening another chapter in the history of the motorcycle when both design trends and the very nature of the market itself were to undergo radical change.

George Stewart performing acrobatics on a Scott during 1915

CHAPTER FOUR
The end of an era

An early Scott advertisement, typical of the approach used during the twenties

WHEN THE production of motorcycles for the civilian market recommenced in January 1919, only a handful of manufacturers had new designs to offer. Those who were in this fortunate position (and Alfred Scott was one) adapted designs originally intended for military use. The origin of the Scott Sociable is but one example of how a wartime development that failed to reach fruition was successfully translated into something new, which it was hoped would appeal to civilian buyers after the war was over. Without authorisation and seemingly quite illegally, Scott had fitted one of his experimental gun cars with a passenger carrying body when he realised that the anticipated War Department contract might not materialise.

THE SCOTT MOTORCYCLE

After the enforced shortage of machines as a result of the war, there now existed a seller's market, which was met only in part by the many ex-WD models released by the armed forces. With the level of demand still unsatisfied, prices rode high and some reconditioned military models sold at £90 or more. Of the few new models that became available, most manufacturers had been content to pick up the threads where they left off in 1916 so that they could get back into production as early as possible. The models they now offered were little more than replicas of their pre-war designs, although they sold at greatly inflated prices. And, if the prospective buyer was able to meet the purchase price, some of the more unscrupulous dealers added their own surcharge, in the form of a non-returnable booking fee to ensure early delivery.

Although during recent years Alfred Scott had given his undivided attention to his three wheelers and had virtually ex-communicated himself from the Saltaire Works, he was nonetheless still a Director of the Scott Engineering Company. This was reflected in his letterheads, in which he described himself as Consulting Engineer to the motorcycle company. Sooner or later the complete break had to occur and it was during December 1918 that Scott took the plunge. He sold out for £55,000 so it is alleged, in conjunction with his brothers. As a result, some reorganisation of the motorcycle company was necessary and on December 21st a new Board of Directors was appointed, headed by two Chartered Accountants. Reginald Arthur Vinter was elected Chairman, his fellow directors being his brother Charles Edward and an engineer named F. J. Allen. A third member of the Vinter family, Norman Odell, became Sales Manager. Of the original subscribers, only Bradford wool magnate A. G. G. Walker retained his interest. Only a few weeks later, on January 13th 1919, Alfred Scott formed the Scott Autocar Company Limited with a capital of £30,000 in £1 shares. £21,000 worth of these shares were held by Scott himself, his brother Herbert and Cuthbert Tunstall, the person appointed Works Manager. He had asked Charles Suddards to join him, but Charles preferred to remain faithful to the motorcycle. Manufacture of the Scott Sociable was at last to become a reality, in newly acquired premises at Lidgett Green, Bradford. Scott purchased the premises, an old building previously occupied by the London Small Arms Company, and the ex-WD machine tools therein.

One of the first employees to return to the motorcycle company after the war was Harry Langman, who was duly joined by Walter Clough to work together in the erecting shop. To most manufacturers it was a slow business getting back into production and the Scott Engineering Company was no exception. Many months were to pass before new Scott motorcycles were to be seen on the roads. On June 16th 1919 some further company reorganisation took place. A new company, known as the Scott Motor Cycle Company Limited was formed to take over the assets of the old company, by raising a share capital of £100,000. Matthew Roley was appointed General Manager, Charles Suddards, Works Manager, and Tim Wood, Racing Manager.

Harold and Willie Wood with a Sociable at Bluehills Mine during one of the classic long distance trials

The address and the general objectives of the company remained unchanged.

Competition events were resumed during the year and two major events in which Scott motorcycles competed with success were the 1919 Scott Trial and the A-CU Six Days Trial. The Scott Trial is worthy of special mention because after the first event in 1914, it was thrown open to allcomers and no longer restricted to those who were Scott employees or closely associated with the marque. This tough trial was run over an 84 mile course, with the organisation entrusted to Norman Vinter, aided by Nellie Suddards, who had joined the company as his Secretary. Vinter made extensive use of arrowed cards for marking the route and it is particularly interesting to note that the colours he used to denote the direction to be followed are still used by trials organisers today. The trial started from the Red Lion at Burnsall and attracted a total of 74 entries.

Although the event was won by an ex-WD dispatch rider's mount, a chain-cum-belt model H Triumph ridden by Geoffrey Hill, Scott riders figured in the results list. J. E. Walker won the Amateur Award and a team comprised of Leslie Guy, Harry Langman and Clarrie Wood took the Team Award. The Amateur Team Award went to Billy Moore, W. H. Sellers and

J. E. Walker, all Scott mounted. Many famous names were associated with the 1919 event, not all of them accomplished trials riders. As anticipated, the severity of the course took its toll and only 35 weary riders crossed the finishing line, most of them on the point of exhaustion. In the A-CU Six Days Trial that followed, which was centred around Llandrindod Wells on this occasion, Jesse Baker, Tim Wood and his brother Clarrie formed the official Scott entry. Jesse was on form and won a Silver Medal.

For some quite unaccountable reason, the organisers of the annual Show at Olympia decided to resurrect the event at the end of 1919, a decision which clearly displeased most manufacturers who had little to show and would have preferred the event postponed for a further year. As a result, detail modifications were the order of the day.

Norman Vinter insisted that his Secretary, Nellie Suddards, should be his assistant on the Scott stand. She was well qualified to help in this manner because she was used to dealing with travellers, customers and other visitors to the Works, dictating all correspondence and handling the many contingencies that arose — often when Vinter was away on extended business trips. She was to be joined by another young lady, Louie Ball, the petite daughter of a Birmingham Scott agent. Louie was a superb motorcyclist who could handle and repair a Scott with the air of the true professional. Not unexpectedly, the two young ladies were besieged with invitations, for they were working in a predominantly male province! Louie wore a velvet gown in Scott purple and Nellie a gown in wedgewood blue velvet which matched exactly the floor rugs on the Stand. Fortunately, both young ladies were well able to look after themselves and despite being frantically busy, managed to visit theatres and restaurants frequently, invariably accompanied by customers and friends. At the conclusion of the Show, Vinter showed his appreciation of Nellie's efforts by presenting her with a most luxurious pair of driving gloves in real sealskin. Without doubt, she had worked very hard and applied herself to the task in a very conscientious manner. The responsibility weighed heavily and for several years immediately prior to the opening of a Show, she suffered a recurring nightmare in which she arrived at Olympia on the opening day only to find that nothing from Saltaire had been delivered. She would frantically run around London, hoping to organise transport that never seemed to be available. Never once did she resolve the problem before she woke up, completely worn out.

Four 532 cc Scotts were displayed at Olympia, three of them in solo form and one attached to a sidecar with cantilever springing of Scott's own design. All the machines exhibited were variations of the same basic model, the shape of the handlebars in the case of the solo models denoting whether the machine was designated touring, semi-sports or sports. The most noticeable difference from the earlier pre-war models was the fitting of a double sight-feed lubricator in place of the single lubricator fitted previously, the use of a Binks three-jet carburettor (although the side flange for the Scott carburettor used previously was still in evidence) and a cast fishtail at

F. W. Scott adopts the one horse power approach whilst negotiating one of the Scott Trial sections. J. C. Suddards can be seen checking progress!

The award of the Amateur Team Cup at the conclusion of the 1919 Scott Trial. F. W. Moore (cloth cap) looks on whilst J. Walker is presented with the cup by Norman Vinter. H. W. Sellers, third member of the successful team, is in the background (bow tie)

The Scott Team at a petrol stop during the 1919 A-CU Six Days Trial. No. 48 is Leslie Guy and No. 49 Billy Moore

Star of the silent screen, Chrissie White, poses for a publicity photograph at the time of the 1919 Olympia Show

the end of the exhaust tail pipe. Other detail improvements included a new honeycomb radiator, telescopic guides instead of rollers for the front forks and more generous mudguards and shields, which necessitated the front forks passing through the front mudguard on account of its greater width. A British-made Thompson Bennett magneto was now fitted as standard, presumably because the designs evolved as a result of the war had reached a stage where they compared favourably with the Bosch magneto, used almost universally before the war. Palmer 26 x 2½ beaded edge tyres and an XL-All saddle completed the specification. All cycle parts were finished in black, with narrow white lining applied to the mudguards and the gear shields. An alternative finish was available, in which the white-lined panels were finished in purple. A new Scott cost 110 guineas, with an extra 30 guineas if a Scott sidecar was required.

Visitors to the Stand included Chrissie White and her husband Henry Edwards, heart-throbs of the silent screen at that time. Chrissie posed on a Scott for an advertisement. Unfortunately, another even more distinguished visitor was whisked away by the Show promoters before any of the Scott sales staff could get near him. He was the Duke of York, a keen motorcyclist who was soon to purchase his own machine.

Here it is pertinent to mention the Kendal Scott, which although not on display at Olympia, nevertheless, represented an interesting adaptation of the standard Scott design at this particular time. The originator was Lancelot Parker, the son of a Kendal motorcycle repairer who held an agency for Scott motorcycles and had ridden as a Scott team member in the 1911 A-CU Six Days Trial. Influenced by the 1913 rotary valve TT models, one of which he subsequently acquired for his own use, Parker made quite a name for himself in local events, riding this and some of the more standard models. One of his more memorable feats was accomplished in a fuel consumption test held during 1914, which he won by recording the incredible figure of over 200 mpg on a specially-prepared machine. Needless to say this figure is disputed even today and has been the subject of much spirited controversy! His own experience with the Scott design led him to design his own spring frame, which formed the subject of two patent applications in 1917 (British Patent Specifications 118,441 and 118,453). Had it not been for the war, his design would have made its debut before 1919. In the design, springs hidden within panelling that enclosed the long twin tubes running from the steering head to the rear wheel controlled the movement of the pivoted saddle tube in the fore and aft direction. A distinctive wedge-shaped petrol tank was suspended from these tubes, immediately to the rear of the radiator, so that at a very quick glance, the model took on the appearance of the 1914 TT model. Both wheels were fully enclosed by discs and whilst the engine was originally fitted in unmodified form, Parker later designed and fitted a chain driven rotary valve by taking the drive from an overhung sprocket on the end of the magneto shaft. Although very efficient, the design was crude and there was no enclosure for the chain. Later, Parker redesigned this attachment,

One of the
early Kendal
Scotts built
by Lancelot
Parker **89**

taking the drive from the right hand crankcase door so that full enclosure could be provided. The parts, which were also marketed separately in the form of a kit, were followed by another well-made conversion — cylinder blocks with detachable heads and separate exhaust ports. At last there was means of adding distinguishing features to the standard Scott design at one's personal whim, whilst gaining the benefit of enhanced performance.

A racing version of the Kendal Scott built by Bert Hill. The saddle tube pivot and the detachable exhaust ports are clearly evident

The Scott Sociable did not appear at the 1919 show because Alfred Scott was having his own problems trying to get into production and the Company had to take out a £10,000 mortgage. Still based at his experimental workshop in Bradford, he was joined by George Halliday, later better known through his involvement with the post-World War 2 Douglas twin. George Halliday joined the Scott Autocar Company as personal assistant to Alfred Scott, having left Beardmore Motors of Coatbridge, Scotland, where he had held the post of Assistant Design Engineer. At Beardmore, Halliday had been involved with the design of a very sophisticated car engine, under the general supervision of John Reith, then General Manager of the company. But he was no newcomer to motorcycling or for that matter to the Scott clan. He had purchased a 1919 Scott from Cuthbert Tunstall, Works Manager of the Lidgett Green factory, before he joined the Scott Autocar concern. It was the third Scott that he had owned amongst a great many other machines, and he recalls that it was a particularly well-finished model with a 'round' exhaust note that often lingered on in his ears for an hour or two after a long ride. The machine was fitted with disc wheels, as was the fashion at that time. Although aesthetically pleasing they had their disadvantages too. A ride across Crawford Moors in a high wind was like navigating a ship in heavy seas, especially when passing the occasional cottage by the roadside.

Derek Cox's Scott Sociable
chassis stripped for a rebuild.
The unusual wheel configuration
is readily apparent from this
photograph

The design of the Sociable closely followed the general lines of the prototype and the experimental gun cars that preceded it. However, several modifications were made, mainly with a view to improving the rate of production. In the main these related to changes in the front suspension by reversing the triangulation to give wider bearing centres for the king pin and by duplicating the tension springs to give some control over rebound. Scott also standardised the lengths of the chassis tubes, so that only four lengths were employed throughout. Originally, the tubes had lugs at each end, which were replaced by eyelets so that the tubes could be bolted together. But problems soon arose due to the geometric formation of the flat triangulation causing the final bolt to misregister, often by a not unappreciable amount. To correct this fault, Scott devised a screwed tensioning device, which pulled the framework diagonally until the bolt holes registered and the bolt could be inserted, a practice which George Halliday considered somewhat questionable in view of the distortion of the triangular construction and the loading on the now redundant member. The greatest disadvantage was that the points on which the body was to seat no longer registered correctly, at least on the very early models.

THE SCOTT MOTORCYCLE

Lightweight plastics suitable for the construction of the body were unknown at that time, otherwise Scott would undoubtedly have used them. Instead, he used the next best thing available, eschewing either metal or wood. His choice was fibreboard, a material that is light in weight and easy to work. Unfortunately, it is also dimensionally unstable and prone to distort badly when damp. This too added to his problems, for local buckling was liable to occur, which in turn gave rise to paintwork failures. During the year, Scott filed four patent applications, all of which were accepted. Three related to the Sociable design, namely British Patent 126,591 (segment starter), British Patent 150,944 (steering wheel forks) and British Patent 153,671 (arm rest design). Quite out of context, the fourth patent (British Patent 129,926) related to a design of strut for an aircraft wing, an indication that Scott still maintained his interest in aircraft as a future mode of transport.

The first event of any real significance to be held in 1920 was the Paris — Nice Reliability Trial. Held during February, an invitation was extended to the Auto-Cycle Union for approximately 20 English riders to take part. Five accomplished Scott riders were amongst those who took part — Jesse Baker, Tim and Clarrie Wood, Leslie Guy and Russell King. The start was at Montegron and it was soon obvious that the going would be tough. The French roads had suffered badly from the war and items such as saddle springs and footboards shook loose and vanished, making progress very uncomfortable. Jesse later claimed he rode most of the event standing up! Punctures were frequent too, although they failed to prevent the British competitors from finishing on time and winning all the principal awards. Clearly this had not been anticipated by the French journal that had sponsored the event, who promptly registered its dismay in a most unsporting manner by cancelling the presentation! The British protested in vain and not one took home a prize.

Jesse decided to stay on in Nice for a few days, encouraged by the fact that the Mardi Gras festival had just started. Whilst talking with some friends, it was suggested that it would be a good idea to explore North Africa before returning to Britain, by taking the ferry to Tunis, riding along the Algerian coast to Oran over a rugged mountainous track and then catching the boat home. In all, a 700 mile trip was involved, with an ascent to 7,000 feet above sea level at one particular point.

Russell King elected to accompany Jesse on the trip, riding pillion because he had damaged his own machine too badly in the trial. All went well initially, until the party encountered a landslide that necessitated abandoning their machines for recovery later. The whole trip took much longer than had been anticipated, but fortunately ended without further incident. It was well reported in the press.

1920 was also Harry Langman's year, for it marked his acceptance as a Works-supported trials rider. Partnered by Clarrie Wood, he rode in every major trials event held that year, winning one of them outright — the Ilkley One-day event. His personal two-speed model (AK 4505) was used almost constantly — for a period that extended over the next ten years!

Billy Moore at the start of an Ilkley Club Trial during 1920. The photograph was taken in Otley cattle market. J. S. Duxbury is wearing the armband, on the left

The Scott Team at the 1920 A-CU Six Days Trial, Leslie Guy, Clarrie Wood and Geoffrey Hill

Although the TT races in the Isle of Man were resumed during 1920, there was no official Scott entry for the company was more than occupied getting into full production. But they did contest the A-CU Six Days Trial with considerable success, winning the Manufacturers Team Prize and Six Gold Medals.

Two young ladies with a sidecar outfit. Nellie Suddards, Norman Vinter's secretary, and a friend prove that women can handle a sidecar outfit too

The Assembly Shop at Shipley. The man in the white coat is Walter Smith, Shop Foreman

In his experimental workshop, Alfred Scott and George Halliday were struggling to complete the Sociable that was to make its debut at the Olympia Show. Somehow the model was finished just in time to be transported to London by road, on a wet day that did little to encourage the fibrework body to retain its shape. By now Scott was almost unapproachable with the tension that had built up as preparation neared the deadline. George Halliday recalls someone leaning on the half open door whilst talking to Alfred Scott, whereupon the door fell off the upper hinge. All conversation ceased abruptly, then Scott made the observation, 'When *I* lean on the door it doesn't fall off!'.

At the Show, the Sociable attracted a considerable amount of attention, despite its very unusual, lopsided appearance. It was priced at £273, a price that did not compare at all favourably with that of the average sidecar outfit. But it had at least one outstanding advantage when this comparison was made. The driver and passenger sat closely together in comfort and had no difficulty in conversing with each other. The passenger was no longer doomed to sit in isolation, a state of affairs that until now had been regarded as acceptable when the ordinary motorcycle was converted into a means of transport for the family by the addition of a third wheel. One of the first production Sociables was purchased by Jesse Baker and it gave him good service during the next few years.

The Scott motorcycles on display at their own separate stand were virtually identical to the machines that had been exhibited during the previous year's hastily arranged exhibition. Best and Lloyd drip feeds were one distinguishing feature, since this design was now standardised for the lubrication system.

1921 marked the resumption of interest in the Isle of Man TT and it was Tim Wood who had the responsibility for providing the Works entry with four special machines, to be ridden by Harry Langman, Clarrie Wood, R. W. Stansfield and Geoff Clapham. The new racing model bore a superficial resemblance to the 1914 TT model on which Tim had set a record lap at 53.50 mph before his enforced retirement. A closer look showed that the engine, frame and gearbox were all of a new design.

The new twin cylinder engine (73 mm x 62.5 mm) had an alloy cylinder block fitted with cast iron liners. The cylinder head was detachable and employed a copper/asbestos head gasket. Both the cylinder block and the cylinder head were water cooled. Each cylinder had a separate exhaust pipe that terminated at a point just beyond the rear wheel hub. Like all Scott two-speeders, two chains transmitted the drive to the two-speed gear, one on each side of the central flywheel. But in place of the usual final drive sprocket, a pinion was substituted which drove the layshaft of an additional two-speed gearbox. A separate foot control locked the final drive sprocket to either the high or low mainshaft gear pinions, between which it was centrally disposed. In consequence, four speeds were obtainable, with gear ratios ranging from 3.3 : 1 to 6.4 : 1. Both engine and gearbox were mounted in a subframe that was readily detachable from the main frame of triangulated construction. A re-arrangement of the frame tubes, covered by a patent granted to Tim Wood (British Patent 151,552 of 1919) permitted greater lateral rigidity by arranging each side of the duplex frame so that no two tubes were in the same plane. The frame was now narrower at the top than at the bottom. An unorthodox feature was the use of a pan seat suspended on quarter elliptic springs that extended to uprights which pivoted adjacent to the rear wheel spindle. The open frame was filled by a triangular shaped three gallon petrol tank and a cylindrical half gallon oil tank was mounted vertically behind the magneto. Crankcase vacuum was used to operate the lubrication system. The compression release control on the handlebars operated the ignition cut-out switch and at the same time closed the throttle by means of an override action. An Amac carburettor and a Lucas twin-spark magneto completed the specification. Harry Langman rode well in this his TT debut and held seventh place in the Senior race until his chain broke at Hilberry and forced his retirement. Of the other Works riders, only R. W. Stansfield managed to finish, in 17th place. The other Scott rider to finish was J. W. Moffat, who rode a standard model and was placed 22nd.

Clarrie Wood with one of
the 1921 Senior TT models

It was about this time that the Company decided to market a new 500 cc sports model, known as the Squirrel, the first time this name had been used. Although there is nothing to suggest why this particular name was chosen for the new model, later advertisements referred to 'As lively as a Squirrel and never sheds a nut'. It has been suggested that the Squirrel was inspired by the 'Stansfield Scott' which Jesse Baker had purchased to ride in the 1921 Scottish Six Days Trial. The machine had been constructed by R. W. Stansfield, the TT rider and Scott employee. It embodied a number of non-standard features, such as disc wheels and a special oiling system. For some unaccountable reason, Jesse incurred Alfred Scott's wrath by appearing on this particular machine, a surprising reaction because Scott no longer had any connection with the motorcycle company. He had once agreed that Jesse should ride an ABC in the annual London–Edinburgh Trial when the latter considered that the experimental three-speed Scott sidecar outfit that was to have been his entry had been too hastily improvised. It is worthwhile digressing to mention that Jesse's account of the 1921 Six Days Trial was somewhat hazy, understandably so because one control point was at a remote croft where an illicit whisky still was in action. A free sample sent him on his way with a hitherto unknown zest and may possibly account for his subsequent crash on Man Rattigan, which left him concussed and out of the running!

The 1921 A-CU Six Days Trial was held at the beginning of September. This year the event started at Brooklands and covered over 700 miles, penetrating into the West Country as far as Lynmouth before returning back to the starting point. Three Scott entrants, all riding solo models, gained a Gold Medal each — Geoffrey Hill (now a Scott convert!), Billy Moore and Walter Forbes Scott, one of Alfred Scott's brothers. None of the trio lost a single mark during the event. Walter Scott caused some amusement when he arrived at Winchester for the lunch stop on the fifth day. He was resplendent in a grey bowler hat, which he had purchased for 1s 9d en route! The Scott team won the Special Team Prize and three Gold Medals.

Whether or not the Stansfield Scott had any influence on the design of the Squirrel, this latter model was revolutionary in a number of respects and represented the first attempt by the Company to market a genuine sports model that had a guaranteed maximum speed of 60 mph and was not just a standard machine fitted with sports handlebars. Engine capacity was 486 cc (70 mm x 63.5 mm) and the general specification included footrests in place of footboards, sparking plugs in the top of the air cooled cylinder heads and aluminium alloy pistons. The twin drip feeds were moved to the front down tubes, where they were more readily observed. Overall weight was about 220 lb and the sale price £105.

A curious diversion during 1921 was the manufacture of some rail inspection trolleys for the Drewry Car Company of London. A 532 cc engine provided the power, with a twin radiator set up for efficient cooling. Not unexpectedly, the main chassis was of triangulated construction! A Scott two-speed gear gave rail speeds of 11 mph and 20 mph, two-up. The complete trolley weighed just over 5 cwt and was completely equipped, even to the extent of acetylene lights. Three of the trolleys were shipped to India, the fourth saw service on the London and South Western Railway and was based at Exeter.

The 1921 Scott Trial marked the end of Jesse Baker's association with Scott motorcycles. Early in the event he crashed badly, but managed to remount and struggle on to the finish by strapping his injured knee to the petrol tank by means of his scarf. Despite the pain, he covered the 89 mile course, with all its usual hazards, in just under five hours, to win a Finisher's Certificate — the ambition of all entrants. Although he had not known it at the time, the fall had fractured his knee, which explains the pain he experienced. Needless to say his determination to finish aggravated the injury and he was subsequently confined to a nursing home for eight months. Although he still retained an interest in competition events after his recovery, he married his fianceé who had managed to visit him every day during his convalescence and directed his attentions to his jewellers business in Wigan and later, his family.

At the 1921 Show, three quite different Scott models were on display, the standard 532 cc touring model, the new 486 cc Squirrel and a 532 cc Colonial model fitted with three inch section tyres and having a ground clearance of no less than eight inches. Two of the Squirrels on the stand were attached to lightweight sidecars fitted with polished aluminium panelling, one of the Zeppelin type and one of slipper design. The cantilever sprung sidecars added an additional £30 to the purchase price, still £105.

The Sociable was also on view at the same Show, although the price was now reduced to £215. Still above the price of the average sidecar outfit, the reduced differential made the Sociable a much better counter-attraction. Several improvements had been made during the year that included slight stiffening up of the transmission, a solid propeller shaft and the use of a spiral bevel to quieten the final drive. The radiator was now enlarged and an ML dynamo used in conjunction with a very neat switch-board provided the single headlamp with a better standard of lighting. Even the engine compartment had received attention to give improved access, ample evidence of Alfred Scott's continual attention to detail. It was once said by those who knew him that he could never leave the Sociable alone; at one stage he had even tried fitting a fourth wheel!

During April 1922 *Motor Cycling* published a road test of the Squirrel which had been conducted by H. Mortimer Batten, a popular writer about motorcycles who still contributes the occasional article today. He evidently approached the test with some trepidation because he prefaced his impressions of the machine by referring to the quite appalling condition of the unmade road outside the Scott works at Saltaire. It would seem that the first few hundred yards were deeply rutted and when wet resembled the very worst type of trials section. A knee-deep quagmire of mud followed, with the additional hazard of a sharp right-angled turn and from this point onwards,

PALM OIL

The Only Lubricant for

COPPERS AND TRAPS

A Sergeant writes--

"It is the only Dope which
really avoids friction."

Supplied (perhaps) by all Banking Institutions.

KEEP YOUR BOYS AT HOME

BUY A

'Woolworth Special,'

THEY WON'T RUN FAR.

Stops and Starts when it likes, A Child could use it.

A grateful mother writes :—" My son was never at home
until he purchased one of your machines, since when,
he has been in (bed) continuously."

Address your Enquiries to
WOOLWORTH, WOOLWORTH & WOOLWORTH,
Lincoln Inn Fields, PUDSEY.

Two typical parodies of advertisements from the 1921 Scott Trial programme

a severe and stoney gradient led up to the main road from Bradford to Keighley, with inevitable cobbled sets and greasy tramlines. Small wonder that even a hardened rider had his qualms when invited to put one of the new models through its paces, especially a 'hot stuff' model with a somewhat high two speed gear and no hand operated clutch!

A combination of fog and quite appalling road conditions led Mortimer Batten to take the road to the north east via Otley, Wetherby and York after he had gingerly edged his way out of the Scott Works. At Otley he paused, for he had actually enjoyed the first stage of the journey, despite the aforementioned hazards. The machine was both comfortable and well balanced and the frame showed not the slightest tendency to whip. Despite the lower than standard capacity of the Squirrel there was complete freedom from chain snatch, even though the chains fitted to the machine were decidedly slack. Plans were hastily revised to include an ascent of Sutton Bank.

The road to Thirsk, via Ripley and Ripon contained some fast stretches and as the fog had now thinned out, speeds of up to 50 mph were possible without overstressing the new engine. At this speed, the exhaust note was little more than a quiet purr, giving little impression of road speed. Eventually the road turned towards Sutton Bank, the notorious test hill that had already featured 100 ascents in one day, by Frank Philipp for Scott publicity. At its steepest point, the long Sutton Bank gradient reached 1 in 4. On questioning a cyclist in Sutton village, Mortimer Batten was told the hill had never been in a worse state and that no motor vehicle had climbed it for several weeks. But although an alternative route was advised, the opportunity to meet the challenge was too good to turn down!

The first attempt to make a non-stop climb failed when a misfire set in and it was necessary to close the throttle so that the engine would not overheat and tighten up. The second attempt was more successful and half of the first stretch was negotiated in top gear before changing into bottom for the 1 in 4 section, which was now climbed with ease. A pause was made in consideration for the new engine, and on the restart, the machine climbed to the top of the hill with ease. From this point onwards the going was again rough, for the fog had returned and the road surface was a mixture of deep ruts, bottomless sand and occasionally, deep sodden snow. Yet the Squirrel continued to pull well, making it possible to remain in top gear, even at low rpm.

In summing up the test, Mortimer Batten considered the Scott to be a most delightful solo mount and had no criticism to offer. Although well received by the sporting fraternity, the Squirrel had shown it was by no means exclusively a sportsman's mount. In short, it was the safest machine he had ever ridden.

For the 1922 Senior TT, the Works entries reverted to a two-speeder that was similar in many respects to the standard production Squirrel. The most noticeable differences were the larger capacity petrol tank, necessary in view of the much higher speeds, a separate oil tank that superseded the oil-in-frame

The 1922 Senior TT riders. The group includes Harry Langman, Jimmy Simpson, Ivor Thomas and Clarrie Wood. One of the TT models is in the foreground

arrangement, and the use of two sparking plugs per cylinder fired by a special Lucas magneto. They were the first to be fitted with small, hub front brakes. Although the specially-prepared engines would run up to 5,000 rpm, tests showed that sustained high speeds were limited by recurring sparking plug troubles, mainly because the plain cylinder heads were still air-cooled. But it was too late to rectify this defect. Fortunately the Scott Team of Harry Langman, Clarrie Wood and Geoff Clapham acquitted themselves well. They won the Manufacturer's Team Prize with their 3rd, 4th and 9th places respectively. It was in the Senior race that Jimmy Simpson made his one and only appearance on a privately-entered Scott. He was entered by Chapmans Garage of Leicester, but failed to finish as the result of a leaking fuel tank. Ivor Thomas, another of the Works entries, also retired from the fray.

The Scott team were staying in Ramsey and they rode back to their digs in order to take a bath, change and have a meal before returning to Douglas for the prize giving. They hired a taxi to take them to the Villa Marina and somehow managed to cram seven or eight inside. Someone suggested a stop for a drink on the way, the taxi driver included. Unfortunately a drinking session developed and by the time they eventually left the bar, time was running short. The taxi driver took the hint and tried to set up his own personal record for the run to Douglas via the coast road. He lost control on a bend at Maughold, crashed and flung his passengers out, causing injuries that prevented the entire Scott team from attending the prize giving. Harry Langman suffered two broken ribs and Clarrie Wood had head injuries. Ironically, the broken ribs represented the only fractures that Harry Langman sustained in the whole of his riding career, and he subsequently obtained £20 compensation which helped offset the incident a little.

As a result of the TT successes, Squirrel orders picked up appreciably and helped stave off the financial difficulties into which the Scott Motor Cycle Company was slowly drifting. Other wins in trials events helped back up this success, the most notable being the award of two Gold Medals and a Silver Medal to Billy Moore, W. L. Gray and G. W. Scott for their performance in the 1922 A-CU Six Days Trial.

It was about this time that a Scott came into the repair shop for overhaul, whereupon it was found that the engine number and the serial number of certain other parts had never been entered in the sales records. Suspicions were aroused and late one night Charles Suddards and other works personnel secreted themselves in the yard near the railway sidings to await the results of a tip-off. Soon shadowy figures emerged who began to search the scrap heaps for hidden parts. All were caught red-handed and some profitable smuggling was nipped in the bud, without police intervention. There was clearly an effective way of dealing with such matters in those days!

At the 1922 Show a new three-speed 532 cc model made its debut. The gearbox was of conventional design (apart from the use of an outrigger final drive sprocket) and was fitted with a hand operated multiplate clutch. It was designed by Harry Shackleton who was now in charge of design and development. The internal arrangements of Shackleton's gearbox included constant mesh gears with one sliding dog on the mainshaft that engaged with overhung dogs on the middle gear pinion. The teeth of the gear pinions were of fine pitch, an excellent arrangement for constant loading because it gives a smoother, quieter drive. Gear changing was effected by a lever mounted on a quadrant, which operated the selector fork by means of a spring-loaded face cam assembly and a short link, the latter connecting the face cam lever with the selector fork lever. The spring loading arrangement was utilised primarily to ensure that the gear lever could be immediately located to select the required gear, even if the dogs on the sliding pinion were not opposite the appropriate spaces in the gear pinion dogs. When they eventually matched up the spring loading pushed them into engagement. This arrangement worked very well when the clutch was disengaged, but if the clutch had been re-engaged and the throttle opened, even a fraction before the dogs had engaged fully, the fine teeth of the gear pinions suffered accordingly. This was why the gearbox had a reputation for giving trouble.

The multiplate clutch used in conjunction with this gearbox had nine steel plates (including the backplate, sprocket and outer plate) and eight plates lined with friction material. Six springs pressed the outer and back-plates together, to clamp the other plates between them. The clutch was actuated by a pushrod through the mainshaft. At the clutch end, a slot through the mainshaft had a key in it, the ends of which engaged with the clutch thrust race. This in turn engaged with the outer clutch plate, to compress the springs and so disengage the clutch. On the offside, the pushrod screwed into a quick thread lever, mounted in a worm housing on the gearbox cover. The quick thread lever was operated by Bowden cable from the handlebar lever.

The gearbox bolted to a substantial aluminium alloy undertray that bolted direct into the frame. The magneto was mounted above the gearbox and was chain driven from a sprocket on the clutch housing. Perhaps the main disadvantage of the new gearbox was that it helped bring the overall weight of the machine up to the 270 lb mark.

An internal expanding hub brake of 5 inch diameter was fitted to the front wheel, similar in design to that fitted to the TT models. The long gear change lever projected vertically upwards, through a slot cut in the shield that sealed the space between the engine and gearbox. With standard gearing, ratios of 4.5, 7.0 and 12.75 : 1 were obtainable. For the first time, the kickstarter appeared in what is now considered to be the conventional position. Priced at £110 solo, the new three-speed model cost £15 more than the standard 3¾ hp model that had been continued virtually unchanged, apart from the fitting of the new internal expanding front brake. The Squirrel, priced at £89 solo, was modified in similar fashion and on all machines it was apparent that attention had at last been given to the position of the twin sight feeds of the lubrication system by repositioning them near the top of the upper frame tube, where they were more visible.

Although the Scott Sociable was again displayed by the Scott Autocar Company, on their own stand, Alfred Scott was having his own problems behind the scenes too. It had already been necessary to raise a second mortgage to keep the Company solvent and the small car 'boom' had started, led by Herbert Austin's famous Seven, which was destined to make heavy inroads into the sidecar market by selling at £225. There was nothing unorthodox about the appearance of this vehicle, which had been designed with the requirements of the family man in mind. As subsequent events showed, it was destined to be made in very large numbers.

The one event that could save the Scott Motor Cycle Company in these troubled times was an outright win in the 1923 Senior TT and on paper this seemed possible in view of the success of the Scott riders who had offered strong challenge in the 1922 event. One of the factors that had handicapped the Works riders and prevented them from gaining higher positions on the leader board was the continued use of the air-cooled cylinder head, which restricted the use of full throttle for any appreciable length of time. In consequence, the engine was completely redesigned to feature a detachable cylinder head that had its own water jacket. At the same time, the opportunity was taken to lengthen the stroke of the engine to 78 mm and to fit a mechanical oil pump to improve the lubrication of the engine. An improved induction system was also devised whilst Geoff Clapham, profiting from his previous experiences, designed a quickly detachable radiator mounting that permitted the radiator to be changed in a matter of minutes. Since the previous year's small diameter hub brake had proved a success, it was decided to employ a brake of similar type but of larger diameter, in the rear wheel. In general appearance, by far the most noticeable departure from existing practice was the fitting of a large capacity petrol tank that completely spanned the hitherto open frame.

The 1923 TT was destined to be memorable in another respect too, for it had at last been decided to include an extra race for sidecar machines as the result of popular demand. Two Scott outfits were prepared for this race, each having a 596 cc engine that was virtually a scaled-up version of the new engine fitted to the Senior TT bikes.

The sidecar race preceded the Senior race and things had already got off to a bad start when Clarrie Wood crashed his outfit during the last day of practice causing sufficient damage to eliminate him from the race itself. He hit a steam roller, of all things! In those days the roads were not closed for practice. Although Harry Langman was widely fancied to win, it was obvious that his greatest challenge would come from Freddie Dixon, provided Dixon could keep going and was not eliminated by the frame breakages that were plaguing the Douglas riders at that time. The unknown factor was Dixon's banking sidecar, which he was finally permitted to use after a special demonstration lap. The A-CU considered it unsafe to use, an attitude that was duly challenged in characteristic manner by Dixon himself, the originator of the design. Knowing full well the capabilities of his Douglas and the masterly way in which Walter Denny, his young passenger, could operate the banking sidecar, there was no doubt in Dixon's mind as to who would win!

Such was Dixon's confidence that he eased off a little after a rapid first lap and was serenading his passenger with 'We won't be home 'till morning' when Harry Langman's outfit closed up behind him on the mountain climb. This signalled a furious chase that ended when Dixon drew into the pits to refuel. Having already made the fastest lap at 54.69 mph, it seemed that Langman and his passenger Ernie Mainwaring were all set for that much needed win, but alas, fate then took a hand. At Braddan Bridge on his last lap, Langman affected by some misjudgment of his passenger's side-to-side leaning, drifted wide and struck the right hand kerb on the exit from the bridge, fortunately without serious injury to either himself or his passenger. He retired on the spot, for amongst other considerations, the front wheel and forks were too badly damaged for him to continue. Dixon tearing along behind him somehow missed the wreckage and won the first ever sidecar TT at 53.15 mph with an outfit that listed badly to port. One of the nearside frame tubes had broken and it was only the handlebar end resting on the sidecar body that prevented a complete collapse. Victory truly hung by a thread. S. E. Longman had taken over Clarrie Wood's rebuilt outfit, but he was out of luck and had to retire for reasons unknown.

Harry Langman rounds Ramsey Hairpin whilst in the lead during the 1923 Sidecar TT

S. E. Longman and passenger at Quarter Bridge during the 1923 sidecar race. Note the triangulated sidecar chassis

THE SCOTT MOTORCYCLE

The two sidecar incidents had serious repercussions on the Scott Works entries for the Senior race, since neither Clarrie Wood nor Harry Langman were fit enough to ride. Of the original team, only Geoff Clapham was able to ride, but eventually the other two Works machines were taken over by Stanley Woods and Jack Watson-Bourne, neither of whom had raced a Scott before! Worse was to follow. The Senior race was run in pouring rain and thick mist swirled around the mountain, making conditions even more hazardous. Two punctures eliminated Geoff Clapham early on, whilst Stanley Woods struck trouble and had to take on water — an ironic twist that eliminated him from the results. Jack Watson-Bourne struggled on to finish a very creditable 11th, a position which he afterwards confessed pleased him greatly. To use his own words he had 'never played the organ before', an allusion to the two-speed gear pedal, the positions of which were irreverently known as soft and loud! Howard Riddell, on a Kendal Scott, finished 15th.

Harry Langman's 1923 TT sidecar outfit as it is today. It has been preserved by Scott enthusiast Ossie Neal and can be seen at the Stanford Hall Museum, near Rugby

It was about this time that a young local rider of no mean repute called at the Scott Works to purchase some spares for his two-speeder. Quite by chance the Service Manager, Bentley Rigg, happened to open the hatch in the spares department where visitors called. He recognised the caller and promptly gave him an entry form for the 1923 Scott Trial, expressing the hope that he would enter. The rider was none other than Allan Jefferies and his entry in the 1923 event marked the beginning of a long and highly successful acquaintanceship with the Company. At that time, most of the locals regarded him as a somewhat wild youth, who was sometimes seen riding his machine hands off whilst he struggled to put his jacket on. This fact fascinated many a bystander for throughout the whole performance the machine barely deviated off line nor lost speed.

> **It was on August 11th 1923 that the cruellest blow of all fell because it was on this day that Alfred Scott passed away after only a short illness, aged only 48. One of his favourite pastimes was that of potholing and he was President and a very active member of the Bradford Gritstone Club. A few days previous he had emerged from one of their potholing sessions around Ingleton, Yorks, with very wet clothes, but insisted on driving home in his own Sociable affectionately known as the 'Crab' before changing. As a result of his soaking he caught a severe cold, but even then refused medical attention. The cold worsened and developed into pneumonia, by which time it was too late. He was laid to rest in Bradford Cemetry on August 14th, thus bringing to a close the career of a very gifted engineer who had a remarkable spread of talents and a divergence of interests, many of which extended far outside the motor industry**

It is alleged that Alfred Scott's interest in potholing was aroused by a chance visit to Stump Cross Caverns, along the road from Pateley Bridge to Grassington, when he was on a motoring excursion. He returned to visit these caverns on several occasions, which today have become one of the more popular show caverns for those who wish to enter a pothole without undue fear of claustrophobia. The Gritstone Club, of Bradford, was formed on January 13th 1922 and although Scott was not a founder member, he soon became involved with the Club's explorations. He made many visits to Newby Moss during the latter half of 1922 and was responsible for the surveys of the Pillar Pots, Long Kill West and certain surface features. To facilitate the descent into Long Kill West, which was 300 feet deep, Scott devised a beam and pulley arrangement as a convenient means of lowering and raising the explorers.

He also explored Alum and Diccan Pots, the latter being especially difficult because it was first necessary to divert water into Alum Pot before a safe descent could be made. Scott gave much attention to this hydrological problem, even to the extent of building a dam and aqueduct, but he was not able to divert sufficient water by these means and had to concede defeat. The Gritstone Club Journal records the fatal caving trip in the obituary published in their second issue of 1923.

Much has been written about Alfred Angas Scott. Some have claimed that he insisted on utter originality and would not profit from the knowledge of others or even from their mistakes, because everything had to be his own from beginning to end. In consequence, they allege, his experience was gained the hard way. But this view comes largely from those who may not have seen eye to eye with him or perhaps were jealous of his abilities. It could be construed that he had already considered many of the ideas put forward, at an earlier date, and had rejected them because he had seen their shortcomings.

It is also alleged, perhaps with more truth, that he never gave consideration to what the public wanted; it had to be his way. Viewed objectively, it would appear that he could have sold many more motorcycles if he had fitted a top tube and tank across in the conventional manner, to break up the illusion of a ladies model. If needs be, this tube could even have been a dummy. As for the Sociable, there can be no doubt that its highly unconventional appearance was a great deterrent to sales, no matter how good the vehicle. Yet he resolutely refused to pander to public taste and change the design because in his own mind it was right.

It is true that Scott designed everything down to the very smallest of details, for as his drawings show, he had great ability as a draughtsman. He could go into the Works and pick up any part, to produce results that even the best mechanic could not equal. Yet he was infinitely patient with those around him who were less gifted and would go to any length to explain things. Although never a person to suffer fools, he had been seen outside a village pub explaining the various features of the Scott design to a simple country bumpkin who had commented on the unusual looking mount. Some go as far as to say that Scott would have made an outstanding professor, such was the depth and spread of his ability.

His hobbies were widespread and included motorcycling and motor boating. He had a marvellous memory and could remember landmarks many years later, so that when he was faced with an alternative of routes to follow, he knew instinctively which one to take. He loved music and greatly enjoyed the works of Gilbert and Sullivan. He could play the piano and could sketch and paint, the latter accounting for his interest in architecture, especially that of cathedrals. By nature he was more or less a vegetarian, although he enjoyed the occasional 'heavy meat meal'. He loved children and was often to be found in their company. One of his favourite games was that of 'heads, bodies and legs', a game in which three persons added their own version of each part of the anatomy to one of three folded portions of the paper on which the caricature was to be drawn. Some of his sketches in this series have survived, all executed with a soft BB pencil. Although always very polite to the opposite sex, he remained a bachelor and expressed no interest in them, always referring to 'the so-called fair sex'. Unlike most other manufacturers, Scott never sought the limelight and in consequence, outside the family, very few photographs acknowledge his presence. Occasionally there is just a glimpse of him in a doorway or the appearance of his head above a crowd — nothing more. It seems all the more remarkable that this quiet, unassuming man had such a formative influence on the design of the two-stroke engine and produced such highly advanced ideas based on theories that still hold good today.

It is said that every dark cloud has a silver lining and to an extent this proved to be true in the case of racing successes that followed the misfortunes of the 1923 TT. In July, Harry Langman showed the potential of the new racing models by winning several speed trials and in the month that followed both the Welsh Tourist Trophy race and the Ulster Grand Prix. He set up a record lap of 66 mph in the latter event and won a Gold Medal. Trials successes also added to the imposing list of awards gained during the latter half of the year and there are few events of any standing in which the rider of a Scott did not win a major award or a Gold Medal.

In September 1923 the first Amateur TT was held, or to give the event its correct title, the Amateur Motor Cycle Championship Race, according to the official programme. It had become increasingly obvious that the amateur rider no longer stood much chance in the June TT races, now that manufacturers were providing special factory-developed machines for the exclusive use of their skilled riders, who had been placed under contract. As far as the amateur was concerned, there was need to return to the splendid air of informality that prevailed throughout the very early TT events on the old St John's—Ballacraine—Peel course when virtually everyone was an amateur, although of course, making use of the much more suitable Mountain circuit that had by now become well established.

No less than seven Scotts were entered for the 1923 races, six of which were standard factory products. The seventh was a Kendal Scott, constructed to the specification described earlier in this Chapter. One rider, J. McGill, was eliminated from the race as the result of a bad crash during practice, and D. K. Mitchell (who was also a practice casualty) had the misfortune to be put out of the race near Ramsey, as the result of a defective magneto. The remaining five machines completed the race, but without any conspicuous success. The Kendal Scott, ridden by H. V. Prescott, finished in 8th place, with A. E. Catt Jnr 13th, A. Howard 14th, F. Coward 15th and P. B. Cheston 18th. Clearly the Scotts were not fast enough, a fact emphasised by the knowledge that Cheston had finished some two hours after Len Randles had won the race on his Sunbeam at an average speed of 52.77 mph!

At the 1923 Show, a three-speed Squirrel was displayed, following the lines of the standard three-speed model offered at the previous year's event.

Both wheels were now fitted with internal expanding hub brakes and at last the oil-in-frame feature was discarded. In its place, a separate, cylindrical oil tank retained with aluminium bands was fitted to the main down tube of the frame, with the twin drip feeds mounted near its base so that they were readily visible yet did not require long delivery pipes. It was painted Scott purple and was lined in white.

In some respects the frame was similar to that of the two-speed model, the main difference being the replacement of the bottom frame tubes from in front of the rear mudguard to the engine mountings at the front down tubes with a long aluminium alloy tray, similar to that used for the 1922 three-speed model described earlier. The tray carried the engine as on the two-speeder and had provision for mounting the gearbox. It was strengthened by two ribs. Unfortunately the aluminium alloy tray still proved somewhat fragile if the machine was used in sporting events of the cross country type and the favoured few were able to obtain a bronze or gun metal tray specially cast in the Works, as a substitute. It was undoubtedly much more robust, but added so much extra weight that much of the advantage of the three-speed design was lost!

The three-speed Squirrel was priced at £89 5s, against the sum of £73 10s required for the standard two-speed model. This latter model had been continued virtually unchanged, apart from the addition of the rear hub brake and the separate oil tank. The standard 532 cc model was also continued, with similar modifications, at £94 10s, whilst for only £5 5s extra, the new 74.6 x 68.25 mm, 596 cc engine could be fitted as an alternative. There was also the option of a two-speed 532 cc model at £78 15s, for those who were working to a tight budget. The 596 cc engine had a detachable alloy water-cooled cylinder head and was based on the unit used for the 1923 sidecar TT models.

Despite the death of Alfred Scott, the Scott Autocar Company continued in business and announced a further price reduction to £135, which placed the Sociable on even more competitive terms with the conventional sidecar outfit. Some of the economies made were reflected in the use of a standard ignition system based on a BTH magneto. The earlier models had used a somewhat complex twin spark system in which a special ML magneto was linked with two sparking plugs per cylinder, a Scott twin pole plug and one of the standard commercial type. Another change was evident in the materials of construction used for the body. There was now aluminium panelling on the front part of the body and steel at the rear. The windscreen no longer had its characteristic 'V' shaped slot either, an innovation that permitted improved visibility in the rain in the absence of a windscreen wiper. On more than one occasion Scott had left a note affixed to the windscreen of his own car, explaining to bypassers that the cut-out was intentional and the windscreen was not broken!

On the credit side, the new price included dynamo lighting and the provision of a spare wheel, previously considered unnecessary. Twin headlamps either side of the windscreen replaced the single, centrally-located headlamp and two small sidelights that had been fitted as standard. The same chassis was employed but the transmission had been improved by the use of a better bearing assembly at the rear of the propeller shaft, that included a large ball thrust race. For an extra £5, it was possible to purchase a new version of the Sociable that had a double dickey seat and was capable of carrying four persons. Detail modifications that applied to both models included a vertical car-type ratchet for the handbrake and the use of a cast alloy offside body sill in the form of a step, to replace the wooden sill used previously. By now the Sociable was beginning to acquire a reputation for its soundness of construction and good reliability as the result of successes gained in trials. D. W. Rhodes was one of several Sociable drivers who was particularly successful in many of the national long distances reliability trials held during the twenties.

During the year, the Wardonia Motor Engineering Co of Carfield Avenue, Bradford, offered the Wardonia one-piece inlet and transfer manifold, priced at 15s 0d complete with packings. It bolted on, in place of the existing transfer port covers. Also available from the same source was an external contracting band brake for the early type open sprocket, priced at 17s 6d complete. These proprietary fittings provided owners of a Scott motor cycle with a convenient means of improving performance and braking efficiency.

A c.1926 two-speed Scott and sidecar restored by Robert Rawlins of the Scott Owners' Club

Transporting machines to the 1925 TT; a view of the deck of one of the
Isle of Man steamers

CHAPTER FIVE
Brighter prospects

NOTHING short of an outright TT win would have alleviated the financial difficulties that now faced the Company, despite a whole string of successes in other events of only slightly less importance. Debts totalled £47,000 and before long an Official Receiver was appointed, a man who, by coincidence, had the surname Norton! He remained in office until R. A. Vinter mounted a rescue operation, with yet another Company reconstruction.

Strangely, little seems to be known about the two Vinters who were on the Board, or for that matter, about F. J. Allen. Nellie Suddards recalls all the Vinters were tall, dark and handsome, with impeccable manners. Reginald Vinter was in his forties, his brother Charles about five years younger, and Norman, the youngest of the three, in his twenties. Reginald Vinter had a model farm and enjoyed both fishing and shooting. Most remember him as a somewhat autocratic country gentleman, who usually wore a well-cut tweed suit. Norman Vinter had just left the Army with the rank of Captain, when he joined the Company. He had a very friendly disposition, but always seemed to be a little in awe of his brothers. Some considered him to be little more than a playboy, but he was far more astute than many would credit. As has been mentioned earlier, Norman Vinter played a leading role in the organisation of the annual Scott Trial. Unhappily, he passed away during 1923 as the result of gassing during the war.

Virtually nothing has been recorded about Charles Vinter, or for that matter the somewhat mythical F. J. Allen. This is hardly surprising since these two directors always seemed remote and were divorced from personal contact with the firm's personnel. There was also a Mr. Elliott, who was appointed General Manager. He was known only to the office staff, as a shadowy figure using the Board room as his office. Apart from the dictation of letters, his sole communication with the office staff was a somewhat curt passing of the day.

The 'hardcore' of the office staff during the twenties included Alex Doverner, a middle-aged bachelor of a thin and somewhat irritable disposition, who was the Company Secretary. He gave enthusiastic, loyal service and worked long hours, surviving on what appeared to be a diet of tea and cigarettes! Matthew Roley was Office Manager, a jolly thick-set man who was always very approachable. He managed the Scott TT entrants each year, aided by his assistant William Grosert. Harry Shackleton fulfilled the role of Head Draughtsman in a very able manner, a quiet but very clever man. Willie Haley was the Office Storekeeper and the Secretary's assistant. Ida Walker managed the typing pool that included Millie Padgett, Kathleen Wheeler, Gertie Raybould and Elsie Hahn. The Filing Clerk was a Mrs Green, whilst monetary affairs were looked after by Cashier Fred Sugden, his assistant Hubert Fortune, and Kathleen Sowden. The atmosphere was friendly, although busy. Hours were from 9 to 6 daily, with morning and afternoon tea provided whilst the staff were still at work. It was customary to stay on at the end of the day, until the day's work quota was complete.

Although the Company worked to a very tight budget as the result of the financial problems, it is fortunate that the cutback had little noticeable effect on the competition programme. As later events would show, 1924 proved to be another turning point in the history of the Company and the five years that were to follow, one of the more memorable periods. Continuing competition successes in virtually every major event ensured the Scott name remained well to the fore. Not many other manufacturers could field a team of such able and highly competent riders.

As far as the 1924 TT was concerned, it was obvious that the 1923 factory racing models had the ability to secure a win in the Senior event, provided their few shortcomings could be eliminated and fate itself did not weigh so heavily against the riders. The engines were modified by reverting to a non-detachable cylinder head, fitted with a water jacket and having only one sparking plug per cylinder. In order to achieve higher engine speeds, the bore and stroke measurements were equalised at 68.25 mm, giving a 'square' engine that was reputed to top 5,000 rpm and yet retain a high standard of mechanical reliability. It is alleged that financial aspects permitted only one Works entry — Harry Langman — for the Company was only just on the point of recovery from the difficulties that had led to the appointment of the Official Receiver. Clarrie Wood now assumed the role of private entrant, for he had now left the Scott Works in order to set up his own motorcycle business in Bradford. But it may be assumed that he had some measure of support from the factory because his machine was fitted with one of the new 'square' engines. In practice, Clarrie set up a record lap with the new engine, but before the Senior Race took place, both riders reverted to the original longstroke engine in the belief that the lower revving engine had better long-term reliability. In Langman's case the gamble paid off, for he finished in second place at an average speed of 61.24 mph — only a little slower than the race average of Alec Bennett's winning Norton. Clarrie Wood was less fortunate. He switched to the machine he had ridden in the 1923 Senior race, which he had purchased from the Works. He managed to hold a position on the Leader Board right up to the last lap, when his engine seized. Fortunately he was able to get going again, to finish in 13th place and help the Bradford Club win the Team Prize. There was no Scott entry in the Sidecar Race.

Mention has been made of the other Scott riders who were particularly successful in reliability trials and other forms of competition events held during this period. It is interesting to take stock of the individuals concerned for individuals they were, each a real character in his own right, destined to become something of a legend in the annals of Scott history. Yet they possessed that unique ability to knit together as a hard, relentless team when occasion demanded, as exemplified by their exploits in the Inter-Club Team Trials held during the twenties. Year after year the Scott-mounted Ilkley and District M.C.C riders carried off awards in all parts of the country and excelled themselves in events such as those organised annually by the Yorkshire Centre A-CU and by the M.C.C. One of the more outstanding feats occurred during an inter-club team trial that centred on the notorious Alms Hill area, near Henley-on-Thames. Apart from the necessity to cover three laps of the very severe course on a non-stop basis, a complicated time keeping schedule had also to be observed. Whilst each rider was permitted to cover the first lap of the course at whatever speed he chose, he had to repeat the time exactly on the second lap and again on the third lap. The Ilkley team perfected their timing by practising for several days before the event, using imaginary check points. H. V. Ebblewhite, the famous A-CU Time-keeper, was astounded when he checked his stop watches after the event. Both Ilkley teams (six riders in total) were so consistent over the three laps that their total cumulative error was only three seconds! Although the make-up of the two teams changed over the years, the most consistent performers were Walter Clough (4 years), Billy Moore (3 years), Alex Duxbury (2 years), J. H. Holmes (2 years), Harrison Town (4 years), Geoff Milnes (3 years), George Gill (2 years), W. M. Mason (2 years) and Harold Wood (4 years). The only person who did not ride a Scott was Fred Marshall. He had an AJS outfit and was usually passengered by Sidney Jayne.

The elder member of the Scott team was Billy Moore, a master builder and contractor who lived in Keighley. He rode in his first Scott Trial during 1920 and won the Amateur Award, a feat he repeated again during 1922 and 1923. Yet he was no youngster, for he was then over forty years old. Much has been written about Billy, a tough, blunt Yorkshireman with greying hair, who always wore a white tie. His machine bore the distinctive registration number U6, which accounted for the diminutive number plates used and the title 'Yewsix of the Moor'! It is reputed that U6 was the number shared amongst the three Scotts he owned, a fact once commented upon by the local policeman who happened to call at Billy's garage. Fortunately, policemen used their discretion in those days and matters were not taken further!

Such was Billy's riding ability that one of his favourite tricks was to ride across the local canal on a plank only six inches wide! He was also seen on occasion riding through town whilst reading a newspaper, seemingly with perfect control over his machine and forward progress. He had a unique knowledge of the Yorkshire Dales, which was put to good effect in later years when he joined Harold Wood for the responsibility of plotting the course

Scott Trial course hunting, circa 1927. Billy Moore pushes Willie Wood out of one of the hazards. Note the exhaust pipe tied across his back

Ken Wilson, an occasional Scott Trial helper, tries to ride across a frozen pond

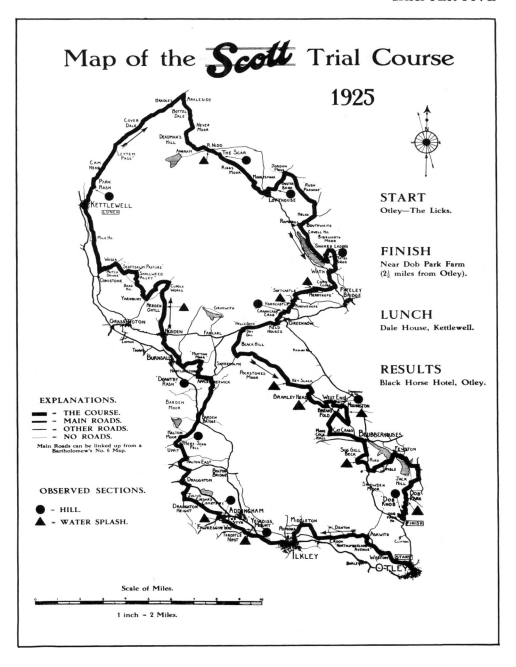

Map of the 1925 Scott Trial course

of the Scott Trial. Both knew most of the local landowners and their gamekeepers and it was only on rare occasions that their request for access was refused.

Harold Wood was a Scott enthusiast from a very early age, for the Wood family lived close to Alfred Scott's lodgings in Spring Gardens, Heaton. Harold used to watch Tim Wood pass by each day, whilst he was on his way to school and by the age of seven had fitted his scooter with a purple disc that sported the two characteristic white bands used on the Scotts of that period. News of Scott trials successes encouraged him to construct a miniature trials course in the back garden, with a representative sample of almost every hazard which he would negotiate on his pedal cycle. Feats such as riding slowly across the rungs of a ladder taught him the art of balance and low speed control, which must have paid dividends during his later years as a very active and successful rider in all manner of competition events. He purchased his first Scott during 1919 when he was aged 20, a move that led to his eventual employment as a fitter and then a road tester at the Saltaire Works.

It was in 1919 that Harold witnessed his first Scott Trial, only the second to have been held. On this occasion he somehow persuaded his father into taking him by train to Otley and walk a distance of 4½ miles to the notorious watersplash at Dob Park. They returned home in similar fashion after the last competitor had struggled through, father no doubt a little wiser about the prospects of undertaking such a journey again! It was not until 1922 that Harold rode in his first competition event, a sporting trial held by the Bradford M.C.C. This signified the beginning of a long and highly successful period as a competition rider, that included entry of the Scott Trial in 1924 and again in 1925. On the first occasion he became utterly exhausted well before the finish and decided to retire from the event there and then. But because it was easiest to follow the course rather than attempt to retrace his steps, he continued with innumerable pauses. The account of his experiences was recorded in a later Scott Trial programme and makes such entertaining reading that it is worth repeating in full:

"I kept retiring all day long and then thinking better of it. Soon after starting, two team mates drowned their engines in Dob Park, so I retired to help them. Then, feeling so late as to be out of the trial, I decided to press on just to see a little more of the course. The rivers were very full that year, but I reaped the reward of careful preparation in waterproofing (my great uncle Harbutt was the inventor of Plasticene, so I had ample supplies!) and after every splash I was delighted to find myself passing fields full of exhausted humanity pushing or kicking lifeless motorcycles. It came as quite a shock to be hailed everywhere as a competitor and I was too self-conscious to explain that really I had retired. I decided to hurry on to some tit-bit and there to sit down and *watch* the trial until my battered brain suddenly realised that there was very little trial left behind me to watch! Feeling that nothing mattered, I went mad and set off to catch up something worth

Harold Wood's 3-speed Super finds a soft spot whilst course hunting for the Scott Trial. The exhaust pipe extension is both ingenious and very necessary when fording rivers

Billy Moore negotiates one of the many streams to be found across the desolate moorland

watching. Re-passing dozens of stragglers and feeling thoroughly happy at last, I reached the old rocky Park Rash and decided to stop there — at the top. The top, however, was miraculously reached feet up and to dump the model and join the spectators after such a glorious and well-applauded fluke seemed out of the question, so on we clattered.

After battling with wheelspin on lonely Arkleside, I gave up altogether and decided to go home. It seemed just as sensible to follow the course homewards as to go back, and dejected observers woke up and seemed so overjoyed to find another little bit of trial coming along that I had not the heart to explain I had retired. At Hardcastle, I pondered for a while whether to go straight home or to nip around by Burnsall to see how many had finished. The old fever won and in a rash impulse I chose to follow the dye rather than the main road. Imagine my amazement when I was welcomed in as a late survivor and I realised I had actually covered the whole course. A finisher! Perhaps even a coveted Scott Trial Certificate hung on the horizon! On Monday morning I opened a newspaper to learn that C. H. Wood (486 cc Scott) had *WON A TROPHY*. I had made second best performance on observation only".

Although now rather rare, the early Scott Trial programmes make very amusing and entertaining reading, for they contain innumerable witticisms, parodies of popular advertisements, cartoons, poems and all manner of contributions that help 'send up' the event. Harold's own part in compiling much of this material when he became involved with the organisation from 1926 onwards, is only too evident, for those who are privileged to know him will be aware of his very keen and impish sense of humour. It is, perhaps, in the naming of some of the Scott Trial sections that he particularly excelled himself. Who else would conjure up names such as Wantas Top, Cummerkroppa, Tawnyscote, Skottskum Pasture and Little Sedbut Allotment! To quote his own words once again, "In 1925 I rode again, but the collection of another Certificate seemed such a simple matter, even for me. 1926, therefore, saw me on the side of the conspirators (organisers), and it is in this cruel role that I have hidden ever since".

The surname Wood has tended to cause much confusion amongst the lesser informed, for it is one that is shared by no less than four prominent Scott riders and personalities. It should be emphasised that Harold Wood is in no way related to Tim Wood, the winner of the 1913 Senior TT, or for that matter to the latter's younger brother Clarrie. Because Harold has the initials C. H. and Clarrie the initials C. P., it is not difficult to understand why such confusion has arisen and it is for this reason that an explanation is given. The fourth person having the surname Wood is Harold's brother Willie (A. W.) who became the motorcycle company's Sales Manager after the Scott Autocar Company closed down.

The third member of the Scott Trial course plotters was Geoff Milnes, a very able and talented rider and mechanic who was one of the Scott Motor Cycle Company's testers in his earlier days. He lived close to both

Special Contribution.

THIS IS A
100%
HE-MAN
CRIMSON-BLEED
TRIAL!!!!!

In " Alice in Wonderland," Lewis Carroll describes a race in which everybody won and everybody got prizes. If he had survived till the motor-cycling era, Lewis Carroll would certainly have been Pluperfect President of the A-C.U. For in the average A-C.U. trial most people get gold medals. This is very bad for the riders, who get swollen heads. Very bad for the manufacturers, who fancy their machines must be perfect, and go off to play golf at 11 a.m. every morning, leaving the mass production to look after itself. Very bad for the public, who suppose it is impossible to smash up a modern machine, and only discover their blunder when they meet two traction engines canoodling round a blind corner. Fortunately, the Scott Trial exists to correct such matters. Our aim is to plan a trial in which nobody shall finish and nobody shall qualify for any awards of any kind. We thus hope to make riders modest, manufacturers energetic, and the public wiser. Hitherto, we have never quite succeeded, because Yorkshire is becoming so absurdly civilised that it is annually more difficult to discover a patch of country fit for a realy sporting motor-cyclist to tackle, and successive Scott Trials have had the effect of toughening up " 'buses " past belief. Still, we live in hope, and if only we get half-a-dozen cloud bursts on September 10th, we may yet achieve our ideal of running a trial in which nobody finishes, and Alex. is able to send the whole of the entry money to St. Dunstan's. So here's to us; and to the poor boobs who will be silly enough to start this year.

" IXION."

Ixion's summary of the Scott Trial, reprinted from the 1927 programme

Middleton and Denton Moors, Ilkley, only a few doors away from Frank Philipp. According to Harold Wood, Geoff possessed the unique ability of being able to relax quite suddenly and go to sleep anywhere at any time. Once, when leading a team of Scott riders en route to an Inter-Club Team Trial in Buckinghamshire he carried straight on at a sharp bend in the road, crossed the grass verge and disappeared into a field through the hedge. He was found still astride his machine, which by some miracle was still in an upright position, rubbing his eyes and enquiring what had happened! Fortunately his machine was undamaged and he helped the Ilkley Club win the Team Prize on the following day!

Geoff Milnes collected innumerable first class awards and cups in most open events, including the Scottish Six Days Trial. His most outstanding success was his outright win of the Leeds £200 Trial, an event sponsored by the local newspaper of which more is related later in this Chapter.

Other riders of note were Walter Clough, another Scott employee who invariably rode a sidecar outfit, passengered by either Geoff Milnes or by a youngster named Frank Varey, of whom much was to be heard in later years. Harrison Town, Foreman of the Repair Shop, was another regular competitor and others such as Allan Jefferies, Harry Langman, Clarrie Wood (until he left the Company in 1924) and the Langton brothers, Eric and Oliver, were all brilliant all-rounders who helped swell the never ending list of Scott successes as the weeks passed by. In retrospect, it would seem doubtful whether any other manufacturer had quite such an abundance of talent on tap at this particular time.

The Scott entry in the 1924 Amateur TT dropped to just two — Prescott's Kendal Scott and one of the 'square' engine TT models, to be ridden by a newcomer named P. Hoggarth. Both machines were well down in speed and the best place went to Prescott, who was 12th. He finished some four minutes after the 350 cc Cotton that was 11th. Hoggarth finished in 16th place, after several long stops for reasons that were not recorded. Prescott's race average was some 10 mph below that of the eventual winner — Len Randles and his Sunbeam for the second year in succession.

The 68.25 mm 'square' engine was fitted to the new Super Squirrel model that had been added to the range and was available in both 498 cc and 596 cc capacities, the latter by increasing the stroke. The 596 cc engine carried a surcharge of £3 3s if it was fitted in place of the 498 cc unit, making the overall cost of the larger capacity Super £76 13s. According to the Show Number of *Motor Cycle* the new Super Squirrel engine, with its polished aluminium cylinder head water jacket, looked decidedly attractive, the whole machine having a very pretty appearance. Prices in general had been lowered, for the industry was about to experience a sharp price-cutting campaign. The standard Squirrel was now priced at only £66 3s, to quote one example.

All models now featured an improved design of curved induction stub, which bolted direct to the crankcase instead of being clamped by a setscrew from a bolted-on frame lug. A cleaner handlebar effect was obvious on all models by the use of inverted levers and the removal of the ignition cut-out, although the latter was still actuated by the half-compression device. Other improvements included the fitting of wider section tyres and the purchaser had the option of either a two or a three-speed gear with the new Super models. The three-speed Super Squirrel was destined to become one of the most revered of all the Scott models and was the favourite mount of many of the competition riders of that era, including Billy Moore.

For those whose financial outlay was restricted, the older two and three-speed models had been retained in the range, giving them a chance to join the ever growing circle of Scott enthusiasts. At £66 3s the standard

486 cc Squirrel was basically similar to the current models in outward appearance, apart from the air cooled cylinder heads of the larger bore engine and a slightly smaller capacity petrol tank. For those who required extras, items such as legshields and a Lucas electric lighting set were also catalogued, the latter adding £12 10s to the overall purchase price.

The Scott Autocar Company were no longer in a position to exhibit the Sociable for in view of increasing financial difficulties, production came to a halt at the end of the year and only a few remaining machines were assembled from the stock of spare parts. Like so many ingenious designs, the Sociable had failed to attract the support of the ever fickle public, who were loud to sing its praise but reluctant to purchase when the opportunity eventually arose. Undoubtedly the advent of the Austin Seven car during 1922 did much to lure away prospective purchasers, who were a little apprehensive about the odd appearance of the Sociable in spite of its many technical attributes. And so the Sociable became yet another of motorcycling's curiosities and the victim of yet another lost cause. It is probable that the industry as a whole has lost more money in attempting to perfect a true 'everyman' model than on any other single project.

The winning team (Ilkley Club) in the 1928 MCC Inter-Club Team Trial, held near Buxton. L to R - Harold Wood (passenger G. Jones), C. Thackray, Geoff Milnes, J. S. Duxbury (reserve), Harrison Town, Billy Moore, Walter Clough (passenger Frank Varey)

THE SCOTT MOTORCYCLE

Although the Scott motorcycle may seem to be a difficult subject to convert into a 'special', it was during 1925 that one or two such machines were in evidence, apart from the Kendal Scott already mentioned in a previous Chapter. One of the more unusual was the Palethorpe Special, which had been constructed during the years 1923–4 by a Captain Palethorpe of Stourbridge. He had taken a two-speed model and fitted it with a shaped 'chair', presenting the rider with a somewhat low but presumably more comfortable riding position, virtually just above the two-speed gear. This necessitated dispensing with the open frame petrol tank and substituting a combined petrol and oil tank that was mounted across the downtube, immediately to the rear of the radiator. The tank was a slabsided affair, not unlike the tank fitted to the ladies models available from other motorcycle manufacturers. Why this somewhat strange layout was adopted is by no means clear, but the model was a familiar sight around Stourbridge at this time, often with a Miss Louie Ball seated in the 'chair'. As some may recall, Louie Ball was a lady trials rider of no mean ability who progressed to even greater fame when she married George McLean and became a member of the Douglas trials team.

The most famous Scott special was undoubtedly that created by the redoubtable Bill Bradley, another of the regular competitors in the Scott Trial and similar events. The machine was, in fact, built as a complete sidecar outfit and was used by Bill as a form of mobile test bed for a whole series of his inventions that extended over a period of ten years. One of the more notable features was the banking sidecar which, unlike Freddie Dixon's design, was operated by the rider and not the passenger. Pressure on a portion of one footboard supplied the necessary power *from the engine* to either raise or lower the complete sidecar chassis so that it was possible to run along a bank with the sidecar wheel raised high whilst the outfit itself remained in the vertical plane. It obviated the need for either the rider or the passenger to indulge in the usual acrobatics when taking corners at speed, yet ensured the wheels remained on the ground. Other innovations included a really practicable inlet valve that materially improved engine scavenge efficiency, a six-speed gear arranged by lining together a Scott two-speed gear with a hand operated clutch to a three-speed Sturmey Archer gearbox. The outfit also had sidecar wheel drive. These latter attributes proved especially useful in events such as the Scott Trial and account in no small way for Bradley's Best Sidecar Performance during the 1926 event. The outfit, appropriately named Felix, soon became an accepted part of the trials scene.

Not all 'specials' were directed to trials and road use. In sprint events, Bert Hill was one of the leading northern exponents, using a Kendal Scott to which he had made his own modifications. He worked with Lancelot Parker but because pressure of business left little opportunity for experimental work, most of the work had to be carried out in his spare time. The very high compression ratios used caused endless problems with either the pistons or the sparking plugs, which would not withstand the high temperatures for

Bill Bradley coaxes 'Felix' up Hepolite Scar. The look of apprehension on the passenger's face is worthy of attention!

long. Some idea of the depth of the problem may be gauged when it is realised that aluminium alloy pistons were not generally available at that time. There is one instance on record where some locally-cast pistons in an unknown alloy needed a 0.025 inch clearance to give satisfactory performance when the engine was hot. The clatter when the engine was cold had to be heard to be believed! One of Hill's major objectives was a crack at the hour record, which at that time was still in the sixties. Although his engine was capable of a sustained 70 mph for the period involved, some over-zealous drilling of the connecting rods led to a disastrous blow-up, which erased completely two years spare time work. Although he was able to reconstruct another engine to similar specification the opportunity for the record attempt had passed by the time the engine was completed. One can only conjecture whether he would have achieved his objective had fate been a little kinder, for sad to relate, the name Scott is not one that appears frequently in the record books.

The reception of the new Super models seemed to augur well for the future and although the Company was still far from affluent, it was decided that support should be given to the 1925 Senior TT and the Sidecar Race, in the form of Works entries. Langman's second place average of 61.23 mph in the 1924 Senior was considered to show great promise, especially since his

125

trouble-free ride was accomplished at an average speed less than half a mile per hour slower than that of the winning Norton. But at the same time it was appreciated that speeds were steadily rising and that this was placing much greater demands on the cycle parts, particularly in terms of roadholding and braking. In consequence, the preparations for the 1925 events included the need for better front forks, brakes and larger bearings together with improved lubrication of the old two-speed gear. Enginewise, it was evident that the 'square' revver engine used during practice at the previous year's event and later in the Amateur TT, would have the ability to provide the much desired win if the new cycle parts improved the machine's handling. It was already in current use on the production models and required only one or two refinements, one of which was the adoption of full mechanical lubrication by means of an oil pump. This would ensure oil was fed to the main bearings and cylinder walls at a pre-determined rate, without necessitating the frequent attention of the rider. Drip feed oiling was retained only for the chains. Strangely enough, the basic problem was one of rider selection. Although Harry Langman remained the number one choice, Clarrie Wood was no longer available and had transferred his allegiance to another manufacturer. Geoff Clapham was another who would have been selected, had he not deserted the Scott camp and elected to ride a Beardmore Precision in the Lightweight Race. And so three sand racers got their chance — Ernie Mainwaring, Harrison Town and a man named J. H. Welsby. All were experienced Scott riders, although only Mainwaring and Welsby had any previous experience of the Mountain course. Welsby had ridden in the 1923 Junior Race on a Wetherall, and Mainwaring had been Langman's sidecar passenger in the ill-fated 1923 race.

By now, the overhead valve four-stroke models were getting into their stride and no one could have predicted that the average speed of the Senior event would shoot up by some 5 mph. The Scott Motor Cycle Company was not the only manufacturer taken by surprise and all three of the newcomers were soon out of the race, eliminated by engine troubles of one kind or another. Once again it was left to Harry Langman to hold the fort and he matched up to expectations. After a very spirited ride that included one lap at 65 mph, he crossed the line in 5th place. He had lost time having to stop for brake adjustments and at one time had encountered such severe frame pitching that the machine was virtually uncontrollable. The brake trouble was subsequently traced to grease getting onto the rear brake shoes and rendering them ineffective.

The Sidecar Race had been put back until after the Senior event, in case one of the riders should be involved in an accident that would eliminate them from the Senior Race, as had occurred on several occasions in the past. Langman had the misfortune to retire early in the race, when the countershaft of his two-speed gear seized at Greeba. It had been widely predicted that he would win, especially since his 1923 lap record was still unbroken. But it was not to be and once again Douglas stole the honours when Len Parker crossed

One of the 1925 Senior TT models, possibly the machine ridden by Harry Langman

the line in first place. The Scott contingent packed up their gear at the Bay Hotel, Ramsey, with an air of gloom.

Although it was evident that the existing, original Scott design had reached the point where the cycle parts would never be capable of handling the higher speeds that were now commonplace in long distance racing events, no matter how much they were strengthened or modified, there was insufficient time to prepare anything new for the 1925 Amateur TT, even if a new design would be entrusted to an amateur rider. It should be appreciated that the event no longer enjoyed quite such an amateur atmosphere as had been envisaged originally, for the 'Shamateurs' were already in evidence, aided and abetted by loads of Works spares that somehow filtered into the hands of those who showed good racing potential. Again, only two Scotts featured in the entry, one a Super Squirrel to be ridden by P. Coward and the other, one of the latest two-speed models that had full mechanical lubrication. This latter model was ridden by P. B. Cheston, who put in two very good laps before the top gear chain broke at Bray Hill, necessitating his retirement. Coward finished 15th after an uneventful ride. Although H. V. Prescott again rode in the event (and finished 10th) he had elected to ride another local thoroughbred on this occasion — a P and M, made in Cleckheaton near Bradford.

Another new series of models made their debut at the Olympia Show, held during September. Designated Flying Squirrel and distinguished by the (optional) TT full frame tank, they were clearly based on the 1925 TT design. The full specification included full mechanical oiling by means of a Best and Lloyd pump mounted on the offside crankcase door, enlarged exhaust ports with polished passages and an improved water-cooled cylinder head that gave better plug cooling. For those who did not wish to pay the surcharge for the TT tank, and wished to retain an open frame layout, the customary oval tank was still available. To distinguish the model from the Supers, the tank had a large red diamond with a silver surround, over which a flying squirrel motif was superimposed. Not unexpectedly the 498 cc and 596 cc Flying Squirrels carried a somewhat high price tag — £86 2s and £89 5s respectively. The Super Squirrel models of similar capacities retained at £73 10s and £76 13s respectively, with a Best and Lloyd oil pump on the crankcase door, whilst the older standard 486 cc Squirrel was retained in the range at £66 3s, as the year previous, the only model now having suction and drip feed lubrication. For the sidecar enthusiast, a special low-compression 596 cc three-speed model could be obtained for £92 8s. All models other than the Flying Squirrel dispensed with the drip feed oiling system, but had a hand-operated pump embodied in the cylindrical oil tank which delivered a charge of oil when the plunger was operated. One welcome modification was provision for adjusting the primary chains in a positive manner by means of modified two-speed gear frame brackets incorporating studs and nuts which abutted brazed-on slotted lugs on the chainstays. One that did not apply until later in the 1926 season was that of wider bearing engines. When they became available much later in the season, they could be identified by the slight belling of the crankcase in the vicinity of the crankcase doors.

For the 1926 season, the gearbox of the three-speed models was substantially improved. Pinions of coarser pitch were fitted and the positions of the low and middle gears were interchanged. This latter modification permitted the overhang to be put on the dogs of the sliding pinion, instead of the middle gear. Clutch operation was changed to a quick thread ring, using three short thrust pins, in the manner that is in use today. This necessitated repositioning the quick thread ring and thrust race between the gearbox shell and the clutch.

The gearchange was also modified. The spring-loaded face cams and linkage were replaced by a spring-loaded thrust rod, operated by a pin at right angles to it, the movement of which was controlled by a longitudinal slot in the hollow gear lever spindle, the ends of the pin being guided by a cam groove in the gearbox shell. The spring-loaded rod operated the selector fork, which was shaped like a double wishbone. The whole of the gear operating mechanism was now totally enclosed within the gearbox shell.

The multi-plate clutch was unchanged, apart from the actuating mechanism as described above. The magneto was no longer mounted on top of the gearbox. It now bolted to a separate platform, mounted on the frame tubes above the gearbox. The drive was still taken from the clutch sprocket housing, provision for adjustment being accomplished by raising the platform to increase chain tension.

As far as racing was concerned, the design team was now at the crossroads, for it was evident that some quite fundamental design changes would be necessary if the inherent handling problems of the original cycle parts were to be overcome in a satisfactory manner. In effect, this meant a further break away from the Alfred Scott era, although there was no doubt that such a break had to occur if the Company was to be in the least progressive. The outcome was a new duplex frame of heavier gauge tubing, arranged in triangulated fashion, a heavily braced plunger-type front fork assembly and a close ratio three-speed gearbox with a gate change lever pivoted on a lug brazed to the offside downtube, adjacent to the petrol tank. The actuating rod was coupled to a selector lever at the front of the gearbox. A separate gate was bolted to the handchange lever lug. The 1926 multi-plate clutch was used, with friction inserts instead of rings. Better brakes were necessary in anticipation of higher speeds and an increase in chain sizes, but as may be expected, all these improvements could be made only at the expense of added weight. Instead of scaling something in the region of 240 lb, the weight was now closer to 315 lb. It is interesting to note that nearly all the subsequent Flying Squirrel models were based on this prototype design, the layout of which remained basically unchanged until production at Shipley ceased during 1951. Harry Shackleton was responsible for these design changes as indeed he was for most Scott development work that took place during the twenties.

Engine improvements were necessary to retain a more favourable power to weight ratio now that the overall weight of the machine had increased so considerably. Separate exhaust ports and a more robust bottom end helped boost power to an alleged 18 bhp at 5,000 rpm. Some early tests are reported to have claimed that the roadholding was not up to that of the well-proven two-speeders, but it is questionable whether in fact this was so because the new model was entered for the 1926 Senior TT in unmodified form. Three machines were produced in time to be ridden by Langman, Mainwaring and Welsby. Langman had his engine blow up at Ballaugh on the first lap and Mainwaring retired soon afterwards. Only Welsby completed the race, albeit with a very troublesome gearbox. 18th place was the best position he could muster under the circumstances. It afterwards transpired that Langman's machine had broken a crank, whilst Mainwaring's retirement was caused by a moment's inattention. Whilst ascending May Hill, he reached down to replace a plug lead that had jumped off, the resulting electrical shock causing his machine to wander sufficiently to hit the kerb and catapult him into a potato field! Fortunately he escaped injury.

Undaunted by this unexpected setback, four Scotts were entered for the September Amateur TT, three of them on the new TI models that were soon to go into general production. The fourth rider proved to be something of a mystery, for the entry was made by a member of the Scott M.C.C under the pseudonym 'A Menace'. Whoever it was (Andrew Leach) failed to materialise in time for practice and was automatically excluded from the race. Two of the riders — Paul Stables and Noel Mavrogordato — were Cambridge University clubmen who were making their first appearance in the Isle of Man. The third member was none other than H. V. Prescott, who had been attracted back to his former allegiance. Senior race day was wet, misty and cold, the penance of holding the races at this somewhat unpredictable time of the year, although the weather in Mona's Isle is always prone to sudden change. All three riders gave a very creditable account of themselves in a race where there were many retirements. Stables rode especially well to finish 6th — the first occasion on which a Scott had appeared on the Leader Board of the Amateur races. Mavrogordato finished 7th, despite an encounter with the padding that protected the wall at Craig-ny-Baa and an engine seizure on the Sulby straight. He had intended to retire, but when the engine freed, he decided to continue in the race. Prescott was 15th, after what he described as an enjoyable joy ride! It was evident that the Scott Motor Cycle Company had decided to give full support on this occasion because Harry Langman and Jim Capstick, the Works mechanic, acted as pit attendants. The late Reg Summers, a great Scott fanatic, was asked by Harry Langman to look after Paul Stables' pit and it is largely through Reg's well-kept diaries that such complete records exist today of each Scott rider's achievements in both the Senior TT and the Amateur TT. Reg evidently discharged his duties well, for he recorded a pit stop of only 35 seconds in which Stables' machine took on three gallons of fuel, about a half gallon of oil and had a quick inspection of the radiator whilst the rider was briefed about his position!

Noel Mavrogordato (right) and Paul Stables (left) just before the 1926 Amateur TT

It was in 1926 that the organisation of the annual Scott Trial underwent a quite fundamental change, largely on account of repercussions from the Leeds £200 Trial that was held the year previous. Sponsored by the local newspaper, the event had been thrown open to both motorcycles and cars, with a measure of publicity that attracted a vast entry that included about every local rider of merit to say nothing of those drawn from other parts of the country. Although the event was run in a very efficient manner, no attempt had been made to consult the Auto-Cycle Union or indeed to liaise with this body in any way, thereby giving rise to a serious breach of protocol. The Trial was therefore regarded as an 'unofficial event' and the outcome was the suspension of several prominent A-CU officials who had helped with the organisation. A complete embargo was also placed on any future events of this nature, unless the organisation was handled by a Club affiliated to the A-CU. As may be imagined, this placed the Scott Motor Cycle Company in an awkward predicament for until this time, the Scott Trial had been organised by the Company, even though most of the officials were A-CU members and had their names as such included in the programme credits. Fortunately the problem was resolved quite easily by transferring the organisation of the 1926 event to the Bradford and District M.C.C. The names of the organising officials shown in the programme were virtually unchanged, apart from the removal of the name of Alex Doverner, former Secretary of the Bradford Club and the Yorkshire A-CU. He was one of the officials of the Leeds £200 Trial and had been suspended. However, he was still much in evidence at the event wearing a badge inscribed BBL which, on enquiry, stood for Bradford's Bad Lad! By the time the 1927 event was held, he had been reinstated in office and his name once again included in the programme.

As events transpired, the 1926 Scott Trial had the doubtful distinction of being the longest ever, for the course covered no less than 105 miles! It attracted a total of 134 competitors and optimistically contained provision for the award of a ladies prize. Such was the severity of the event that only 30 survivors completed the course — even Bill Bradley's Felix called it a day at West End after putting up a simply incredible sidecar performance. As Stanley Woods said afterwards, "I could not have moved another yard for £10,000!" yet he considered himself at the peak of physical fitness.

Another local event that attracted great attention in the middle and late twenties was Hepolite Scar, a shingle hill of severe gradient located just off the lower main road from Shipley to Bradford. Although no longer in use, the twin tracks leading to the summit are still visible today and can be seen across the valley when descending from the Heaton district to the main road. Hepolite Scar was the scene of numerous hill climbs, in which both cars and motorcycles took part. Ropes wrapped around the rear tyre or some other means of obtaining extra grip on the loose surface were an essential requirement if a solo rider was to reach the summit. Such was the severity of the gradient that officials stood by with a chock on the end of a long pole so that the rear wheel could be scotched immediately forward motion ceased.

This obviated the risk of a backward somersault like that filmed in some of the more spectacular American events. Bill Bradley's Felix provided a number of demonstration runs for the general entertainment of the spectators and it was Harold Wood who was one of the more successful local riders. Needless to say the two local products — the Scott motorcycle and the Jowett car — drew the greatest cheers when they were successful. Harold Wood recalls a day when the hill proved unclimbable by even the most powerful cars, yet a small two cylinder Jowett in full road trim made a slow and unhesitating climb to the summit, with the driver looking as though he was out for a leisurely afternoon drive!

As had been expected, a new series of models featuring the redesigned cycle parts used in the 1926 TT models, were on display at the October Olympia Show. In effect, the new 498 cc Flying Squirrel could be regarded as the actual TT model put into production, with the option of a 596 cc engine for those who required more power. The most noticeable differences from the previous models, apart from the new duplex frame, comprised a larger radiator, separate exhaust pipes from each cylinder to a forward-mounted expansion box, an improved hand-operated gear change control complete with gate that was fitted to the front downtube, larger diameter brakes, heavier gauge chains, adjustable footrests and the addition of a transmission shock absorber. This formidable list of modifications necessitated an increase in price, which brought the latest Flying Squirrel models up to £93 9s and £96 12s respectively, the additional 3 guineas being required for the 596 cc engine. The 498 cc and 596 cc versions of the two-speed Super Squirrel were still catalogued at the previous year's prices, although both models now incorporated a number of modifications that included a mechanical lubrication system and better brakes. Also catalogued was the original two-speed 486 cc Squirrel with narrow forks at an unchanged £66 3s and two 596 cc touring models, with the choice of either a two or three-speed gear. The option of a three-speed gearbox similar to the 1926 design, was also open to the purchaser of the standard Super Squirrel models and for those who required a sidecar, a range based on the Scott triangulated chassis or a rectangular tube chassis in two types, was available from £15 15s upwards. All Super Squirrel, Squirrel and standard models were fitted with wider front forks having sloping shoulders.

During March 1927 there was news that a supercharged Scott was being constructed by J. Shuckburgh Wright for use at Brooklands. Based on the Flying Squirrel model, it was intended to run the machine in both the solo and sidecar classes by the simple expedient of interchanging cylinder blocks and pistons. This would permit the machine to compete in the 500 cc solo class and yet gain from the benefit of the permissible increase in engine capacity when sidecar races were contested. The supercharger was of the centrifugal type, located below the saddle and driven by chain from the magneto platform area. It developed a pressure of 5 - 6 psi at the intake of the 1¼ inch Amac carburettor used, which was fitted with only a single float

A good clean sport! Tommy Hatch and Frank Varey after a motor cycle football match

chamber. The BTH magneto had received special attention from the manufacturer and incorporated a specially-made contact breaker. The engine had a compression ratio of 8.5 : 1 and was claimed to develop maximum power at 4,700 rpm. Anticipating cooling problems, Shuckburgh Wright had fitted a thermostat to the radiator so that a water temperature gauge would give visible warning of overheating when the level in the radiator dropped more than two inches, causing steam to heat an internal tube.

In an attempt to overcome the noise problem, two separate long exhaust systems were employed, each of which terminated in a Derrington silencer fitted with a regulation Brooklands fishtail. At this time, the whole future of racing at Brooklands was in the balance as the result of the ever growing level of complaints from local residents, whose gardens backed on to, or were adjacent to the giant concrete saucer. It was clearly in the interests of both competitors and officials alike to do all they could to help mollify the situation.

It was on April 20th that the Scott made its Brooklands debut, for an initial try-out. It was in full race trim, but had the supercharger temporarily disconnected as the result of some teething troubles. When the engine was started, the officials present took exception to the noise and only one practice lap per half hour was permitted. This in itself was a severe handicap, for the engine required at least one lap before it reached the correct running temperature. Whether the outcome of the tests proved disappointing or whether the attitude of the officials was resented is not known. The Shuckburgh Wright Scott was not seen again and it passed into obscurity.

Spurred on by the failure of the Works entries in the 1926 Senior TT, Harry Shackleton and his design team set about reducing the overall weight of the TT models, whilst at the same time giving further attention to the handling problems. The new 7 inch forks were lightened by dispensing with some of the girder work, so that they more closely resembled the earlier Super type. But they were much stronger than the originals and had an open centre spring and Hartford friction dampers. To achieve better weight distribution, the wheel base had been reduced by one inch between the rear wheel spindle and the rear engine bolts. The engine itself was shortened too, and moved back in the frame. This necessitated the use of a shorter gear tray. A duplex Pilgrim pump, driven from the magneto sprocket looked after engine lubrication. It was supplemented by a hand pump, to provide cylinder wall oiling. A two-into-one exhaust system was carried on the left hand side of the machine. The completed machines were much lighter in weight and benefitted from the short wheel base.

The 1927 Works entries comprised Harry Langman, Ernie Mainwaring and a newcomer to the event, Eric Langton, another of the locals who had achieved a great reputation as a competition rider, in company with his brother Oliver. Third place in the team was originally allocated to Geoff Milnes, but near the time of the race, he stood down and Eric took his place. Although hopes ran high on race day, they were soon dashed to the ground. Harry Langman's engine lasted for only two laps, whilst Ernie Mainwaring was forced to retire after lying 5th on the sixth lap, when float trouble caused his machine to run out of fuel. Eric Langton went out after six laps too, with the same trouble. In his case, the petrol tank itself had ruptured.

Again it was hoped that amends could be made in the 1927 Amateur TT and both Harry Langman and Jim Capstick went over to the Bay Hotel at Ramsey to give their full support to the Scott entry. This year there was a total entry of eight. Three of the runners, Stables, Prescott and Mavrogordato, already had experience of the event, but for the others — J. Nash, D. de Ferranti, G. Limmer, J. E. Lomas and D. G. Bird — it was the first time. Stables and Lomas were allocated two of the TT models, one of which was fitted with girder forks in place of the special Super forks that had been used previously. This was to be the machine ridden by Lomas. Little is known about the other machines, except that Ferranti rode a standard Flyer and Mavrogordato had a specially-built two-speeder. It was a replica of the 1925 two-speeder TT model, built by Harry Langman.

Lomas on his 1927 TT Scott, the forks of which snapped off on the approach to Hilberry during the 1927 Amateur TT

Race day was simply appalling. It rained so heavily that it is doubtful whether a race has ever been run under worse conditions. On the first lap, Limmer held third place and Lomas was sixth, but on the second lap the latter's forks broke at Hilberry, fortunately without incident. Stables was even more unfortunate. On the fourth lap a Norton rider fell heavily just above the Gooseneck, directly in front of him. He had no chance to take any evasive action and hit the Norton, which caused him to crash through a wire fence and sustain injuries that kept him in hospital for a while and terminated his riding career. Nash crashed at Cruikshank's Corner in Ramsey and Prescott came unstuck at Greeba, when he lost his steering damper. Meanwhile, Limmer had managed to retain his leading position on the fourth and fifth laps, whilst Ferranti drew closer and closer to him. They were separated by only two Nortons, ridden by Tim Hunt and W. Provis. The question in everyone's mind was, could Limmer and Ferranti pull off the seeming impossible and give Scotts the long-awaited one-two win?

Never before had there been such tension in the two Scott rider's pits, as the race neared the closing stages. Ferranti made a supreme effort and turned a six minute deficit into a two second lead as he snatched third place from Provis. Limmer maintained his lead at the start of the last lap and fought every inch of the way to retain it. But his brakes were fading and he eventually overshot at Governers Bridge which let Hunt into the lead with no chance of reclaiming it back. And so the two Scott riders had to be content with a very creditable second and third place, with the honour of

135

the fastest lap by a Scott going to Ferranti, at a speed of just over 59 mph. Hunt put up the fastest lap at 60.46 mph, which gives some indication of the conditions under which the race was held. Needless to say there was great jubilation amongst the Scott clan at the Prize Giving Ceremony and the riotous celebrations that followed.

Mavrogordato was a non-starter. On the last day of practice the two-speeder he was riding shed its front mudguard at the bottom of Bray Hill. It fouled the wheel and gave rise to a spectacular crash at over 80 mph; Mavro injured a knee sufficiently badly to keep him out of the race.

1927 was the last year the Scott contingent used the Bay Hotel, Ramsey, as their base. Henceforth, the Howstrake Hotel in Douglas was to be the new venue, a much more convenient siting on a number of counts. Apart from the possible need for privacy and perhaps some road testing on the more remote parts of the Mountain circuit, it is difficult to understand why the Ramsey location had been used for so long.

1927 was also the last year in which the roads remained open during the practice periods that preceded the races. Archie Birkin had been killed during practice for the June races, when he swerved to miss a fish cart near Kirkmichael. It seems incredible that this state of affairs had been tolerated for so long; the consequences of meeting any slow moving vehicle when travelling at over 80 mph are too dreadful to imagine.

Whilst writing a recent series of articles about his career with motor-cycles, Bob Holliday mentioned the Humfrey Symons monocar, a curious vehicle constructed during 1927 at the whim of Ernest Perman. Perman was a member of the Temple Press board and had come to the conclusion that a monocar was the solution to Britain's growing traffic density problem. The design he evolved was based on a Scott engine, used in conjunction with a three-speed Sturmey Archer gearbox. A Weymann-type body was fitted to the vehicle, having a wooden frame filled in with wire netting that was covered by rexine. To obviate starting problems, a Rotur dynamotor was fitted, which performed the dual role of starter and battery charger. Not surprisingly, the experiment proved little short of a disaster, not the least of the problems being chronic overheating. The monocar lapsed into obscurity and there was no attempt to revive it.

Once again the Company found itself in financial difficulties and in an endeavour to ease commitments, R. A. Vinter floated a number of separate companies, each of which handled the sale of Scott merchandise in the larger provincial cities. A typical example was Scott Motors (Manchester) Limited, which was destined to be taken over in a few years' time by another company more closely associated with the Scott factory.

The 1927 Scott Trial, held on Saturday, September 10th, was run over a course that had been reduced in length to some 70 miles. The starting point had been moved to Threshfield, much further up the Wharfe valley, so that some of the newly-exploited terrors along the edge of Malham Moor could be included. It was generally considered that the previous year's event had been just a little too severe, although there could be no question of relaxing the hazards encountered in each section since it was the aim of the organisers to maintain the reputation the event had built up as the toughest of all trials. On this occasion, heavy rain fell for several days preceding the event, which helped encourage spectator interest but did little to ease the burden on the competitors. Even Geoff Milnes was seen at one point with both crankcase doors removed, bailing out the contents of the crankcases! Oliver Langton put up the Best Performance and registered the first Scott victory in this event for a couple of years.

At the 1927 Olympia Show, held during the early part of November, attention was focussed on the Flying Squirrel models, the engine of which incorporated the TT model lubrication modifications. Externally, there was little difference from the models currently in production, apart from a new exhaust system that discharged into a cast aluminium alloy manifold, from which a single pipe led to a Howarth silencer attached to the nearside chainstays. Not so apparent was the use of taper tubes for the lower portion of the girder forks. Wired-on tyres were available as an optional extra now that they were coming into fashion. Another optional extra was a twist grip, another fashionable fitting that would soon completely replace the old lever operated throttle that had been so popular in the past. Prices remained unchanged.

The Super Squirrel models fitted with a three-speed gearbox now featured the new gear change lever and gate that had been available on the Flying Squirrel range only. Two-speed versions of the Super were also available, even though many considered this type of gear to be outdated. The main advantage was lightness in weight, a factor that was fully appreciated by the more discerning rider. Again prices remained stable. Even the original 486 cc Squirrel was still catalogued at £66 3s, along with a fully equipped touring model of 596 cc capacity that was slightly more expensive. By the end of the 1928 season, these two models were to be discontinued.

As far as the design team was concerned, it seemed that a Scott still stood a reasonable chance of a Senior TT win if only a little extra speed could be obtained without any sacrifice of engine reliability. Since the new cycle parts had already given a good account of themselves under racing conditions, apart from the tendency to brake fade, work commenced on a new longstroke engine with bore and stroke measurements of 66.6 mm x 71.4 mm. The short wheel base of the previous year's models was retained, and the shortened gear tray, so that the gearbox could be brought closer to the engine. This necessitated recessing the rear vertical faces of the crankcase to assist in clutch removal and primary chain fitting. A recessed rear crankcase wall was also required, to give clearance for the gear operating lever and to give access to the clutch and primary chain. Obviously the Works were more optimistic about the chance of success since no less than six machines were entered for the Senior event. All were identical, apart from the machine to be ridden by Eric Langton, which was fitted with Webb girder forks in place

THE SCOTT MOTORCYCLE

The 1928 Flying Squirrel model

of the Scott forks with taper bottom tubes and straight top tubes. The other riders comprised the two evergreens, Harry Langman and Ernie Mainwaring, who were backed by G. Limmer, Oliver Langton and Tommy Hatch. Limmer had clearly earned his place in the team as the result of his splendid effort in the 1927 Amateur TT. Tommy Hatch was the only newcomer to the Isle of Man of the latter trio. Oliver Langton had ridden a New Hudson in earlier events, but had ridden Scotts in other competitions.

Pouring rain heralded race day, with conditions near identical to those experienced by Limmer when he came second in the 1927 Amateur TT. However, Limmer was a non-starter on this occasion and his place was not filled by a reserve. Ernie Mainwaring was forced to retire on the third lap, when his engine packed up at the Gooseneck. Eric Langton was in trouble too and was seen riding into Ramsey with a flat back tyre, where he dumped the bike and caught the bus back to Douglas! Oliver Langton was one of several riders who fell at the Gooseneck and it was subsequently found that a patch of grease was responsible for the crop of incidents at this point. He was in good company, for Freddie Dixon parted company with his machine at the same spot. Fortunately, Freddie's comments were not recorded! Tommy Hatch pressed on to finish third, averaging 60.89 mph, whilst Harry Langman finished a very creditable twelfth after riding for most of the race without goggles. This was to prove his last ride in the TT for the rain and wind damaged his eyes and ever after it was necessary to wear spectacles. Hero of the race was a Triumph rider named Harry Hobbs, who struggled on to finish 19th without footrests, front mudguard and no means of disengaging the clutch! When Mainwaring and Oliver Langton went to collect their machines, they were horrified to find they had been picked clean by souvenir hunters, leaving only the major components that were not so easily removed.

Weather conditions had not permitted the new longstroke engine to be fully extended, for it was alleged to develop 24 bhp at 5,000 rpm. One of the first opportunities did not occur until the Ulster Grand Prix, when Harry Langman led the unlimited event for the first seven laps before engine troubles set in. In the 500 cc class, Ernie Mainwaring finished 9th.

Earlier in the year, a new motorcycle sport had come to Britain, following its successful introduction several years earlier in Australia. It was at High Beech in Epping Forest that the Ilford M.C.C decided to stage the first properly organised dirt track meeting to be held in Britain, aided by two Australian riders of experience, Keith McKay and Billy Galloway. The date was Sunday, February 19th 1928, the first date the A-CU would grant under a restricted permit. Such was the success of the gamble that long before the event started, every single programme had been sold. No one knows exactly how many spectators attended, but it could not have been far short of 20,000 since they lined the inside of the track as well as the outside. No other sport enjoyed such a splendid start and within a matter of weeks tracks were springing up in all parts of the country. Jack Hill-Bailey, Secretary of the Ilford Club, was well-pleased that he had continued to badger the A-CU so that an event of this nature could be held. Practically any type and make of machine was eligible to compete and in due course, manufacturers found it worthwhile adding a dirt track model to their range, such was the level of demand.

The Scott Motor Cycle Company's involvement with dirt track racing occurred in a quite unexpected way. When Frank Varey was detailed to join the Scott riders party to the Isle of Man in the capacity of machine cleaner,

Frank Varey, the 'Red Devil' astride the original 1929 dirt track model that brought him fame

139

Allan Jefferies begged him for the loan of his three-speed Super whilst he was away. Unfortunately, the Super was written off completely in a road accident that followed, when Allan was run into by the rider of a Scott sidecar outfit whose sidecar wheel lifted on a left hand bend. The crash did not do Allan much good either, for he suffered a fractured skull, cheekbone and jaw. When he ultimately emerged from hospital it was obvious that a machine would have to be built from scratch, since even the Super's crankcase had been cut in two by the force of the impact. Putting their heads together, Frank and Allan decided they might as well build a machine that could be ridden on the cinders. And so, from a quite calamitous beginning, a dirt track Scott began to take shape. To assist with the finances, Allan promoted two meetings at the nearby Greenfield Dog Track and at various tracks in Lancashire.

According to Allan, it was Frank's superhuman strength and courage, coupled with their complete ignorance of steering geometry that made Frank such a spectacular favourite with the crowds! His lurid style of riding and the scream of the Scott on full power drew spectators in large numbers and soon word got around to Harry Langman, who took such an interest in the project that it was decided to add a dirt track model to the official Scott range. Cecil Knowles of the Frame Shop organised production, using a frame that was a cross between that of the Flyer and the Super, a formula worked out by Frank and Allan the hard way.

The dirt track model neared completion one Saturday lunch-time, on the day when Frank was due to ride his own model at Bolton the same afternoon. Anxious to give the new model an early try-out, Allan agreed to remain at work so that the new model could be completed in time for

The production version of the dirt track model, fitted with Webb forks

delivery to Rochdale Town Hall Square by tea-time, to enable Frank to try it at an evening meeting in Salford. In return, Allan would take over the old machine, so that he could have a ride at Rochdale.

Like all deadlines, the completion of the machine was met with some difficulty, but Allan eventually set off for Rochdale, just in the nick of time. Both riders agreed to meet up towards midnight at a much-favoured steak pudding shop in Littleborough, where there was a parrot they were teaching all kinds of quite unmentionable phrases! When they finally got together, Frank was clutching a Golden Helmet, the major award presented to the star of the meeting at Salford! The parrot learnt much that night during the session that followed!

Frank Varey became a star rider almost overnight and promoters all over the country clamoured for his entry in their meetings since this would guarantee a packed stadium. Allan acted in the capacity of tuner, mechanic, chauffer, valet, masseur and on one occasion, dentist! Soon the two partners were travelling over 1,400 miles a week to various meetings and there were few tracks where Allan did not whip off the crankcase doors to clear out the excess oil before the next race. Although many other riders bought Scott dirt track models in the hope that they could emulate Frank's passage to the top; none ever had anything like the same measure of success. Anyone who was privileged to see Frank and his beloved Scott roar around the deserted track at High Beech early on the morning of the 40th year of dirt track racing celebrations will understand why. Although the year was 1968 and Frank had long since retired to become a promoter, the old style was still evident. None of the other dirt track veterans present that day could have enjoyed themselves so obviously, as the memories came flooding back.

Wilf McClure makes the dirt fly with his banking sidecar outfit

The view seen by most competitors of McClure's banking outfit

As far as the 1928 Amateur TT was concerned, the Scott contingent intended to make another strong bid. Seven riders entered, including Paul Stables, who was now fully recovered from his injuries. But he did not arrive in the Island. Whenever he sat on a motorcycle he was confronted by the image of a Norton just in front of him, which persisted no matter how hard he concentrated. The six remaining riders comprised J. G. Hall, J. Lambert, J. Nash, Noel Mavrogordato, 'W. T. Carlisle' (W. T. Steel of that town) and once again, H. V. Prescott. Only Nash failed to start, as the result of an accident in Douglas.

The weather was again bad and only 11 riders finished, out of a total of 44 starters in the Senior race. Mavro retired on his second lap, when the petrol pipe on his two-speeder broke and the radiator worked loose. Lambert came off at Ramsey hairpin on the second lap and both Prescott and Webb retired for reasons unknown, after their third and fourth laps respectively. 'W. T. Carlisle' was the only finisher of the Scott team, 11th and last. His greatest claim to fame was a record 150 yard skid along the Sulby straight when his back brake jammed! Once again Tim Hunt was the winner, on a Norton.

Other successes in the year were recorded by Geoff Milnes, Harrison Town and Harold Wood, who won the Yorkshire Centre Trial for the fifth year in succession. G. Sheppard made Best Performance in the sidecar class at the Scottish Six Days Trial and Harold Wood won the Ilkley Non-Stop Trial. Geoff Milnes won the Calder Valley Grand National and a team composed of Sheppard, Billy Moore, Walter Clough, Allan Jefferies and Harold Wood did well in the International Six Days Trial, each member winning a Gold Medal.

Although the racing models had not shown quite the measure of success that was expected from them, they led to the introduction of one of the most beloved of all Scotts — the TT Replica model introduced towards the end of the 1928 season. As the 1929 catalogue stated, 'Designed essentially for the speedman, the TT Replica is the outcome of years of racing experience. The engine has a longer stroke and for power is in advance of any previous Scott engine. It is a replica of the machine finishing third in the 1928 Senior TT race. In its design are embodied many original Scott features and like all Scott machines it is built to an ideal. Its roadholding and cornering abilities are a revelation'. Available in either the 498 cc or 596 cc version, this is the model that drew most attention at the 1928 Olympia Show. Every two-stroke user queried whether it was really fair that four-stroke design should have received such attention at the expense of two-stroke development so that such a handsome machine was now in danger of being completely outclassed in long distance racing events.

As far as the other models in the 1929 range were concerned, it was obvious that the Company had decided to make a real effort to produce a range of machines that would compete more satisfactorily with some of the low priced models offered by other manufacturers. A price cutting campaign

A great moment. Tommy Hatch finishes in 3rd place during the 1928 Senior TT

had started back in 1924 by Rudge Whitworth, which had been followed by both Triumph and Douglas. So for the forthcoming season, it had been decided to drop the 486 cc Squirrel and the 596 cc standard model, together with the three-speed Super Squirrels.

A new version of the Flying Squirrel was introduced, shorn of a number of refinements and renamed the Flying Squirrel Tourer. This was priced at £67 10s (the Company had ceased to price their machines in guineas) or if the 596 cc engine was specified, £70 10s. There was also a De Luxe version of both models, priced at £76 and £79 respectively. The Tourer used Webb forks and a Webb rear hub with a 7 inch diameter brake, but there was no cush drive. A tank similar to that of the 1927 models was fitted, distinguished by white side panels and a white diamond on the top, in place of the purple used previously. The short-stroke engine was fitted, which could be regarded

143

Geoff Milnes negotiates a watersplash in the Calder Valley Club's Grand National

as a slightly detuned version of the engine used in the 1928 Flying Squirrels but without provision for cylinder wall oiling. The new shape crankcase was utilised, together with the short wheelbase frame, following the practice adopted for the TT models. The exhaust system comprised an expansion chamber close to the exhaust ports, with a pipe on the nearside leading to a Howarth silencer and fishtail. Overall weight was 310 lb, without lighting equipment. The De Luxe versions differed in the use of Scott girder forks and the fitting of leg shields and a rear carrier. An Enfield cush drive hub was fitted to the rear wheel, with an 8 inch diameter brake. These modifications raised the overall weight to 327 lb, without lighting equipment.

The two-speed Super Squirrels were retained in the range, but with a price reduction of 20 guineas in each case, bringing the prices down to £52 10s and £55 10s for the 498 cc and 596 cc versions respectively. All the 1929 models used a Pilgrim pump, mounted on the magneto platform, for lubrication of the engine.

The TT Replica, mentioned earlier, replaced the 1928 Flyer and used the TT long-stroke engine. They could be regarded as virtually the 1928 TT machines with a silencing system fitted. They had one unique feature that applied to this year only. A long rear brake anchor arm was used, which terminated close to the magneto platform. Unlike the other models in the 1929 range, the Replicas had cylinder wall oiling in addition to the standard system. Later in the year, a few Replica models had the Pilgrim pump mounted on the crankcase door. Prices were £88 (498 cc) and £91 (596 cc).

Sidecars again added to the general display and the dirt track model made its first appearance on the stand. Wired-on tyres were common throughout the whole range; the beaded edge tyre had finally gone out of fashion.

Although the price reductions gave the somewhat impecunious enthusiast an opportunity to purchase a Scott without a too heavy financial commitment, there was still nothing available at the lower end of the range for the man who required a really cheap utilitarian lightweight that was capable of providing good reliable service. When the price war reached its peak, many manufacturers found it advantageous to add a lightweight machine of this nature to their range, often based on a proprietary two-stroke engine unit such as the Villiers. This extended the spread of their models to the lower end of the range and brought in some useful additional revenue. Some experiments with a machine of this category were made at the Scott Works, using a conventional frame from one of the twin cylinder models into which a Villiers engine was grafted. The completed machine looked somewhat strange, especially without the radiator, and led to many ribald remarks when it was encountered on the road. Eventually, a single cylinder Scott engine was designed to take the place of the Villiers engine used in the test bed, an air cooled engine of 298 cc capacity having bore and stroke measurements of 73 mm x 71.4 mm. A special frame was built that resembled that of the twin cylinder models in certain respects, namely in the form of duplex downtubes and a six tube support for the rear wheel spindle.

The two-stroke engine was of conventional construction, with large crank webs to give good crankcase compression. The crankpin was gripped between these two webs and held in position by means of setscrews. The big end bearing used long rollers and the connecting rod supported an aluminium alloy piston fitted with a deflector. The piston skirt was ported, so that the gases transferred across the underside of the crown would help provide additional cooling. A chain from the crankshaft drove the magneto and a peg was attached to the magneto sprocket to drive a Pilgrim pump attached to an outrigger in front of the magneto sprocket. Oil was carried in a separate compartment of the petrol tank. If required, an additional reserve petrol tank could be provided as an optional extra for £1 10s. Cylindrical in shape, it was mounted below the saddle and extended the range of the machine to 300 miles on one filling.

Harold Wood was entrusted with the testing of the new Scott lightweight and even today he has a whole stack of test reports which record such a multitude of problems that it is kinder to let them remain forgotten with the passage of time. Suffice it to say that the prototype lightweight single proved extremely unreliable and did not even have good performance to give rise to optimism. Whilst the ultimate production models were very much better as the result of his tireless efforts, they could never be compared favourably with the twins, even if the reduced capacity was taken into account.

Other experimental work included a chain driven rotary valve attached to one of the twin cylinder models, the drive being taken from the left hand side of the engine. It was whilst testing this machine on Grimwith Moor, near Appletreewick, in the Yorkshire Dales, that Harold Wood had his riding coat catch in the exposed chain and derange the timing. Dusk was falling at the time and he afterwards claimed he learnt more about the timing of a rotary inlet valve on that occasion than he would have thought possible, as he struggled to get the machine running in time to return to Shipley! The design never went into production.

As far as the 1929 Senior TT entries were concerned, no fundamental design changes were made to the existing racing models. The frame was modified to accommodate much larger oil and petrol tanks, with the filler caps located on the left hand side of the machine to facilitate pit work. The magneto was repositioned closer to the crankshaft, so that the chain run could be reduced. It was mounted on a plate welded between the duplex tubes from the saddle. In keeping with the repositioning of the oil and petrol tank filler caps, that of the radiator was also transposed to the left.

Six machines were entered, to be ridden by Tommy Hatch, A. Franklyn, Syd Gleave, Ernie Mainwaring, Phil Vare, and Oliver Langton. Oliver Langton holed a piston on the first lap and toured back to the pits and A. Franklyn retired after the fourth lap when he came off and bent the handlebars. Syd Gleave managed to complete four laps and Ernie Mainwaring only three, before both retired from the fray. Phil Vare continued long enough to

Jumping the boards on a Scott at Belle Vue, Manchester

'Felix' - Bill Bradley's ingenious six-speed model in full touring trim, circa 1928

complete six laps, leaving only Tommy Hatch to complete the course in 13th place. Although it was not known at the time, this was to be the last occasion on which a Works entered Scott completed the course in the Senior TT. A post mortem conducted afterwards showed that the spate of retirements were caused by engine failures resulting from either holed pistons or disintegrating big ends. Vare had been particularly unlucky. A fall at Quarter Bridge damaged the twist grip of his machine so he used the cut-out button when changing gear. This caused the holed pistons that forced his retirement.

As far as the Amateur TT was concerned, there were seven Scott entries, Noel Mavrogordato, J. A. Fleet, R. D. Long, H. V. Prescott, J. C. Short and J. G. Hall. Mavro had intended to ride a Coventry Victor but it did not match up with his expectations and so he reverted to his faithful Scott. Hall retired on the second lap and Mavro came off at Governor's Bridge but restarted, only to retire at Sulby, on his third lap. Long and Fleet also retired, as did Prescott, leaving J. C. Short to finish in 13th place as the sole survivor of the Scott contingent. There were no wild celebrations this year.

As expected, the 298 cc Squirrel made its debut at the December 1929 Olympia Show, priced at £39 with an extra £5 10s if electric lighting was required. There was also mention of a 350 cc version. As far as the Sports and Super Squirrels were concerned, both ranges now featured a frame in which the steering head had been shortened to give a lower riding position. There were four stages in the development of the Sports Squirrels which were first introduced during March/April 1929. Initially a short seat tube was used giving a low saddle position. A full frame petrol and oil tank was fitted to match and the long steering head was retained, with adjustable handlebars. The 1929 Show models had a short steering head with no top sidecar mounting lug. Early 1930 models used a different head lug and the angle of the front downtube was changed so that a different tank design was necessary, more round and smooth in profile. A four point crankcase fitting was employed on the last few models made during late 1930 and early 1931. This necessitated a shorter petrol tank of only two gallon capacity on the Super. The adjustable handlebars featured on the previous year's Flying Squirrels were now employed more widely and there was a fourth fixing for the front of the crankcase whilst at the same time the sidecar lug was removed from the steering head. The Sports Squirrels were listed at £55 and £57 respectively, depending on whether the 498 cc or 596 cc version was ordered. The latter price also held good for both capacities of the Super Squirrel model. The Flying Squirrel Tourer three-speed models cost £66 and £68 respectively, with an additional £7 surcharge if the De Luxe versions were preferred. These latter models had 26 x 3.25 inch section tyres, Scott girder forks, leg shields and a cush drive hub as added improvements. The Power Plus TT Replica models (Power Plus related to the slightly more potent engine) were priced at £84 and £86 and had B & D dampers fitted to the forks. The most expensive machine in the range was the dirt track model at £95, which could be obtained in either capacity. An attractive feature that applied to the Flyers was a neatly cast aluminium alloy cover that filled in the gap between the end of the crankcase casting and the gearbox, it also helped protect the magneto chain. It was not as voluminous as that fitted to the three-speed Super Squirrels up to 1928.

The model that unquestionably attracted most attention in the range for the 1930 season was the Sprint Special, to many the most sleek and handsome of the open frame models to leave the Saltaire Works. It was described as 'for the elect of speedmen who, despite the obvious costliness, demand a machine built to their special order to embody all their pet fancies, hitherto divided among our various models, the Special is our gratifying answer. Designed for grass track racing and hill climbs, this intriguing Scott is equally fitted to any purpose where speed, liveliness and sure-footedness are essential'. It was listed at £95.

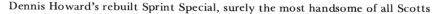

Dennis Howard's rebuilt Sprint Special, surely the most handsome of all Scotts

THE SCOTT MOTORCYCLE

Perhaps the chief advantage of the Sprint Special, apart from its appearance, was the lightness in weight, for a frame of the single downtube variety, derived from the dirt track bike, was used in place of the heavy duplex tube frame employed on all the other models. The old three-speed Super had previously been regarded as the lightweight of the range, although the model had some inbuilt weaknesses too, as mentioned earlier, which could only be overcome by adding more robust parts and thereby adding to the weight. This related mainly to the substitution of a bronze undertray by the elite few, in place of the long aluminium alloy tray that acted as the lower frame member and was fitted as standard.

The high cost of the Sprint Special was attributed to the fact that it was carefully assembled in the Competition Department and was in no sense a standard production model. The prospective purchaser had a choice of wheelbase, wheel size, three types of tank and two types of fork, irrespective of complete freedom to specify gear ratios, engine compression ratio, carburettor and exhaust system. This was quite definitely one Scott of which there were no two models identical.

Despite all the claims, the Sprint Special was not the lightest model in the current range, excluding the 298 cc single. It weighed 300 lb, some 25 lb heavier than the dirt track model and 35 lb heavier than the Super and the Sports two-speeder models. But the overall styling gave the general illusion of lightness in weight, especially when the 1½ gallon fuel tank was fitted. To many, it was the absolute epitomy of everything that was good in the Scott design, even if the high cost tended to put it out of reach and on a pedestal.

An all-original 1930 Flyer owned by Scott registrar John Underhill

CHAPTER SIX
Another relapse

ALTHOUGH the end of 1930 is today regarded as the end of the so-called vintage era, it was in 1929 that motorcycling reached its peak in the UK. By the end of that year, the figure for the number of motorcycles in use was 731,298, an increase of 18,715 over the previous year's total which was itself a record. The effects of the economic depression, amongst other factors, was to bring about a decrease in numbers of just under 7,000 by the end of 1930. The whole scene was about to change, and with it, the outlook of the industry itself.

At Saltaire, Harry Shackleton and the Competition Department had commenced work on what was to be their most ambitious design project to date — an entirely new racing Scott for the 1930 Senior TT. It was unlike any Scott that had been built previously and showed little allegiance to earlier Scott practice, apart from the retention of a two-stroke parallel twin engine with cranks at 180° and a rear frame section reminiscent of that fitted to the 1909 model.

The crankcase of the engine was made in two halves, split horizontally. It was shaped something like a cross between a sphere and a barrel and had detachable end plates, each retained by three studs. Cast in Elektron metal, to save weight, the crankcase was divided into three separate chambers, one for the centrally disposed flywheel and one for each throw of the crank. A four-piece built-up crank was used, having a central flange to which the flywheel was rivetted. It was supported on four roller bearings, the one on the drive side being of the double row type. Crankcase compression was maintained by the customary Scott glands at the inner journals and by long bushes on the outer journals. From this description it will be appreciated that the traditional overhung crank arrangement no longer applied. The primary drive was taken from the nearside of the crankshaft by means of the customary overhung engine sprocket. A bevel drive was taken from the offside of the crankcase, contained within a separate compartment, to drive the magneto and the duplex Pilgrim pump. The oil pump supplied oil to the two outer main bearings and to the big end bearings via internal oilways in the crankshaft. Oil was also fed direct to each cylinder wall by external pipes, whence it was distributed by a narrow groove running around each bore. Oil drainback was collected in reservoirs and used to lubricate the inner bearings.

The water-cooled cylinder block was now arranged in a vertical position and differed considerably from earlier designs. It had a detachable, water-cooled head of cast iron, secured by nine studs. It was claimed that the design of cylinder head gave improved efficiency; the tops of the combustion chambers were almost conical in shape and had centrally mounted sparking plugs. The cylinder block was deeply spigoted into the crankcase and was retained by four studs, making a very rigid assembly. Two exhaust ports were employed, each of large diameter. They had square flanges at the manifold joints. The transfer ports were formed in the cylinder casting and had two small detachable plates to permit access. The induction passage was also formed with the casting and carried a twin float Amal carburettor.

Although the overall design was virtually unchanged, the separate three-speed gearbox had been altered to provide cross-over drive. The shell was cast in Elektron and had a flat base which served as the mounting. The gearbox bolted to a platform behind the engine, to permit primary chain adjustment. It was fitted with foot-operated gearchange.

A 4½ gallon petrol tank was fitted that had cutaways in the underside to facilitate access to the sparking plugs. The radiator was set lower and was mounted a little nearer the vertical position. In most other respects the machine followed what may be regarded as conventional Scott practice, apart from the use of strutted Webb girder forks. There was not much that could have been done with the cycle parts since time was already at a premium.

Two of the new models were built in time for the 1930 Senior TT. The Works entered two riders, Phil Vare and Bill Kitchen, the latter another rider destined to achieve far greater fame on the cinders in later years. Ernie Mainwaring was entered by A. E. Reynolds on this occasion, the Liverpool Scott agent and enthusiast. He had left the Scott Works to join Reynolds during 1929. Although the machines were taken over to the Isle of Man to be seen by the chosen few at the Howstrake base, they were not used in the race, mainly because excessive vibration problems could not be eliminated in time. Both Kitchen and Vare used the previous year's TT models, the former's having Webb girder forks in place of the originals.

In the race, Bill Kitchen fell at Craig-ny-baa, but remounted to continue for another four laps before he came off again at Braddan. Phil Vare was equally unlucky. He came off at Governor's Bridge, remounted and continued for another couple of laps until a holed piston relegated him to the role of onlooker. Just to round things off, Ernie Mainwaring came off at Ballacraine and was forced to retire, suffering from shock. This proved to be his final ride in the Senior TT and it is questionable whether any rider had been quite so unfortunate. Although his riding showed signs of brilliance he could also be rather rash and in six successive years he had failed to finish in any Senior race.

The marketing of the single cylinder model brought in its wake further developments that included a three-wheel tradesman's delivery vehicle known

Ernie Mainwaring sorts out his TT
model after one of the 1930 TT
practice sessions

as the Trivan. In general outline it was reminiscent of the Walls Ice Cream
tricycle that was such a familiar sight before the last war, with a box-like
body mounted between the two front wheels. The rider sat on a motorcycle
saddle behind the box, above what was virtually the rear end of the single
cylinder model containing the engine and gearbox, the former in a horizontal
position. Steering was accomplished by pulling or pushing on the appropriate
ends of a rail mounted across the top rear edge of the box, mounted on
brackets. The throttle control was mounted on this rail. Two small headlamps,
one each side of the box mounted low down, permitted the vehicle to be used
after dark, although it is doubtful whether the standard of illumination was
very good. Petrol and oil were carried in a cylindrical tank with separate
compartments and fillers, mounted immediately below the nose of the
saddle, in transverse fashion. It resembled the optional reserve petrol tank
of the lightweight model.

The Trivan chassis. Note the unusal type of silencer fitted

It was intended to use a trial open to commercial sidecars for the official launch of the Trivan, but delays in assembly prevented the strange looking vehicle from reaching the start of the event on time. Special dispensation was obtained for the Trivan to join the run on the second day, at Hereford. Willie Wood was the rider on this occasion, resplendent in a spotless white coat! The box body had been painted in the livery of an ice cream purveyor and Willie feigned the role of salesman. A separate company — S.A.V. Light Cars Limited — was formed to market the Trivan, but the venture was not a success and the Company soon faded from the scene. It has been claimed that the performance of the early single cylinder Scott engine was about half that of a 250 cc Villiers engine at its best, so it is not difficult to understand why the Trivan met with such an early demise! Other forms of the single cylinder engine also appeared around the same time, some in a water-cooled guise. There is record of these engines being used as starters for diesels and for powering domestic lighting sets and farm pumps. They were marketed by the Scott Engineering Company, of Abbey House, Victoria Street, London, SW1, in conjunction with similar adaptations of the twin cylinder engine.

The 1930 Scott Trial, held on September 20th, is worthy of special mention because a new feature had been included. Controversy had raged in the motorcycling press as to the merits of Northern and Southern competition riders and it was decided to offer an open challenge by selecting two teams from the list of entrants, each of which would represent their particular section of the country. The scores of the best three in each team of six riders would be totalled so that the three with the best aggregate of marks would determine whether the North or the South had won. The selection was good, since both teams were very evenly matched. The South won easily, due to the unforeseen retirement of three of the Northern veterans. Surprisingly, the Scott lightweights showed up well for the second year in succession, for they had made their debut in this event a year earlier. There were a few that did run well, as Allan Jefferies once found out when he rode the lightweight used by Harry Langman in an earlier International Six Days Trial event. No doubt the experts had their own secret ways of making them go!

1930 marked the end of the Scott Trial in the form it had always followed. Organisation was now becoming a mammoth task and in order to simplify course marking, liaison with local landowners and other factors that made heavy demands on the 'spare time' organisers and officials, the venue was changed to a more compact course centred around Blubberhouses and Denton Moor. To many, this was a sad blow, for to them the event was never quite the same afterwards. No longer would Wharfdale, Airedale, Coverdale and Nidderdale echo to the sounds of the struggling competitors and their machines as they pitted themselves against the clock and against some of the worst hazards ever to be encountered in a long distance trial — a trial of both man and machine alike.

A demonstration version of the Trivan with 'period' signwriting

During July 1930 the Government finally gave way to the pressure that had been exerted by the industry and agreed to raise the lightweight machine weight limit from 200 lbs to 224 lbs, as had been requested. This concession gave fresh incentive to produce lightweight models that would qualify for the £1 10s road tax and because the 298 cc lightweight Squirrel tipped the scales at 230 lbs it was decided to reduce the weight so that the new version of this model would follow suit. The opportunity was taken to enhance the appearance and improve performance at the same time, the most noticeable difference being the use of Webb girder forks in place of the original Scott design. The wheelbase was shortened, the saddle lowered, lighter weight mudguards fitted and a centre stand replaced the original rear stand, although the 1931 catalogue showed front and rear stands. A chain guard of polished aluminium alloy superseded the pressed steel version used initially and the exhaust pipe was of increased diameter, dispensing with the cylindrical expansion box mounted close to the cylinder barrel. This and the use of an enlarged cylindrical silencer that no longer terminated in a fishtail, gave a more sporting outline and a deeper exhaust note.

The late Reg Summers examines Peter Waring's very unusual 1930 model whilst judging the Concours at the 1971 Scott Owners' Club Rally

Harold Wood riding one of the 300 cc single cylinder models at Pomona, near Ilkley, during the 1930 Bradford Sporting Trial

Engine changes included improved balance of the flywheel assembly and a direct oil feed to the cylinder barrel from the oil pump in addition to the feed to the main bearings and big end. A Maglita could now be fitted, if desired, to perform the dual function of magneto and dynamo, as an alternative to the Lucas Magdyno. It is alleged that the engine modifications provided greater power, but this is open to conjecture because the same brake horsepower figures were still quoted — 5 bhp at 2,000 rpm and 10 bhp at 4,000 rpm. By far the most important feature was the overall weight of the Maglita-equipped model, which was now down to 220 lbs. The new 298 cc Squirrel retailed at £38 with lighting or £35 without, a reduction of £1 in the former case as compared with the 1930 prices. A 350 cc engine was to be available for an extra £2.

Attention was also given to the production of a road going version of the ill-fated vertical engine TT model, to be known as the Chieftain. The same basic design concepts were used apart from the use of split big-ends and a one-piece crankshaft with integral crankpins. The crankshaft was still supported on four bearings, but in this instance the two inner bearings were of the white metal type. Outwardly, the model retained its somewhat unorthodox appearance, but items such as a Lucas Magdyno, a battery and a polished aluminium alloy chainguard for the primary drive formed necessary additions for the changed role the machine had now to play. The price was fixed at £95, with an additional surcharge if a Magdyno was specified in place of the standard magneto, or if a speedometer was required. One prototype was constructed late in the year but sad to relate, it suffered the same fate as the two TT models and never went into production.

As far as the 1930 Amateur TT was concerned, some quite fundamental changes in the regulations were made because the Auto-Cycle Union had decided they could no longer issue a permit for a race that had grown so far away from its original objectives. 'Shamateurism' had reached a peak and it was patently apparent that few of the entrants could be classified as amateur riders or private owners. Even so, the A-CU did not close the door completely. It was suggested that if the race organisers cared to reframe the regulations so that the factory-assisted expert was debarred, they had no objection to the above-board payment of an amateur competitor's expenses by a club or sponsor, if either so wished. And so the Manx Grand Prix was born, the regulations of which included a provision that required the entrant to be the rider and holder of an open competition licence. Entries would be accepted only from riders who had not entered any International road race since 1920 nor have held any world's motorcycling record. No reserve riders were permitted and it was further stipulated that the machines used in the races must be standard models, as listed in the manufacturer's catalogue, which must have been published prior to January 31st that year. The A-CU were satisfied, and the races went ahead as planned.

Scott entries comprised Noel Mavrogordato riding one of the new Sprint Specials, fitted with his own positive stop foot gearchange, and

R. Stobart. As usual, Mavro got away to a good start and was lying third on the second lap at an average speed of 68.62 mph until he came off at Sulby, when the fork spring broke, and retired. Stobart continued, to finish 15th. There can be little doubt that the change in nature of the event proved attractive to the amateur rider, for the total Senior and Junior race entry totalled just 100. Because the experts were barred, several familiar names disappeared from the programme and it is interesting to note that in their place, the newcomers included F. Frith and H. L. Daniell.

As the year drew to a close, the Company put on a brave front and announced their 1931 programme at the annual Olympia Show — a continuation of the two-speed Super Squirrel and the Sports Squirrel, together with the addition of the new version of the Flying Squirrel Tourer and the Flying Squirrel De Luxe, both of which were based on the Sprint Special and had single downtube and seat tube frames. They featured Replica-like tanks that sat on the top frame tube containing 4 gallons of petrol and ½ gallon of oil. A chromium plated finish was available. The 498 cc version cost £66, with an additional £2 surcharge if the 596 cc engine was fitted, or the addition of £10 if the Power Plus engine was specified. The remainder of the range comprised the Power Plus TT Replica, virtually unchanged with a duplex frame but with the option of Webb girder forks and a tank with either white or purple panels, the Sprint Special, still built to special order but reduced in price to £85 and fitted with Replica brakes, and the revised version of the 298 cc lightweight Squirrel as mentioned previously. The De Luxe Flyers and Replicas had Scott girder forks and Enfield rear hubs; the Tourer had Webb forks and a Webb rear hub. Both the Tourer and the De Luxe models used a small centre stand in place of the usual rear stand. Pilgrim oil pumps were mounted on the crankcase doors. Although the new 650 was included in the announcement, none was made. Whilst the 1931 programme suggested that production would continue much as before, behind the scenes all was far from well. The economic depression had caught up with the Company at last, which was rapidly heading for financial disaster. Early in 1931, G. F. D. Walker was appointed Official Receiver. Mercifully, the Company did not go under completely, although it was touch and go. Somehow it survived enough to continue in business, albeit at a very low level for some time. Many famous names disappeared altogether around this period, and it is fortunate that the Scott Motor Cycle Company Limited did not become yet another of motorcycling's cherished memories.

One of those who attempted to come to the rescue was Albert Reynolds, the Liverpool Scott enthusiast and one of the Company's foremost agents. For many years A. E. Reynolds Limited had specialised in Scott motorcycles and as far back as 1923 had commenced to market accessories such as legshields, special exhaust systems and pillion footrests that were designed especially for use with any model in the Scott range. Frame and fork repairs at very competitive rates were also a speciality whilst many an impecunious

The home workshop. An unknown enthusiast prepares his machine for a forthcoming event, perhaps the Scott Trial

enthusiast managed to keep his machine running by the purchase of Reynolds good quality secondhand spares. The Liverpool address incorporated the words 'Scott Hospital' in the postal address, for it was at Berry Street that all major overhauls and rebuilds were carried out. As the Reynolds catalogue 'Better Scotting' stated, "There are two ways of doing that repair — the way A.E.R. does it — and the wrong way".

Predictably, the saviour of the Scott name was again Reginald Vinter, whose financial expertise was used to good effect. The Scott Motor Cycle Company Limited was now in liquidation and many of the employees had left. So he decided to abandon the original company and in its place, formed Scott Motors (Saltaire) Limited in May 1931 from what was originally Scott Motors (Leeds) Limited, the local distributors who had the same directors. At the same time he raised some much needed capital by selling Scott Motors (Manchester) Limited to Albert Reynolds, thereby permitting the latter to open showrooms in Manchester and to take on the Scott distributorship for the whole of Lancashire. It may seem strange that

Reynolds was able to take advantage of the situation at this particular time, for it was hardly an opportune time to expand when such an acute trade depression existed. Yet he was in a very strong position, so much so that he was able to strike a deal with Vinter for the Scott Works to build machines to his own specification, in addition to the standard production models he would stock and sell. This marked the beginning of the Reynolds Special, or as it was originally known, the Aero Special, from a play on Reynolds' initials. Without doubt, Albert Reynolds played his own part in helping keep the Scott name alive.

When the Scott factory issued their revised 1931 catalogue, it was seen that the Scott Motor Cycle Company had been formed to market the new models for the Proprietors. Reference to the contents showed the 650 cc vertical engine model had been dropped completely, as had the 298 cc lightweight. Of the remaining models, the prices and general specifications remained much the same. In the case of the Sprint Special the list of optional extras had been extended to include a chromium plated tank of welded steel, similar in outline to that of the TT Replica type. Chromium plating was coming into general use at this time and gave machines a much more attractive appearance in contrast with the nickel plating that had been used for so long in the past.

In passing, it should not be inferred that A. E. Reynolds had the sole monopoly in Liverpool when it came to parts for Scott enthusiasts. Another Company, J. Hemmings and Sons Limited, of Hale, marketed their own brand of Scott merchandise and specialised in replacement parts that included some specially-designed exhaust systems, developed to boost engine performance. They were best known for their own design of replacement cylinder block, sold under the trade name Paramount. The main feature of the design was a detachable, light alloy cylinder head which, when used with the Hemmings block, made an admirable replacement for the blind head assembly that was still currently employed throughout the Scott range. Made in 596 cc capacity only, they could be used to 'stretch' the 498 cc engine without any further modifications. They also made decarbonisation much easier, since it was no longer necessary to first detach the radiator or to disturb the cylinder base assembly. Engine performance was enhanced, because it was possible to machine the combustion chambers all over. By far the most noticeable feature was the superb quality of the castings and it is largely on this point alone that Hemmings earned their reputation amongst the more discerning enthusiasts.

The depression itself was not the sole reason for the near collapse of the Scott Motor Cycle Company. After 1930, the much loved lightweight twins had been dropped from the range and the more heavy models that had replaced them were better suited for the fast road rider. The Sprint Special was the exception and whilst this remained the mainstay of the range for a while, it weighed 300 lb without lights, far more than the earlier Super and

Sports Squirrels. The Scott no longer showed up well in racing events either, for the Isle of Man results had shown that as race speeds rose, the Scott engine no longer possessed the standard of reliability to complete the course at high average speeds. It can be inferred that Harry Shackleton had realised the original basic engine design had some inherent weaknesses and for this reason embarked on the quite revolutionary but short-lived vertical engine project. The hard fact remained that the Scott was beginning to lose something of its image and compared less favourably with many of the contemporary four-stroke designs of the day that were more realistically priced. It was not the Scott enthusiast who lost faith, but the person on the fringe of buying a Scott who knew little of its endearing charms.

Harold Wood with passenger C. Shaw at Dob Park watersplash during the 1931 Ilkley Trial

A. W. Hitchens takes delivery of a Scott from the Derby premises of Scott agent W. H. Jones

The Aero Scott was first launched during May 1931, at a price of £105, making it the most expensive Scott yet to be marketed. It could be likened to an improved version of the standard production Flying Squirrel De Luxe which was some £30 cheaper. The specification embraced a specially assembled engine of the TT Replica type in either 498 cc or 596 cc capacity and fitted with either high or low compression pistons. In addition to the duplex Pilgrim pump fitted to the offside crankcase door, a spring-loaded hand pump was fitted to give additional lubrication direct to the cylinder walls, in a manner similar to that first used on the 1928 Flyer.

The most noticeable additions took the form of Brampton bottom link forks and twin headlamps à la 1929 Brough Superior, and the fitting of a Velocette positive stop foot gearchange mechanism to the Scott three-speed gearbox. The chromium plated radiator had a Boyce thermometer incorporated in the cap and twin exhaust pipes were used, each terminating in a Howarth silencer. Other features included a twin float Amal-Binks three-jet carburettor, a 100 mph Smith Jaeger speedometer, and a superbly enamelled petrol and oil tank fitted with TT-type snap fillers. The finish of the tank was enhanced by purple side panels that carried small winged motifs in gold with the words 'Aero Special'.

A Lucas Magdyno supplied the electrics and worked in conjunction with a nickel - alkali battery mounted beneath the pan-top saddle. There was even a stop lamp, that operated from the heavy duty brake cable on the nearside — the Velocette footchange precluded the use of the customary brake rod arrangement on the offside. It was not difficult to see why the Aero Special cost an extra £30 over and above the price of the Flying Squirrel De Luxe.

There were no Scott entries in the 1931 Senior TT, although both Harry Langman and Ernie Mainwaring went across in the unfamiliar role of spectators. In the Manx Grand Prix that followed in September, Noel Mavrogordato appeared again on his Sprint Special, now fitted with a new engine erected by the Scott Competition Department. It also had Brampton Monarch bottom link forks. A particularly attractive feature of this rebuilt model was the specially-made petrol and oil tank that had an unusual flared appearance. This was the classic occasion when someone suggested to Mavro that he could quite easily win the race if he elected to ride a Norton, whereupon Mavro said, "I know — but I would rather lose on a Scott!" And lose he did, for after the usual brilliant start, the front fork spring called it a day at Baaregaroo, causing a real tank slapper and his ultimate retirement at Sulby, the same spot with the same trouble as the year previous! The two other Scott entries were doomed to disappointment too. Trevor Battye had his gear linkage fracture, which caused the gearbox to jam in top gear. Somehow he managed a lap at 58.9 mph, then had to retire when the machine ran out of fuel. Stobart, making his second appearance in this annual event, came off at Quarter Bridge on the third lap and lost bottom gear as a result. He too was forced to retire soon afterwards. One item worthy of note is the fact that Mavro was again using his own version of the Velocette positive stop foot gearchange, which he had modified and linked with the Scott 'gate' so that it would prove equally effective when used in conjunction with a Scott gearbox. His adaptation was even earlier than that of A. E. Reynolds, for it was used on his Sprint Special in the 1930 Manx Grand Prix Senior Race, as mentioned previously. Harry Langman expressed an interest in Mavro's conversion and it is almost certain that it was this that led to the adoption of foot gearchange along somewhat similar lines for the 1934 season.

Towards the end of the summer, Albert Reynolds established a licencing agreement with a Mr Gordon Barnett of Wembley for the right to use the latter's vertical plunger spring frame attachment which was marketed under the trade name Master (British Patent 373,635). In essence, it was a form of rear suspension using undamped coil springs that could be incorporated into a frame during its manufacture or used (in a modified form) to convert a rigid frame. Each cylindrical plunger unit contained two springs, a short lower spring that controlled rebound and a longer, upper spring that absorbed the road shocks. The springs abutted on each side of a plunger, that extended through a slot in each cylinder and carried the wheel spindle. The slot through which the plunger extended was sealed to prevent the ingress of dirt or the leakage of grease with which the unit was filled. Each complete cylinder unit bolted direct to the frame of the machine and had a braced upper extension to preserve rigidity. In the case of the bolt-on attachment for a rigid frame, this took the form of a separate torque arm. The springing functioned quite satisfactorily and added a touch of luxury at the time when such fitments were relatively uncommon. It had the minor disadvantage of adding something like 16 lbs to the overall weight of the machine and promoted increased wear of the rear chain, but this was a small price to pay for the added comfort. It also slightly extended the wheelbase if employed in the bolt-on form, in conjunction with a rigid frame. Nonetheless, it proved an added attraction for the prospective purchaser of an Aero Scott and gave the Scott Works some experience of building a spring frame, albeit not on their own models!

At the end of 1931 there were no Scott exhibits at the annual Olympia Show, due to the financial situation that prevailed and the fact that the existing range was to be continued with only detail modifications. One noticeable change related to the Flying Squirrel De Luxe model, on which Brampton Monarch forks replaced the original Scott braced girder forks. The price remained unchanged, as did that of the other models. Only the Sprint Special was dropped altogether, to reappear in a new guise as the Flying Squirrel Sports Model. This too had the single seat tube, single main down tube frame and the new Brampton Monarch bottom link forks. The Power Plus engine was retained. All models, except the Replica, had an open frame.

Because he did not qualify as a manufacturer in his own right, A. E. Reynolds was automatically debarred from exhibiting at the Show. He had announced two new models, based on the Flying Squirrel Sports model that was now available from Shipley. Both were Reynolds' own versions of the same model, one with a spring frame and the other without. Reynolds' new Easiflow radiator made its appearance on these models, a more squat design that did not have to be removed before the engine could be decarbonised, yet held an extra quart of water. Another innovation was the inclusion of a switch panel for the lighting equipment in the nose of the tank. A Bosch horn was interposed between the twin headlamps and some models were fitted with a balance pipe that interconnected the two crankcase drain plugs, to equalise the oil content of the two oil wells in each crank chamber. The new models carried a revised design of winged transfer that embodied the words "The Reynolds Special"; the word Aero had been dropped. The spring frame model cost 110 guineas and the rigid frame version just £10 less.

A rare Reynolds Special model seen at the 1971 Scott Owners' Rally

To attract the sidecar man, Reynolds fitted a Noxal launch-type sidecar body to a Swallow spring wheel chassis and enamelled the body in a rich purple to match the colour of the tank panels of the machine to which it was attached. Wilmot Breeden bumpers, resplendent in bright chromium plate, were attached to the front and rear of the sidecar body, serving a purely decorative function. The launch body had all the trappings of the day such as a handrail around the 'deck' and imitation ventilators of the foghorn type found on ships. The outfit was priced accordingly, at £160.

THE SCOTT MOTORCYCLE

There were no Scott entries in the 1932 Senior TT, but in the September Manx Grand Prix, both Noel Mavrogordato and Trevor Battye again entered for the Senior event. The race was run under quite appalling conditions — torrential rain and mist swirling around the mountain. Mavro crashed heavily on the first lap, at Quarter Bridge, only a short distance from the start! He bent the handlebars and wiped off the right hand footrest, but gamely decided to press on with one foot in the air. He managed to complete the course and finish fourteenth, at an average speed of just under 60 mph. Throughout the race he had suffered from constant plug troubles, due to the atrocious weather conditions. He was on his last plug at the finish, having used all the eight spares he carried in two leather pouches strapped around his waist. Trevor Battye had similar ignition problems, but in his case they forced his retirement.

When the Scott range for the 1933 season was announced, it was virtually a continuation of the same models which, for convenience, could be subdivided into four categories — Touring, De Luxe, Replica and Sports — each with the choice of either a 498 cc or a 596 cc engine. One important feature applied to all models fitted with the Power Plus engine. It had been decided to fit this type of engine with a light alloy cylinder head that was detachable and retained in position by no less than sixteen studs. It was water cored, had hemispherical combustion chambers with central plug holes and relied upon a copper/asbestos gasket to maintain the seal between itself and the cylinder block. The modified engine showed an increase in power; it was now capable of giving 27 - 28 bhp at 5,400 rpm (498 cc) or 31 - 32 bhp at 5,200 rpm (596 cc). This in turn necessitated stiffening the crankcase of the larger capacity engine and providing more efficient lubrication in the form of a throttle controlled oil pump. This latter device worked on the swash plate principle, and was capable of infinitely variable delivery. A mechanism coupled to the throttle gave the swash plate varying angles of tilt, thereby imparting a variable stroke to the four plungers it contacted. Each plunger delivered oil to a quite separate lubrication point. The pump bolted to the offside crankcase door and was much bulkier than the standard Pilgrim pump that had been used for lubrication in the past. The somewhat complicated assembly of parts within the pump gave the impression that the pump was more complicated than the engine itself and there were disparaging remarks about fitting the engine to the pump!

The Flying Squirrel Tourer featured a new type of rear stand, in which a clock spring was enclosed within a recess of the stand leg. This enabled the stand to spring up when the machine was pushed forward and engage with a toggle clip so that it would not rattle whilst the machine was in motion. The standard engine used, if the Power Plus unit was not specified, reverted to the longstroke specification — 66.6 x 71.4 mm (498 cc) and 73 x 71.4 mm (596 cc) and still retained the blind head. A positive stop gearchange that was foot operated was also listed as an extra at £4 10s. It was the Velocette design originated by Harold Willis, which had been acquired under licence. Despite the various detail modifications, the 1932 prices were maintained.

As far as A. E. Reynolds was concerned, he continued with the existing rigid and spring frame Reynolds Specials and was able to maintain the same price structure.

Early in 1933, the Auto-Cycle Union announced they hoped to revive the Sidecar TT by including a sidecar race in the 1933 TT programme. One of the first to take note was Harry Langman, who had remained faithful to the Scott Works and had hung on throughout the worst of the depression. He decided to make a come-back if the Works would build a suitable outfit for him, to make amends for the race he lost ten years previously when victory was virtually within his grasp. Meanwhile, Albert Reynolds was trying his best to get Tommy Hatch to enter with a separate outfit that was based on a Reynolds Special. An imposing specification was drawn up for both machines since they were to be built under the same roof. It included a specially strengthened frame, a larger capacity radiator capable of running at a higher temperature, a crankcase cast in Elektron, more robust taperless cranks, a bevel driven magneto, a tachometer drive from the nearside crankcase door and a special version of the throttle controlled swash plate oil pump. In addition, a four-speed close ratio gearbox was deemed necessary that had fully enclosed foot change and used needle roller bearings wherever practicable.

Unfortunately the project was still-born, for there were other projects on hand at the same time that precluded the completion of the outfits in time for the races. Perhaps it was as well, for the 1933 Sidecar Race never took place. It was cancelled much nearer the intended date, due to lack of entries.

Determined to have an entry of some kind in the 1933 TT, Albert Reynolds decided to change allegiance to the Senior event and substitute a solo 498 cc Reynolds Special. Tommy Hatch was not too happy with these revised plans — quite understandably too — for he knew he would be hopelessly outclassed now that the ohc four strokes had established their supremacy. But Reynolds was a good diplomat and eventually Tommy Hatch gave in on the understanding that his main objective would be to give a demonstration of high speed reliability — no more!

The Reynolds Special attracted great interest, for it represented the return of a Scott to the TT races after a gap of three years, even if it had a different transfer on the tank. It did not appear until the fourth morning practice session because completion had been delayed at the Works. Tommy Hatch had commenced practice on a five-year old Scott, but on the first morning practice the rear wheel spindle broke whilst he was rounding the 33rd milestone, a happening that caused him much concern! The new machine was the answer to his problems, or so he thought, until the front forks bottomed as he descended Bray Hill, punching a hole in the mudguard and temporarily locking the steering. He cannoned off a garden fence on the bend at the bottom of the hill, somehow ended up back on the road and proceeded, suitably detuned! Alterations to the forks followed and the trail was changed, but to little effect. The approach to Craig-ny-baa needed a half-nelson to keep the machine on course, which hardly inspired rider confidence. There was not even the excuse that the machine was reaching hitherto unexpected speeds!

On the last day of practice, fate dealt another blow, which fortunately occurred when Hatch was riding the machine along Broadway on the way to the start. Both rods broke simultaneously, without fracturing the crankcase. Jim Capstick was hauled out of bed upon Hatch's return to the hotel at which they were staying and conducted an immediate post mortem. The rods had fractured just above the big end and had flailed around making plenty of noise but not causing too much damage. There was only one answer. Out came the engine and Jim caught the first available boat back to the mainland, en route for Shipley where a telegram had told the Works to await his arrival. Jim worked round the clock and was back with the rebuilt engine just four days later. It is alleged he snatched but two hours sleep during this period, such was his determination for the machine to be ready for the Senior race.

As far as the race was concerned, Tommy Hatch had a fairly uneventful ride, his only stop being on the third lap to change the plugs. He was lapped by the winner, Stanley Woods, as he started his sixth lap, but eventually finished in a very creditable 15th place with an engine that had been barely run in. So although the demonstration of high speed reliability had been achieved, he was unable to fulfill his other ambition — to qualify for a replica with this machine.

Several points of interest relate to the engine, which were not apparent from the original descriptions given in the motorcycling press. The throttle-controlled swash plate pump was mounted on the right hand crankcase door and delivered oil at a far higher pressure than the standard pump now in use on the modified Power Plus engines. This enabled the magneto to be mounted on the left hand crankcase door, using a bevel drive to dispense with the customary chain drive. The detachable cylinder head was cast in a silicon alloy and had 14 mm sparking plugs; it was retained to the block by sixteen steel studs.

For his personal transport in the Island, Albert Reynolds used one of his Reynolds Special sidecar outfits, which caused a minor sensation wherever it was seen. Dr Enrico Parodi, the Moto Guzzi designer, avowed it was the most beautiful motorcycle he had ever seen!

During the early thirties, at least two attempts were made to fit a Scott engine to a Rolls Royce, although for what purpose it is difficult to imagine! The first attempt to come to the attention of the press was that made by Messrs Cutlaw of the North Circular Road, London. Although very few details were published, it was claimed conversions could be effected for £70. Later, John B. Paddon of Crawley, Sussex, and the Scott London Depot combined forces to convert a 7 seater Rolls Royce that weighed 2 tons. With a 596 cc Scott engine fitted, it was claimed that 37 mph was possible and that 30 mph could be achieved, seven up, at 22 mpg! The engine achieved a 1 : 3 reduction via the fan pulley to which it was coupled and permitted the

THE GHOST TRAIL.

By G. STUART WHITE.

The riders' looks were sad,
And the riders' speech was low
Darkly looked they at the sky
And at the mud below.
" The snow will be upon us
  " Before we've gone a mile,
  " And if we once get lost out there
" What hope to win the Trial ? "

Up spake a veteran rider,
  An ancient Scott rode he :
" Say, who will ride on either side
  " And cross the Moor with me ? "
Then up spake Eddie Sliptoff,
  A Sunbeam man was he :
" Lo ! I will ride on thy right side
  " And brave the Moor with thee."

And up spake Harold Broadside,
  A Norton proud rode he :
" Sure ! I'll abide at thy left side
  " And cross the Moor with thee."
Now, while these three were buckling
  Their spare tubes on their backs,
A cunning watcher slipped away,
  And in his hand an axe.

With trees and rocks and bushes
  Spectators dam the streams
Until the splash is six feet deep ;
  At least, that's what it seems !
Brave Harold with his Norton
  Fell to the river bed,
While Eddie struck some three-ply
  And landed on his head.
The watchers laugh and shout
    with glee
  As each man takes a toss,
And ruefully gets up to find
  His bike a total loss.
At ten o-clock next morning
  The searchers all returned :
" There's still one poor soul missing "
  Was all the news we learned.
So if you're crossing Denton Moor
  Some dark and stormy night,
Be careful lest your hair be raised
  By a grim and gruesome sight.
A ghostly rider and his bike,
  Struggling onward still ;
Of course, I've never seen this sight,
  And trust I never will !

The Ghost Trail, typical of the many poems that appeared regularly in the Scott Trial programme. This comes from the 1933 programme, and was composed by one of the regular competitors

vehicle to be taxed at £6 per annum. Needless to say none of these conversions caught on!

At the Manx Grand Prix in 1933, two 'Works' prepared Scotts appeared, in the hands of Allan Jefferies and Noel Christmas. Known as 'Grand Prix' models, they were based on the Reynolds Scott that Tommy Hatch rode, but used the four speed close ratio gearbox that had originally been specified for the Scott TT entry that failed to materialise. It was claimed the engine used developed 27 bhp at 5,300 rpm and was capable of over 90 mph. It is interesting to note that Allan Jefferies had returned to the fold, for he had ridden for a number of other manufacturers during the intervening period and for a time had been away in South America with Frank Varey, when the latter agreed to introduce dirt track racing to Latin America. A whole book could be written about the hilarious experiences of that inseparable pair. Just one of many amusing incidents was the occasion when Allan Jefferies was asked to demonstrate the capabilities of a standard Scott for police work, against a number of other machines to be shown by their local distributors. Just prior to the demonstration, Allan fitted Frank's dirt track engine to the machine he was going to use, with the result that the scintillating performance amazed everyone. A quick change back to the original engine escaped detection and Allan took the order for 24 Scotts to be delivered to the Buenos Aires police! Needless to say, Frank got a wonderful reception everywhere he went, for his lurid and fearless riding style quickly earned him the nickname 'Red Devil'. It was not until 1932 that both returned home.

THE SCOTT MOTORCYCLE

On his return home, Allan rejoined the Scott Works as a rider, on an expenses and bonus basis. Unfortunately Reginald Vinter was not at all happy with this arrangement, for wins were achieved far too frequently! Some of the money was paid on an instalment basis, creating a situation like that faced by Harry Langman after his second place in the 1924 Senior TT, all quite illegal and doing little to retain the loyalty of the rider concerned.

Alas, once again the luck of the Scott riders was out. Noel Christmas made a spectacular leap over the hump at Ballig Bridge and landed heavily, causing the back wheel to collapse. He was not the most petite of riders! Allan Jefferies' footchange mechanism started to stiffen up on the first lap and became almost unmoveable on the second, so that he was forced to start the third lap with the gearbox hopelessly jammed in top gear. This put him out of the running too — the odds were too great. There was a keen sense of disappointment, for the 'Grand Prix' models appeared to have some potential. Even Harrison Town had come across to the Island for the last three days of the TT period.

Noel Christmas leaps Ballig Bridge during the 1933 Manx Grand Prix. The rear wheel collapsed on landing, putting him out of the race

Back at Shipley, development work was well advanced on another entirely new project, a three cylinder Scott that had been designed by William Cull, the development engineer who had taken over from Harry Shackleton. Albert Reynolds had been privileged to see the prototype during one of his visits prior to the TT and was so impressed he made an immediate order for what was to form the basis of his 1933/4 Reynolds Special De Luxe. He anticipated adding Master rear springing and hoped to get the overall weight below 400 lbs, fully equipped.

The new engine followed car practice in outline and comprised a rigid, box-like crankcase cast in Elektron which was machined through from one end. A 120° crankshaft of the built-up type carried four alloy drums and was built up with the main bearings so that the whole assembly could be slid into the crankcase tunnel. The light alloy drums formed the walls of the three crank chambers and provided a gas-tight seal. They were retained in position by long bolts that passed right through the crankcase casting. The connecting rods were of light alloy and had split big end eyes to enable them to be fitted through the open mouths of the crank chambers. Normal Scott deflector pistons were fitted and the cylinder block lowered into position. The cylinder block had a detachable, light alloy head; both were cored for water cooling. The gearbox was integral with the engine and was fitted with a transverse car type clutch that ran at engine speed, again closely following car practice. Ignition was by coil and distributor; a single Amal carburettor supplied the mixture. Oil was contained within a compartment of the sump and was distributed by a swash plate oil pump that had a variable setting. An unusual feature was the fitting of an oil pressure gauge, just above the oil filler. The prototype had hand gearchange, but this was subsequently changed to a rocking pedal arrangement. The exhaust system took the form of a three branch chromium plated pipe carried just below the saddle on the left hand side of the machine. It terminated in a single, cylindrical silencer. The frame was of the duplex tube type and was somewhat reminiscent of that used for the larger capacity Douglas twins. The engine unit was retained by six long bolts that passed through transverse lugs along the lower cradle tubes. Brampton bottom link forks provided the front suspension; the rear end was rigid. A radiator mounted in the customary position and a comparatively small, wedge-shaped petrol tank completed the ensemble.

The prototype weighed 448 lbs with fuel and oil and had a 59 inch wheelbase. Ground clearance was 5½ inches and the saddle height 26½ inches. Maximum speed was claimed to be in the region of 90 mph plus; the engine had a capacity of 747 cc. It is alleged that Albert Reynolds took the prototype on a trial run soon after its completion and was delighted with the performance. However, this would seem to conflict with Allan Jefferies' own experiences in the capacity of official tester. He found the navigation left much to be desired. At high speed on a straight road he had the greatest difficulty in keeping the machine from wandering from kerb to kerb, a quite frightening experience! Design changes were made, some of them quite

The original three cylinder prototype

Engine unit of the original three cylinder prototype

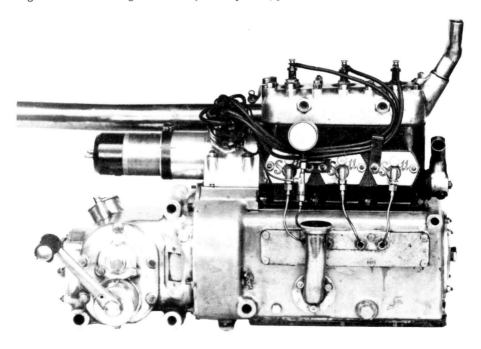

fundamental, for when the three was unveiled at the 1934 Olympia Show, it had changed considerably and now had a capacity of 986 cc. Not one of the 750 cc threes left Shipley, despite the advance publicity given in good faith by Albert Reynolds.

The Scott Motor Cycle Company did not exhibit at the 1933 Olympia Show. It was decided to continue the 1933 range into the next season, but to cut prices as the market was still in a very depressed state. Even the catalogue was unchanged, apart from the amended prices; the addition of a label showed it applied to 1934. On average, prices were cut by £5 10s per machine, bringing the price of the 498 cc Tourer to £59 10s. This was the lowest priced model in the range. The Replica, at the other end of the scale, was offered with the option of a four-speed gearbox that added an extra £5 to the purchase price if specified when the order was placed. One may presume this was to have been the production version of the four-speed gearbox designed originally for the TT models, and ultimately used on the 'Grand Prix' Scotts raced by Allan Jefferies and Trevor Battye. It would seem likely, however, that few 1934 Replicas left the Works with this fitment, which lapsed into obscurity. Later, a revised catalogue showed the substitution of the duplex tube frame throughout the entire range for the single downtube version that had been employed on all but the Replica models of late.

Albert Reynolds was caught unawares, for he had banked on being able to introduce the 'three' into the Reynolds Special range for the 1934 season. Although the three-cylinder model still showed great promise, it was undergoing extensive modifications at Saltaire, as subsequent events will show. In consequence, Reynolds had to continue his 1933 range into the 1934 season too. It was about this time that he began to give serious thought to his marketing weaknesses, for he still had only two models to offer. His ambition was to extend the range considerably, so that he had something to offer from as low as 125 cc, since the cheap, lightweight two-stroke was very popular in these hard times. With the knowledge that the 298 cc Scott single engine of the 1930/31 period was in many respects virtually half of one of the 596 cc twins, he reasoned that if a two stroke engine could be designed and built so that most of the parts were standardised, the engine could be doubled, tripled or even quadrupled to give the desired increase in capacity and some variety of cylinder configuration. Indeed, it would be possible to work quite a number of permutations if he got his sums right. However, this was looking far ahead, with what were still only ideas. The 'three' seemed to offer the best prospects for the immediate future.

1934 was a somewhat quiet year as far as the company was concerned. There were no Scott entries in the 1934 TT or for that matter in any of the future Senior TT events. Sadly, Tommy Hatch's Reynolds Special was to prove the last Scott ever to perform in this historic event. Fortunately, the dedicated few still contested the Manx Grand Prix and 1934 was no exception. There were three entries — A. L. Howitt, L. F. Ivin and Noel Christmas —

THE SCOTT MOTORCYCLE

Mavrogordato had at last decided to retire. All were out of luck and were forced to retire early in the Senior race. Howitt's engine seized at Ramsey when he was on his first lap and Ivin's machine ran a big end soon after. Noel Christmas was unable to make amends for his previous year's performance too. The crankshaft key sheared whilst he was still on his first lap, permitting the cranks to twist so that they were no longer in correct phase.

The Scott motorcycle engine has been used in many diverse applications, some far removed from motorcycling. It was during 1934 that one of the most interesting of all applications took place, which deserves due mention. It started when John Aldington of Fraser Nash cars bought a Morgan Super Sports model and wished to give it a hitherto unknown standard of performance that would make it the most outstanding three wheeler on the road. He took his problem to J. Granville Grenfell, one of the acknowledged Brooklands tuning wizards, and a plot was hatched to replace the original vee-twin ohv engine with two twin cylinder 596 cc Scott Replica engines. The biggest problem was to mount the engines in the form of a vee and to interconnect them in some way to a common mainshaft despite the fact that they would run in opposite directions! Having no wish to modify the crankcases, Grenfell hit upon the idea of having a centre shaft supported by a pair of Austin Seven main bearings which was mounted in a pair of huge engine plates that bridged the gap between the two engines. The shaft was coupled to the standard Morgan clutch and transmission. The shaft also carried two sprockets, in line with the engine sprocket of each engine. The nearside engine ran clockwise in its normal direction and the drive was taken direct to the centre sprocket. The offside engine was reversed and ran in an anti-clockwise direction, which necessitated taking the drive chain under the central sprocket but engaging with about one-third of its circumference. The chain continued around two idler sprockets and relied upon a Weller-type tensioner to even out any slackness in the return run. Although this method required the use of quite long chain runs, it worked and permitted the engines to run in opposite directions. A third chain drove a modified twin spark magneto, which fired the cylinders in diagonal sequence. Two duplex Pilgrim pumps looked after the lubrication requirements and two Amal carburettors, the carburation. These latter instruments were synchronised by means of junction boxes in the control cable layout. Heavy duty ball races were specified throughout and the whole chain assembly was enclosed with sheet metal covers, to provide what was virtually an oil bath.

The 1,200 cc vee twin thus formed produced some 50 bhp at 5,000 rpm and had very good low torque characteristics. Unfortunately, the engine unit was still new when the Morgan was road tested by C. P. Read of *Motor Cycling*, who had no wish to jeopardise the £200 spent on the conversion. Even so he found the acceleration was like driving an aeroplane with the power on, as he put it, and he foresaw that the driver would be able to pass a rival at 70 mph, then change up! As luck would have it, the Scott-powered Morgan has survived and is in the process of being restored to its former glory.

A full road test may yet prove a possibility and show some very interesting performance figures.

At the end of the year, the decision was made to rationalise production and market only the one basic model, which would be available with either a 498 cc or 596 cc engine. This was to be the Flying Squirrel, which would have the words De Luxe appended when the larger capacity engine was fitted. Both machines were to be supplied fully equipped, with lights, horn, speedometer and licence holder. They would also have the detachable head engine and a right hand exhaust system of the two-into-one type, setting the style that was to continue for a great many years. Prices rose to £75 for the 498 cc Squirrel and £78 10s for the 596 cc De Luxe version. Options included hand change or foot change for the gearbox.

Virtually on the eve of the 1934 Olympia Show, the Scott Motor Cycle Company sprang their greatest surprise. They decided to exhibit the latest version of their three-cylinder prototype, which was wheeled in just prior to the official opening time! It caught both the press and the trade completely unawares, the ideal scoop that received more than a good measure of publicity. Anyone privileged to have seen the earlier prototype 'three' would have immediately recognised the many design changes that had been made as a result of the ever-continuing development programme. Not so apparent was the increase in capacity to 986 cc.

The model exhibited at the 1934 Olympia Show, after extensive redesign

THE SCOTT MOTORCYCLE

The cylinders were formed in a single casting, radiator connections being taken from the front of the detachable cylinder head. The crankcase was now split horizontally along the axis of the crankshaft, each of the crank chambers being separated by light alloy 'drums' as before. They were kept gas-tight by the simple expedient of flooding the main bearings with oil maintained at a pressure higher than that of crankcase compression. Pistons were of the split-skirt type, with deflector crowns and one-piece connecting rods were used. The outer wall of the transfer ports was made detachable and the inlet tract was recessed into the cylinder block. An R.A.G carburettor looked after the mixture. The main oil supply was supplied by a throttle-controlled swash plate pump, as before. This was now augmented by two gear pumps driven off the end of the crankshaft, to deal with scavenging. The inlet ports were cut in a small liner, fitted to the lower portion of each cylinder bore. Oil fed through internal passageways in the engine collected in the joint between this liner and the bore, to act as a gallery for lubricating each cylinder wall. Three separate oil filters were fitted.

The radiator was now blended into the front of the 'tank' to give the complete machine more pleasing lines. Detachable, louvred panels, reminiscent of a car bonnet, gave access to the plugs. The exhaust pipe was led away on the left hand side of the machine, at high level. The three-branch manifold from the cylinder block was now heavily finned. The petrol tanks on the Show model were located across the top frame tube. Later, a dummy 'tank' was fitted, which contained only an instrument panel. Fuel was carried in two pannier tanks, slung across the rear mudguard rather like two large-capacity toolboxes. As these tanks were mounted below the carburettor level, it was necessary to fit an SU petrol pump that was switched on at the same time as the ignition circuit. It was obvious that attention had been given to the earlier navigational problems too. Webb girder forks superseded the Brampton bottom link forks which were specified in the original design.

The appearance of the 'three' in public provided Albert Reynolds with the necessary confidence to attend the Scott stand in person and take orders. It was not realised that the very exhibit that drew so much attention was little more than an empty set of castings! No price was available — the classic words 'depending on specification' were applied whenever a feature article appeared. As for the remainder of the Scott range, it was again a policy of one model — one price. Prices had now increased to £80 for the 498 cc model and £83 10s for the 596 cc version of the Flying Squirrel. Later, when a special 3S catalogue was issued in the form of a preliminary announcement, a price of £115 was quoted. Surprisingly, there was the option of a 747 cc or 986 cc engine capacity.

Once again Albert Reynolds had to continue his existing range, with the hope that he could eventually fulfill the orders he had taken for the three cylinder model. The importance of being able to add to the range in the manner he had envisaged became even more important, and he entered into negotiations with the Scott Works for further development along these lines.

176

Unfortunately, the Scott Motor Cycle Company were not able to consider his proposals in any depth, for they were on the verge of becoming involved in other activities that would take up all their surplus production capacity. Reynolds began to realise that if his plans were to reach fruition, he would have to go it alone and not depend solely on the Scott Motor Cycle Company for the range of machines he would sell.

It was about this time that the Scott Motor Cycle Company became interested in aviation. During 1934, a young Frenchman by the name of Henri Mignet had designed and built his own light aircraft, powered by a motorcycle engine. Such was his enthusiasm that he saw a vast backyard industry springing up, where the amateur enthusiast could purchase a set of plans and then construct his own aircraft from all manner of materials that were both cheap and readily available. Mignet's book *Le Pou de Ciel* (Flying Flea) was translated into English and was written in such an infectious style that anyone reading it could not help being fired with the enthusiasm that the Frenchman projected. Because it was possible to build a 'do-it-yourself' light aircraft for something like £50 - £90, the new craze caught on in Britain too, which was heightened by Mignet's visit to this country in his own Flea on August 13th 1935. Everyone wanted to take up flying and all manner of variations of the basic Flea began to appear. William Cull, the Scott designer, had been following the progress of the Flying Flea with great interest and was working on a two-cylinder air-cooled two-stroke engine he considered would make an ideal power unit for these light aircraft. On completion, his engine took the form of an inverted twin cylinder engine, in

Scotts at Elstree. Dennis Howard's Sprint Special alongside a Flying Flea powered by the Scott aircraft engine

which the separate cylinder barrels shared a common crankcase casting, with separate crank chambers. This same casting also contained the 2 : 1 reduction gear for the propeller. Bore and stroke measurements were 73 x 78 mm, giving a cubic capacity of 652 cc. Compression ratio was 6.8 : 1 and the engine developed 16 hp at 3,200 rpm and a maximum of 28 hp at 4,000 rpm. In flight, the engine ran at a steady 1,350 rpm at 50 mph. During 1935, the first tests were carried out at nearby Yeadon airfield and Allan Jefferies was called in to help, one of the problems being the tuning of the TT carburettor that provided the correct mixture to the engine. Initially, the machine would not lift off the ground, until it was discovered the propeller was too large! The Flea had a wing span of only 22 feet and was fitted with neither ailerons nor elevators. Control was effected by altering the angle of incidence of the main wing, which had a distinctive upswept shaping.

The Scott Flying Flea engine, designed by William Cull

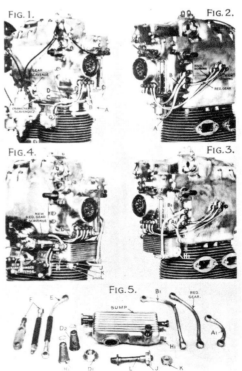

The auxiliary sump conversion kit for the A2S Flying Flea engine

Although the diminutive machine eventually flew quite well, the prospects for long term endurance in the air seemed a little doubtful. Allan was never happy about a two-stroke engine that ran at constant speed for long periods, which was bound to give rise to problems sooner or later. Even so, quite a number of these engines were manufactured and sold before the Flying Flea craze came to an abrupt halt. Several unexplained crashes with resulting fatalities led to an investigation by the authority responsible for aviation safety. They discovered an inherent design fault in the airframe. If a dive of more than 15 degrees was attempted, excess lift on the rear wing initiated a steeper dive from which the unfortunate pilot would be unable to extricate himself. All licences for this type of aircraft were revoked and the Flying Flea died overnight. With it went the Scott aircraft engine, a small but nonetheless interesting divergence from the manufacture of motorcycles. At least one Flea fitted with a Scott engine has survived and can be viewed at the Newark Air Museum, where it has been fully restored.

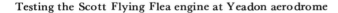

Testing the Scott Flying Flea engine at Yeadon aerodrome

A fully reconditioned Scott-engined Flying Flea that is part of the Newark Air Museum collection

Another interesting activity about this time was the construction of a two litre, six cylinder car engine that was virtually a doubled-up version of the three cylinder motorcycle engine. Many of the parts were interchangeable and even the same basic lubrication system was adopted. The crankcase took the form of an aluminium alloy casting about 22 inches long, to which was attached a sump that carried 2½ gallons of oil. The sump was held to the crankcase by 26 studs and nuts. The crankshaft was virtually two three-cylinder crankshafts mounted end to end and arranged so that the throws of numbers 1 and 6 cylinders were at 180° phasing, giving a firing order of 1 5 3 6 2 4 and therefore six power strokes per revolution. Most other features followed the practice that had already been adopted for the three-cylinder engine, doubling up where necessary. The six cylinder engine employed four oil pumps, two of the swash plate type, a main oil pump to feed them, and a scavenge pump. It was alleged to develop 86 bhp, a figure that could be boosted to 126 bhp by port modifications. Initially, the engine was fitted in an Aston Martin sports car, but when the car was eventually scrapped, the engine was salvaged and found its way to the Birmingham Science Museum, where it has been preserved and displayed. Those who witnessed the early tests claim the engine would run so slowly and evenly that it was possible to count the individual fan blades.

The supreme test! A Scott stationary engine running at speed with a penny and a pencil balanced edgewise on the cylinder head

The six cylinder car engine that was originally fitted in an Aston Martin car

A twin cylinder marine engine

THE SCOTT MOTORCYCLE

There was only one Scott entered in the 1935 Manx Grand Prix, by A. L. Howitt, who hoped to better his previous year's record. This year he managed to complete just two laps before a piston melted and forced his retirement. Even in the Manx Grand Prix the Scott now stood little chance of success as race speeds increased steadily.

1935 marked the termination of Harold Wood's long association with the Scott Trial as the route finder and Clerk of the Course. Such was his relationship with the local landowners and their bailiffs that only on one occasion was he refused the use of land on the day of the Trial. Some, like Sir Arthur Hill, had put off a grouse shoot rather than spoil the trial and it seems ironic that just one awkward person should have proved to be so inflexible. In point of fact, the laugh was on the dissenter in the end because the re-routing necessary took riders along public roads that bordered the land he owned. The noise of the machines effectively prevented the shoot from taking place as planned whereas had the riders been allowed access, they would have passed through in an area remote from the shoot!

To celebrate his emancipation, Harold decided to have a final ride in the Scott Trial and entered on a 172 cc SOS powered by a Villiers engine. He was duly rewarded by winning the award for the best performance by a machine of under 200 cc capacity — his first and only ride in a competitive event on a machine other than a Scott.

It was about this time that *Motor Cycle* carried a report about a super-charged Scott that had been built by Graham Kirk, of Norwich. The basis of this private venture was a 1928 TT model, reputed to be one of the actual TT machines of that year, that was linked by means of a U-shaped manifold to a Cozette No 4 vane-type blower. Earlier attempts to couple the blower to the crankcases had shown indifferent results and it was found preferable to pass the mixture straight into the combustion chambers via the special manifold and the upper transfer ports. The blower was mounted on mild steel plate over the gearbox, so that it lay between the rear mudguard and the twin seat stays. The standard magneto drive was retained, but a heavier gauge chain was employed and used also to drive the blower. A huge SU carburettor looked after the mixture. In most other respects the machine was standard, even to the retention of the original sprockets and a hand gear change. Although not tested to the full at the time of the report, Graham Kirk estimated the maximum speed to be about 100 mph and fuel consumption approximately 45 mpg at 60 mph.

Again, the Scott programme for 1936 was one model — one price and the two Flying Squirrel models continued in production unchanged. The three-cylinder model was still no nearer production, although it was listed in the 'buyers guide' sections of the two weekly motorcycle magazines whenever the special buyers guide issues appeared. The twin rear-mounted petrol tanks, mentioned earlier, were now standard fittings.

As far as Albert Reynolds was concerned, the wholesale cancellation of orders for the Scott three, as a result of the interminable production delays, caused him to place more emphasis on his own design of machine. Plans were made for the manufacture of the first prototype design, which would mean that he would no longer be wholly dependent on the Scott Motor Cycle Company for the machines he wished to sell. There was no question of a break with the Company after so many years close liaison — it was just a question of extending his range so that he could gain a foothold in the lower end of the market.

There was even less to record for 1936, the year that not a single entry was made by a Scott rider for the Manx Grand Prix. There had been a Scott in one or other of the Isle of Man races since 1909 and the absence of this famous name was felt by all true enthusiasts. Had the marque at last become so uncompetitive that this was the end of the road? Certainly it would seem so, for the Scott was becoming a rare sight in all other forms of competitive event; even in the annual Scott Trial the number of Scott entries was down to two. A light machine with a punchy motor and high ground clearance was now essential for any real success.

1937 marked the introduction of Albert Reynolds' own AER twin, the prototype of which appeared in the Isle of Man during the TT period. Reynolds had effectively used this method of introducing new models in the past, for the gathering of a larger number of motorcycle enthusiasts in one location presented an opportunity for displaying a new model that simply could not be missed. The Scott factory continued their one model — one price policy, with prices unchanged and only detail modifications. This was to prove the last year of the three cylinder model, for it was quietly dropped from the range towards the end of the year. Of the small number made, only two of what was to have been the production version have survived.

One of those concerned about the demise of the Scott, especially in competition events such as the Scott Trial, was Harold Scott, nephew of the inventor. He had written to the motorcycling press to encourage Scott entries in these events that was not entirely unsuccessful. One of his inducements was the provision of the Herbert Scott silver cup, which was donated by his father, one of Alfred Scott's brothers. Without Harold's encouragement, it seems doubtful whether the Scott Trial would have had any Scott entries at all, for in the middle to late thirties the number had dwindled to only two or at the most three entries in this annual event. Later the cup was awarded each year to the best first-timer, thus helping to encourage new entrants riding any make.

J. K. Kermode decided to show the Scott flag in the 1937 Manx Grand Prix, even if he was the sole Scott entry. But he was doomed to early disappointment like many of his predecessors. Cooling troubles caused the engine to overheat and on the third lap the radiator burst, giving no option other than to retire on the spot. This Scott too had failed to finish the course.

Once again Scott Motor Cycles announced no change in specification or prices. Sales were now handled by Scott Motors and Kitson Limited of

Ridgemount Street, off Gower Street, London W1. This firm had been appointed the official UK Distributors for the two versions of the Flying Squirrel, using the Charlotte Street premises formerly occupied by Scott Motors (Southern) who had taken over the old London Scott Depot.

It is not often realised that it was during 1938 that the Scott Motor Cycle Company became actively involved with the autocycle, a form of cheap, low powered lightweight that was rapidly gaining prominence as a convenient and economic means of transportation for the commuter. Basically, the autocycle comprised a strengthened bicycle frame often fitted with some form of front suspension and having a pedal assisted 98 cc two-stroke engine. One of the pioneers of this mode of transportation had been the Cyc-Auto concern, which had produced a prototype design as early as 1931. The inventor in this instance was a Mr Wallington Butt, who had evolved a quite novel design in which the small engine was mounted transversely in front of the bottom bracket of the frame, transmitting the drive to the bottom bracket itself by means of a worm and pinion arrangement. Thereafter, final drive was by means of the customary chain and sprockets. Initially, engine units of Cyc-Auto manufacture were fitted, but during 1938 a change was made to the proprietary 98 cc Villiers engine. When the company got into financial difficulties during 1938, Wallington Butt sold out to the Scott Motor Cycle Company, who promptly redesigned the engine unit and moved Cyc-Auto Limited to new premises at 381, Uxbridge Road, West Acton. Although a cheap version of the Cyc-Auto was still available with a Villiers engine, the choice of a slightly more expensive version fitted with the Scott engine provided an alternative. A tradesman's carrier model was also listed, with the same choice of engines. The Scott engines were made at Shipley, and tested alongside their twin cylinder counterparts. They were always referred to as MAJs, an abbreviation for motor assisted juniors.

The autocycle was just another passing phase in the history of the lightweight two-stroke, although interest continued after the war and into the fifties. The combination of a low powered engine and a single gear made use of the pedals necessary whenever a sharp rise was encountered, whilst the standard of comfort was quite primitive. Like the scooter of the early twenties, the autocycle eventually passed into oblivion, to re-appear at a later date in a very different concept.

It was during 1938 that the most remarkable of all Scott entries was made in the Manx Grand Prix. A young Yorkshire lad by the name of Herbert Smith was a real Scott fanatic and had one burning obsession — to ride a Scott in the Manx Grand Prix. Being only a working lad, he had no capital, so he had to realise his ambition the hard way, by cycling to work and saving every penny he could for seven long years. Harrison Town, the former Scott employee who had left the Works to start up his own motor-cycle business in nearby Keighley, got to hear of Herbert Smith's determined effort and was so impressed that he decided he would personally build the best possible machine for this aspiring entrant. And so Smith's ambition became a reality when he pushed off from last position on the grid in the

A 1936 Cyc-Auto, as found. The engine is of Cyc-Auto and not Scott manufacture

A later pre-war version of the Cyc-Auto, fitted with the Scott MAJ engine unit

A Scott water-cooled industrial engine

The twin cylinder TSE starter unit used for starting diesel engines

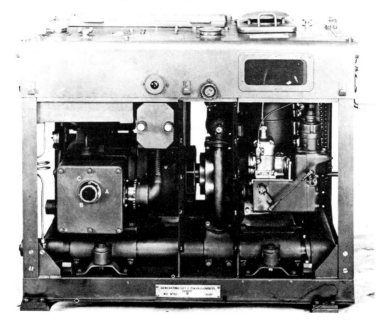

A Scott-engined generating set produced during 1938/9

1938 Senior event. No one rated his chances very high, for it seemed unlikely that he would even finish the course, if the Scott results from previous years were taken into account. But they under-rated the lad from Airedale who had already shown the extent of his determination when he had a fixed objective in view. Although well down in speed compared with the race leaders, he pressed on and turned in a lap at 70.03 mph on his third circuit, the fastest lap ever on a Scott! He eventually finished a very creditable 12th, at an average speed of 67.78 mph, which proved to be the fastest finishing speed of any Scott. Although unknown at the time, it also proved to be the last occasion on which a Scott would finish in an Isle of Man race for many years. Apart from Herbert Smith's riding ability, much of the credit for this remarkable performance must be credited to Harrison Town, who clearly knew a thing or two about machine preparation.

Another interesting experiment that came to light during the year originated from a Company known as Mercury Motors, of West Croydon, Surrey. One of the partners in the business, a Mr L. Jenks, decided to convert a 1930 596 cc engine to rotary valve operation by incorporating a rotating, ported disc in each crankcase door. The disc was mounted on a double roller bearing and was driven by the peg on the big end nut that is normally used for the oil pump drive. The normal inlet passage was blanked off and an Amal carburettor attached to a stub on each crankcase door, the whole assembly being held in position by the usual retaining strap. The engine itself had been adapted previously to run on petroil, so there was no problem caused by the removal of the oil pump. The engine was mounted in the Mercury frame, a somewhat heavy duplex loop frame of channel section duralumin fitting into cast iron lugs and fitted with rear suspension and a form of duplex steering, all part of the somewhat unorthodox specification of the Mercury Special. It was claimed the rotary valve permitted a maximum speed of approximately 90 mph at something like 4,000 rpm, and showed an improvement in fuel economy. Most advantage was gained in acceleration and the ability of the engine to pull well at low speeds on hills. Overall weight was 450 lbs and it is alleged six of these machines were made.

During October, an announcement was made about a new addition to the Scott range — the Clubman's Special. Two versions were to be marketed, one having a rigid frame and the other a spring frame of the plunger type that was entirely of Scott design. Both models were fitted with a 596 cc engine that had been specially tuned and was capable of giving a maximum speed in excess of 90 mph. Internally, three ring pistons were fitted and provision for cylinder wall oiling was made by fitting another duplex Pilgrim pump on the left hand crankcase door. Improved transfer ports and a large bore carburettor aided the boost in performance. Other features of the new models included fully enclosed footchange mechanism, a four-start worm to improve clutch withdrawal, a four gallon fuel tank and a half gallon oil tank combined, both with snap fillers, a separate oil tank for chain oiling and a chromium plated radiator. Most of these improvements, with the exception of the engine

187

modifications, were also included in the specification of the Flying Squirrel models, one of which could also be obtained with a spring frame.

In order to rationalise production, the 498 cc engine was dropped completely, so that the intending purchaser of a Scott now had the option of two rigid frame models and two fitted with a spring frame. The standard Flying Squirrel cost £85, or £95 10s if the spring frame version was required. The rigid frame Clubman's Special was listed at £105, with an additional £10 if the spring frame version was preferred. Tyre sizes remained unchanged in the case of the Flying Squirrels apart from an increase to 3.50 inches in the section of the rear tyre. The new Clubman models had 19 inch wheels, fitted with tyres of 3 inch and 3.25 inch cross section, respectively. Obviously the Company was now on the way up again, for they took space at the 1938 Show, now held at Earls Court. There were many who welcomed their reappearance, for they had exhibited at this annual event only once since they reached their all-time peak during 1929.

The 1939 Clubman's Special springer

One important factor that was not too apparent was the ever increasing weight of the Scott. The rigid frame Clubman's Special scaled no less than 411 lb, whilst the spring frame version weighed a quite incredible 490 lb. It was not surprising that some criticism was levied at the brakes, which were hopelessly inadequate for high speed work. As the guarded words of *Motor Cycling's* road tester stated, "The front stopper could be improved if the lever were a little longer and curved to bring it more easily within reach". An understatement indeed when trying to brake 411 lbs of motorcycle from the very high speeds attainable! The test was conducted at Brooklands and in most other respects the machine acquitted itself well, taking into account that it was the rigid frame version. Even so, there was a hint of consternation about handling, which left something to be desired at speeds in excess of 60 mph. The tester attributed the instability to the arms that extended from the forks and held the headlamp some distance away. The unsprung weight tended to promote a pendulum effect which made the steering light as the machine traversed a series of bumps.

To many, the Clubman's Special represented the very peak to which the Scott engine had been developed, whilst still retaining a high degree of mechanical reliability. It was unfortunate that this model should have such a short production run, for in little more than a year's time the production of all motorcycles destined for the civilian market was to come to an abrupt end. Britain was once again at war with Germany.

Of the few production figures available, it is particularly interesting to note that the total production of machines during 1929 was fractionally more than the total produced during the years 1931 - 1940 inclusive — a good indication of the dramatic effect of the economic depression and the slow recovery of the Company. For those interested in the actual figures, they were 1,398 and 1,356 respectively.

Close-up of the Clubman's
Special rear suspension

The rigid frame version of the Clubman's Special

CHAPTER SEVEN
Last days at Saltaire

DURING the war, the Scott Motor Cycle Company was fully occupied with work to help the war effort, much of it contract work on behalf of the Admiralty. No motorcycles were manufactured during this period, since the requirements of the armed forces were met by several other manufacturers capable of producing their machines in considerable volume. All were single cylinder designs of the type that had proved very popular before the war. Although not ideally suited to active service conditions, they had the advantage of requiring only the very minimum of maintenance to keep them in good running order.

Towards the end of the war, there was a growing interest in old machines, which was influenced in part by the late Graham Walker's 'flashback to the past' articles in *Motor Cycling*, of which he was then Editor. The late J. J. Hall took things a stage further by presenting a whole series of quite light-hearted articles based on his tour around the country seeking out old machines and often acquiring them at amazingly low prices or even as a gift. Letters began to appear on this theme in the correspondence columns that ultimately led to thoughts about forming a club that would cater for this specific area of interest. Foremost amongst the correspondents was C. E. (Titch) Allen, who was at that time still serving in the forces. Not unexpectedly, the odd Scott or two appeared and it was not long before Cyril Quantrill — a young journalist with *Motor Cycling* — began to take a special interest in them himself. Encouraged by his boss, Graham Walker, Cyril invested in a 1924 Scott two-speeder and was sufficiently impressed to write a two and a half page article about it during January 1946. The seeds were sown!

Interest in old machines grew and it was not long before Titch Allen took it upon himself to form the Vintage Motor Cycle Club. This historic occasion was marked by an inaugural rally and meeting at the Lounge Cafe, on the Hog's Back, near Guildford. The date was April 28th 1946 and despite the inclement weather, there were enough present to prove there was a need for the Club and to send it off to a good start. Of the dozen or so machines present, two were Scotts.

A few months later, there was evidence that the Scott Motor Cycle Company was beginning to think about producing motorcycles once again,

191

and Cyril Quantrill seized the opportunity to pay them a visit on his 1924 two-speeder. It proved to be a very interesting visit, for he was shown some drawings of a projected new design by William Cull, even though he was not permitted to disclose details. More important, he was loaned one of the first pre-production models that were to represent the return of the Scott motorcycle to the civilian market. It was virtually an updated version of the pre-war rigid frame Flying Squirrel, the most noticeable difference being the use of full-width hubs, the front one of which was fitted with a dual brake assembly operated through a self-compensating balance box. The machine tested was fitted with Brampton girder forks and it is understood that about six of these models were made, along with six that had Webb girder forks, forming the first of the post-war production. The machine tested gave a good account of itself, although surprisingly the brakes did not quite match up to expectation. Performance-wise, it was virtually identical to its pre-war counterpart, and handled just as well.

Whilst he was at the Works, Quantrill was given a ride in a car that was fitted with an in-line three cylinder engine, virtually the old three cylinder Scott motorcycle engine that had been adapted to run on petroil through a metering device. The engine was housed in a somewhat battered Morgan four-wheeler chassis that formed the mobile test bed. The car gave a good account of itself too, but it was stated that at that time there was no intention of using the engine in a motorcycle.

Before motorcycle production got under way, it is interesting to note that in common with several other manufacturers, the Scott Motor Cycle Company had been giving thought to new designs of racing engine. During 1945, V. Stohansel of the Scott Motor Cycle Company projected a 500 cc TT engine in the form of a supercharged vee-four, with provision for fuel injection. The cylinders were arranged at a 30° vee-angle, each pair sharing a common combustion head located axially along the crankshaft. Each pair of working cylinders was offset to each side of the shaft, in order to give the assymetrical port timing necessary for the supercharger that was fitted. This necessitated the use of a four-throw crankshaft arranged in the up-down-up-down sequence. The flywheel attached to the end of the crankshaft carried a hollow shaft to which two eccentrics were attached, phased at 180°. Each eccentric operated a rocking lever which caused a piston to reciprocate in the large pumping chamber across the rear of the engine. The chamber had a dividing wall at the cylinder centre, each piston being of the double-acting type. Intake and delivery was controlled by a rotary valve that was chain-driven from a cross shaft. The shaft itself was skew driven from the shaft to which the eccentrics were attached and formed the drive for the magneto at the other end. Wet sump lubrication was employed, using a gear pump that also drove the water pump necessary for the cooling system. The clutch was incorporated in the flywheel, as in car practice, and the drive shaft was taken through the hollow crankshaft of the blower. Although the drawings showed a conventional carburettor, provision was made for fuel injection as an alternative by incorporating injector nozzles just above the inlet ports of the rearmost cylinders.

Apart from the few girder fork models made towards the end of 1946 or early in 1947, the Scott post-war production models embodied one further change. Dowty Equipment Limited had designed and patented a new type of telescopic front fork, based on their wide experience of manufacturing hydraulic and pneumatic equipment for the aircraft industry. The forks were of unusual design in the sense that they had no internal compression springs but relied upon air as the suspension medium in their place. The advertising literature at the time made clear the reasons for this departure from current practice by stating that air springs are impervious to fatigue failures common to metal springs and give far smoother action. Steel springs have a constant deflection per increase of unit load whereas air springs, given suitable compression ratios, provide soft springing over the normal range of movement. But they will also absorb a considerable amount of energy for a very small movement at the extremes of the compression stroke; air cannot bottom like a helical spring.

The author's 1946/7 post-war prototype, fitted with Webb girder forks and full-width hubs

Externally, the fork assembly was very similar in appearance to other telescopic designs, although somewhat slimmer in profile in view of the absence of internal compression springs. Telescopic forks were the very newest trend in motorcycle design, following the successful introduction of Associated Motor Cycle's 'Teledraulic' fork on some of the late Matchless G3 models used by the Army. Although not the originators of the telescopic fork, the Teledraulic fork represented the first successful application of an hydraulically-damped unit on a production basis. Credit must go to Alfred Scott, who designed the first forks to operate on a sliding or telescopic basis!

The complete fork unit weighed about 22 lb and had a total movement of 5½ inches, equally divided between the fully extended and fully compressed positions. Static pressure with the rider seated was approximately 42 psi, a rating that rose to some 250 psi on full compression and fell to 20 psi on full recoil. Oil provided the damping medium. Each fork leg was provided with a valve close to the top which provided the means of inflation from a normal tyre inflator. A Kilner valve provided the seal, that was similar to the familiar Schraeder tyre valve, but was shorter in length. Each leg was interconnected by means of an air balance pipe, carried in a recess below the upper fork yoke. The Scott Motor Cycle Company was not alone in using this proprietary fork assembly. The P & M Panthers also used a somewhat similar design, as did Veloce Limited, when the manufacture of Webb girder forks was discontinued during 1947.

In service, the Dowty forks performed well and it was claimed that up to 20,000 miles could be covered before any 'topping up' was necessary. However, air is an intangible medium to keep in any confined space, especially when it is under pressure. Sooner or later leakage occurred as the synthetic rubber seals began to wear and there was always danger that the forks would subside until they remained in the fully compressed position, for there were no conventional compression springs to keep them extended in an emergency. Amongst other things, the Dowty fork depended upon perfect cleanliness for satisfactory working, and it is probable that air was lost prematurely if the person inflating the forks did not first ensure his pump and connector were completely free from dust or dirt that may otherwise work its way into the system. It should be mentioned that the use of telescopic forks necessitated repositioning the front wheel speedometer drive. It was moved to the gearbox area and taken from the outrigger of the final drive sprocket.

The basic purchase price of the 1947 Flying Squirrel was £194 10s, to which had to be added an additional £52 10s 3d, representing the Purchase Tax now applied to all new vehicles. Even then it was necessary to add a further £4 for the obligatory speedometer, which itself carried an additional £1 1s 8d Purchase Tax! Only the 596 cc version was available, but as the sales leaflet put it, it was "the finest machine that money can buy". Sadly, it was still very expensive when compared with other machines, some of which could be considered in the thoroughbred category. You had to be an enthusiast to buy a Scott with so many cheaper counter attractions. Even the 350 cc International Norton was less expensive.

Performance-wise, the post-war Scott was capable of about 75 - 80 mph and would cruise quite happily in the 60 - 65 mph range. If ridden without a too heavy hand, petrol consumption was alleged to work out at 70 - 80 mpg, although in practice, most owners found it to be somewhat lower. Oil consumption averaged out around the 1,000 mpg mark. The overall weight was now 376 lb, a figure not included in the sales leaflet. Power output was rated at 16 bhp at 2,500 rpm and 30 bhp at 5,000 rpm. Somehow it seemed the Scott just came back into production, for there was no notification about the return to the civilian market in either of the weekly motorcycle magazines.

When racing got back into its stride after the war, the most exciting news was the introduction of a series of Clubman's races, to be included in the 1947 Isle of Man TT programme. There had been pressure for some time to give the average clubman a chance to ride a standard production motorcycle in race meetings, no doubt prompted by the success of *Motor Cycling's* Donington Day, held as an experiment during 1939. On this latter occasion, the average private owner had been given the opportunity to use his 'ride-to-work' machine on a racing circuit, so that he could try his hand without having to come up against the experts. The meeting had proved to be a great success, but since the Army still occupied Donington, there was no hope of being able to use this famous circuit. However, to most the Isle of Man appealed even more and there was a total of 64 entries for the three Clubman's races — Senior 33, Junior 23 and Lightweight 8.

There was one lone Scott rider in the Senior race, J. H. Marshall of the Sunbeam M.C.C. Unfortunately, he was in trouble right from the very start. The A-CU regulations relating to the Clubman's races stated that the exhaust pipe must terminate within a square that bounded the rear wheel rim, an arrangement that suited the four-strokes quite well but not the Scott, which functioned most efficiently on an exhaust pipe only 23 inches long. During practice, it was found that the extractor effect of the ultra-long pipe was too great, drawing most of the charge through the engine and giving rise to over-heating problems. Jet sizes were increased to the maximum, but whilst this helped, another problem appeared — high fuel consumption which gave rise to doubts whether the machine would be able to carry sufficient fuel for the compulsory two laps before a pit stop could be made. An appeal about the exhaust system was rejected, so there was only one answer — to fit a silencer in order to cut down the extractor effect. In consequence, the Scott proved one of the quietest machines in the Island.

On race day, the Scott had covered only 1,200 miles since new and was capable of holding more than 90 mph on the straights. By the time he had reached Ramsey, Marshall had already passed five Senior competitors and was going well, until he ran into a patch of mist at the Waterworks, on the climb up the mountain. He misjudged the bend, grounded a footrest, and ended up in the wall, fortunately without serious injury. But the crash had burst the radiator and he was out of the race. Many were sorry to see him tour in to the Grandstand and retire, a fate that had befallen so many of his predecessors.

Another Scott was entered for the September Manx Grand Prix races, this time by Major Hilary Iremonger-Watts, who had ridden a Triumph twin earlier that year in the Senior Clubman's TT. The machine he used was basically a 1928 Flyer that had been extensively modified by the late Philip Smith. Even the Shipley factory took an interest and supplied the full-width hubs and Dowty forks that formed part of the new specification. Philip Smith's basic objective was to beat the highest average speed for a Scott set up by Herbert Smith in 1938, when he finished 12th in the Manx Grand Prix of that year. Smith reasoned that if he could build an engine that would give a maximum of 5,500 rpm this should produce a maximum speed of just over 90 mph and would permit lap speeds in the region of 70 mph, with the aim of finishing rather than challenging any of the faster machinery. Externally, the most noticeable modification to the engine was the cross-over oiling system used in which lubricant from one crankcase well passed through a finned oil cooler mounted transversely across the engine to the opposite cylinder wall, and vice-versa. The Pilgrim pump was used to supply the main bearings alone. Specially-made tanks gave the machine a somewhat unusual appearance, for the petrol tank was mounted well back from the steering head, permitting the radiator to be raised to a more vertical position. The right-hand exhaust system terminated in a small diameter megaphone.

Quite by coincidence, Iremonger-Watts drew number 40, the same number that Herbert Smith's machine had carried in 1938. But he was not to be so fortunate. When he started, Philip Smith was quick to notice the absence of oil smoke and anxiously awaited further news from around the course about the machine's progress. At Ballacraine, it was reported the Scott was travelling very fast, but again there was no evidence of any smoke. Kirkmichael was reached at an average speed of over 70 mph, then the score-board indicator moved no further after progress at this point on the course was recorded. Soon the news filtered through. Iremonger-Watts had retired with a broken crank, just short of Ramsey. The Pilgrim pump had given trouble and the resultant lack of lubrication had done the rest.

There was no Show at Earls Court for 1947 and the Scott programme continued unchanged. It was broadly suggested that the model was so perfect, why change it in any way?

There were no Scott entries in the Clubman's TT, but in the Manx Grand Prix, R. G. Phillips contributed the sole Scott entry. He was even more unlucky than his predecessors because the A-CU officials decided his machine infringed the new ruling that all machines must have fully-enclosed primary chains! Obviously none of them had ever experienced trying to fit a new primary chain on a Scott without using the old chain to draw it into position, a task that has brought many an enthusiast to a very distraught state! Phillips' remonstrations passed unheeded, for he ultimately started

Ossie Neal at a Prescott hill climb with his racing outfit. He has done much to ensure the Scott name is not forgotten in racing circles

the race on a Rudge and was forced to retire on the first lap.

The first post-war Motor Cycle Show was held at Earls Court during the last week in November, but there were no Scott exhibits on this occasion. An announcement made a couple of weeks earlier related to the 1949 programme and stated that for the new season, coil ignition was to be adopted. The advantages claimed were easier starting and better slow running, plus the elimination of the long magneto chain. The space now available permitted the fitting of a separate five pint oil tank on the right hand side of the machine, and an air cleaner to the carburettor air intake. To replace the dynamo of the Magdyno unit used in the past, a new Lucas dynamo of the 'pancake' type was bolted direct to the left hand crankcase door, taking its drive from the left hand crank. The right hand crank drove the duplex Pilgrim pump, but there was now a short skew gear interposed between the driving dog of the crank and the pump, to drive a car-type distributor mounted vertically to the rear of the cylinder block, on the outside of the crankcase casting. Two other useful features included a roll-on centre stand and a quickly-detachable rear mudguard to facilitate removal of the rear wheel. The price of the new model was £194 10s, as before, the addition of Purchase Tax and speedometer etc, bringing the grand total to £247 0s 3d.

When the 1950 programme was announced during the end of September, only detail improvements were made to the 596 cc Flying Squirrel, which was to be continued virtually unchanged. In the main, these consisted of wider 'D' shaped mudguards, with heavier stays and the use of the latest 7 inch Lucas headlamp. The basic price had been increased to £198 10s, which came to a grand total of £252 1s 11d, after the addition of Purchase Tax.

The Company decided to exhibit at the 1949 Earls Court Show and displayed five solo models, together with a combination using a Watsonian sidecar. Although the reappearance of a Scott at the annual show was appreciated by all true enthusiasts, there were very few purchasers. At a price of over £250, the Scott was indeed in the luxury category.

During March 1950, it was announced that the weekly magazine *Motor Cycling* proposed to stage the long delayed second road race meeting at which Clubmen could ride standard production motorcycles. It was to be the follow-up to the highly successful 'Donington Day' held during May 1939, an event that would undoubtedly have been repeated the following year had it not been for the war. Since Donington was no longer available, the meeting was renamed 'Silverstone Saturday', in honour of the new venue. The date selected was April 22nd, so that the meeting would signify the opening of the 1950 racing season.

'Silverstone Saturday' was a great success too, attracting more than 45,000 spectators. The organisation of the meeting was entrusted to the very capable hands of the British Motor Cycle Racing Club and one of the highlights of the meeting was a race for vintage machines, all of which had been manufactured prior to 1931. For Scott enthusiasts, this was a very memorable occasion, for the race was led from start to finish by Noel Mavrogordato on the 1930 Sprint Special he had last used in the 1932 Manx Grand Prix. It was like turning back the pages of history, for Noel dressed for the part in his famous yellow sweater (over his leathers) and wore the leather plug pouches around his waist that also formed part of his characteristic attire. The familiar Yowl of an open frame Scott brought a lump in the throat. Mavro had won his first race, riding a Scott!

Sadly, only a few weeks later *Motor Cycling* carried a simple announcement to the effect that following a meeting of creditors, Scott Motors (Saltaire) Limited had gone into voluntary liquidation. Noel H. Kitchen and Miles G. Burrows had purchased the assets on the behalf of the shareholders of a new company, which it was anticipated would be formed shortly. The new board would comprise Messrs Kitchen and Burrows, with the addition of William Cull and J. C. Armitage. The blow was softened a little by news

Mavro with his 1930 Sprint Special on the grid at Silverstone. He won the vintage machine race, the first of its kind to be run at this venue

that the services of the principal executives of the old company had been retained and that it was hoped to maintain the old Scott tradition and to continue the manufacture of motorcycles. It was expected that Works repairs of existing models would continue, as would the supply of spare parts. A total of just over 600 machines had been made since the war.

There followed a long silence, until December 14th 1950, when *Motor Cycling* carried a column about the 1951 Scott range. The 596 cc Flying Squirrel was to be continued, unchanged, at a price not at that time available. Manufacture had been transferred to the Aerco Jig and Tool Company of 2, St Mary's Row, Birmingham — a company owned by Matt Holder, who had been a Scott enthusiast since a young man. The old Works in Saltaire was sold to Hepworth and Grandage Limited, the automotive piston specialists.

Matt Holder (prototype number 2), Bernal Osborne (*Motor Cycling* - prototype number 5) and a 1954 production Flying Squirrel

CHAPTER EIGHT
Carrying on the tradition : Birmingham and Derby

FOLLOWING the acquisition of the Scott Motor Cycle Company by the Aerco Jig and Tool Company, for a sum believed to be around £10,000, the Scott motorcycle was still regarded as though it was in production. Although a new prototype model was being developed, none were for sale until several years later. Matthew Holder, the head of Aerco who had come to the rescue, had to cope with all the problems of moving tools, parts, drawings and other equipment to his premises in Birmingham, an old and somewhat unimposing building at 2, St Mary's Row, almost in the City centre. He also had some difficulty in obtaining craftsmen, for it was not easy to find men of the right calibre to carry on the old Scott tradition. In consequence, the only machines sold during this period were those that had been completed and were in stock at the time of the purchase. It was Matt's sheer enthusiasm, business acumen and technical know-how that kept things going through this very difficult transitional period.

Although in no way connected with the company, one of those who helped to keep the Scott name in the news was John Catchpole, a Scott enthusiast and active competitor who was also Chairman of the Sidcup Club. In July 1951 Catchpole had already been in the news when he was timed at 100 mph on his 1929 vintage model in a vintage road race event at Boreham. Previously, the magic three figures had always eluded Scott riders; the best on record had been 95.6 mph recorded by L. C. Williams during a Flying Kilo attempt at Brooklands during 1935. He too had used a 1929 model, in this instance a Replica named 'Zip IV' stripped of all but its basic essentials.

Apart from his solo rides in vintage events, John Catchpole was no mean hand with a sidecar outfit either and could be seen at most South Eastern Centre trials and grass track meetings, always Scott mounted. In 1949 he became the Southern Expert in the South Eastern Centre sidecar class and it was probably this that inspired him to construct a very special outfit to his own design, based on the Scott engine.

The new model was a beautiful piece of engineering that would have appealed to even the most hardened of the Scott purists. The frame, which was built from one inch diameter tubing using Sif-bronze welding, was of the duplex cradle type and had a rigid rear end. Modified AMC Teledraulic forks were fitted, carrying a 21 inch diameter front wheel and hub from an AMC competition model. A cut-down 2½ gallon BSA petrol tank permitted the Scott radiator to be fitted in the customary position and a 3½ pint Norton oil tank, mounted above the gearbox, provided the container for the lubricating oil. It contained a bleed-off for chain lubrication.

The engine was based on a vintage crankcase that had been modified in the vicinity of the left hand crankcase door to permit bevel drive to a BTH magneto mounted in an inclined position. A Pilgrim pump on the right hand crankcase door followed conventional practice and was driven from the other end of the crankshaft. The two-in-one exhaust pipe was upswept and was carried on the right hand side of the machine, to terminate in a barrel-type silencer. Although a 596 cc engine was used, it could easily be converted to 498 cc form, a peculiar advantage of the Scott engine that endeared it to special builders. Bolted to the rear of the crankcase in semi-unit form was a four-speed Velocette gearbox, which had been modified internally to give ratios of 5.99, 7.97, 12.58 and 16.65 : 1, with an 18 tooth final drive sprocket. It was mounted upright and created no additional lubrication problems.

The sidecar chassis was also Sif-bronze welded and incorporated a rubber shock absorber, so that the wheel spindle could pivot about a lug on the rear cross tube. Previous experience with sidecar wheel spindle breakages dictated this innovation. With sidecar attached, the complete outfit weighed only 298 lb and had a wheelbase of 53½ inches, which gave exceptionally good handling characteristics. Christened the J. C. Scott Special, it is hardly surprising that John Catchpole took the Sidecar Award in the Sanderstead Club's Loughborough Cup Trial on its very first outing.

In July 1953 a Scott Sociable came back into the news again, but only because *Motor Cycling* had the opportunity to road test one of the very few survivors, a 1924 model. The Sociable formed part of a large collection of motorcycles owned by John Ellis (which included a Scott three cylinder model too!) and was in fully restored condition. The 40 mile run showed that passenger comfort was of a surprisingly high standard and that even a six feet driver had more than sufficient headroom with the hood raised. The unorthodox appearance of the little car, with one wheel 'missing' like a sidecar outfit, provoked the customary looks of sheer astonishment from other road users, and provided much additional entertainment for the passengers. One item appreciated during the rainy conditions under which the test was conducted was the 9 inch by 2 inch slot cut in the driver's windscreen. The slot compensated for the lack of a windscreen wiper and permitted the driver to maintain clear, if somewhat limited vision, in the pouring rain.

By now, the Scott was no longer listed as a current production model, especially since the long-awaited price had still to be quoted officially. But in July 1954 the silence was broken, when the Aerco Jig and Tool Company released the first details of their new prototype designs. At last some changes in frame design had been made and the old rigid frame was finally discontinued.

Birmingham Scott prototype number 2, 1954

Birmingham Scott prototype number 3, 1954

In its place was a new duplex tube frame, fitted with swinging arm rear suspension. Armstrong rear suspension units were used to control the rear wheel movement. At the front end, Scott telescopic forks had been substituted for the original Dowty units. Although somewhat similar in appearance, the Scott forks contained internal springs in place of the pneumatic system that formed the principle of the Dowty design. The engine remained virtually unchanged, although the crankcase and cylinder head were now diecast, an innovation which it was claimed gave improved cooling due to the improved water passages. Apart from the use of a restyled petrol tank, the remainder of the machine specification was unchanged.

Bernal Osborne, *Motor Cycling's* Midlands man, had the opportunity of a brief run on the 498 cc version; it had been decided to re-introduce the 500 cc engine as an alternative to the 596 cc, the only engine available in the past. Although a 596 cc model had been completed, it was having the petrol tank modified at that time. No performance data was available, or for that matter prices, other than a statement that the 596 cc model was capable of over 80 mph. It was explained that the preview of the prototypes did not infer that manufacture was imminent. The prototypes had been seen on test around Birmingham by the more observant motorcyclists and it seemed advisable to make some statement at this time. After all, how can one disguise a Scott! It was especially pleasing to note that one of the old Scott employees who had joined Matt Holder in Birmingham was none other than Harry Langman, continuing in his capacity as Development Engineer.

It was not until June 1956, however, that the Scott motorcycle was announced to be back in production once more. Minor changes had been made in the intervening period, the most noticeable being a new twin front brake unit of 7 inch diameter. The old balance box compensator had been dispensed with and in its place a simple device on the handlebar lever ensured an even pull on both drums. Only a 596 cc model was listed, priced at £298 inclusive of Purchase Tax. There was still the option of a rigid frame model, however, based on the new frame design. This cost £275, inclusive of Tax. Surprisingly, the rigid frame model proved to be the heavier at 406 lb. The spring frame model weighed 11 lb less.

During September 1957, the Scott programme for 1958 was announced. The old Lucas MC45 pancake dynamo was to be replaced by a new crankshaft-mounted alternator of larger diameter, but mounted in approximately the same position. The production models were now using the new Miller nacelle-type headlamp unit, which contained provision for mounting the speedometer head in the shell. A very minor price increase raised the price of the swinging arm model to £299 8s, including tax. No price was quoted for the rigid frame model, although it was later apparent that the original price of £275 still applied.

It was during May 1958 that even more interesting news came from St Mary's Row. Whilst production of the 596 cc models had been continuing, attention had been given to the design of an entirely new engine, similar in

Birmingham Scott prototype number 5, 1955

A new Birmingham Scott photographed at the old St. Mary's Row factory during the early '60's

outline to the traditional Scott layout but having many internal modifications. Of 498 cc capacity, the new engine had bore and stroke measurements of 66.5 x 71 mm and employed flat top pistons. A three port system was employed, utilising loop scavenging for the first time. An interesting feature was the use of side transfer ports like Alfred Scott's 1904 patent! Extensive redesigning of the crankcase and cylinder block had proved necessary, in order to provide the new transfer passage layout. It was also found possible to increase the compression ratio of the engine to 8 : 1 by using a more efficient combustion chamber. The most noticeable external difference that made the new engine instantly recognisable was the finning around the mouth of each crankcase, into which the cast iron cylinder barrels were deeply spigoted. Each bore carried a slipper-type piston, fitted with three pegged compression rings.

In view of the increased compression ratio, the bottom end of the engine was stiffened up. Larger diameter crankpins were fitted and tougher connecting rods. Whilst the old, familiar central flywheel had been retained, together with the customary overhung cranks, the diameter of the former had been reduced from 9 inches to 7 inches, in order to improve acceleration. Lubrication was by means of the usual duplex Pilgrim pump, driven from the right hand crankcase door. The distributor also took its drive from this point.

Twin Amal Monobloc carburettors looked after the mixture, on the ends of long induction pipes, cranked at the end nearest the inlet ports so that the carburettors were kept horizontal. Some experiments had been conducted with twin Amal GP carburettors, but the Monoblocs gave the best, all-round results. The cycle parts were virtually unchanged, although it seemed unlikely that a rigid frame version would be marketed as an alternative, now that the accent was on machines sprung at both ends.

It was not possible to give the new model a rigorous test because it had covered only 250 miles and was not fully run in. It was claimed that the new model, to be known as the Swift, would achieve 91 mph under favourable conditions, which compared it favourably with the pre-war Clubman's Special. Missing was the familiar Scott 'yowl' however. The large diameter exhaust pipe and silencer needed to give the extractor effect for loop scavenging gave the new engine a much deeper exhaust note that was pleasant and not over-loud. No prices were quoted and there was no indication when the Swift would go into production.

An event of significance that also occurred during the month of May 1958 was the formation of the Scott Owners' Club now having over 500 members. The date chosen was particularly apt, for it was exactly fifty years to the month that Alfred Scott had ventured into the manufacture of motorcycles in Bradford, bearing his name. Fittingly, Harold Scott, nephew of the inventor, was elected President of the Club.

Although the Scott Motor Cycle Company did not exhibit at the 1958 Show, production for the 1959 season was to be limited to a continuation of the standard spring frame Flying Squirrel only. The Swift was destined never to go into production and of the six models made, the first is now on permanent display in the Birmingham Science Museum.

Later in the year a somewhat unusual application of the Scott engine came to attention. The BRD Company Limited of Aldridge, Staffordshire, announced plans to market a range of inboard and outboard motor boat engines, under the trade name Bermuda, based on existing Scott designs. A Scott twin cylinder engine was modified to serve as an outboard engine by fitting the crankcase with outrigger main bearings so that a full crankshaft could be fitted in place of the arrangement hitherto employed. There was also provision for fitting a starter ring to the central flywheel so that an electric starter could be included in the specification, if required. The inboard engine was none other than the Scott in-line three, mounted in a vertical position. It will be recalled that a petroil version of this engine had been built after the war and used for development work, with the prospects of a car engine in mind. Presumably, both types of engine were to be purchased, suitably modified, from the Aerco Jig and Tool Company; the BRD Company (Blade Research Development) was a subsidiary of GKN, one of the industrial giants.

Three versions of the twin cylinder outboard engine were listed, the 2/40 fitted with an electric starter and generator, at £260, the 2/40 with hand starter only at £255, and the 3/60 at £375, which also had an electric starter and generator, but gave a higher power output. Two three-cylinder inboard engines were listed, a 40 hp version at £275 and a 60 hp version at £385. Although the engines were displayed in London at the 1959 Boat Show, the whole project failed to materialise and little further was heard of these unusual adaptations of Scott engines. It is alleged the in-line three proved especially troublesome because it had not been designed to work in the vertical plane that was now essential.

It was not until November 1961 that the Scott motorcycle made a welcome reappearance at the London Motor Cycle Show, held at Earls Court. Although still in limited production, the spring frame model was shown in unmodified form, with the standard Flying Squirrel engine. The price was £291 5s, a price that had remained stable for the past few years. It was claimed that a unit-construction version was planned, which would supplement the model on display. It should be noted that at this time the Scott Motor Cycle Company had two official depots, one in Leeds run by Geoff Milnes (who had been joined by Harry Langman) and the other at Sutton, Surrey, run by Ted Murphy. A number of machines were constructed at both premises.

Late in 1963, news filtered through about a very special Scott that was being built by Matt Holder for his personal use. Basically, it comprised one of the spring frame models fitted with a Swift engine, which had a twin ignition system giving the option of either a magneto or a distributor and coil — for comparative tests only. The most distinctive features included a five gallon fuel tank and the use of a pair of Norton Roadholder forks to improve handling. Matt intended to use the machine on holiday, as a pre-production prototype.

Almost a year later a new 344 cc twin cylinder Scott racer was unveiled. The project originated when it was considered that the introduction of a racing machine would pave the way for a new line of roadsters to carry on the Scott tradition, benefiting from the rigorous testing the new engine would undergo in competitive events. It may seem strange that a 350 cc twin had been designed in this instance, although the reason was logical enough. At that particular time this appeared to be the best capacity class in which to offer challenge.

Outwardly, the machine appeared somewhat conventional in appearance. Indeed, according to one contemporary report, when it was first started up at the St Mary's Road premises, an onlooker assumed it to be of Japanese origin! The engine was air cooled, with forward inclined cylinders and an outside chain drive to the five-speed Albion gearbox. A duplex tube frame fitted with Earls-type forks and an 8 inch diameter twin leading shoe front brake looked after the general handling. Brian Wooley had been responsible for the engine erection and development; Brian Bulmer had designed and assembled the cycle parts.

Internally, the engine used a built-up crankshaft assembly in place of the familiar overhung crank design that had been characteristic of Scott design for so long. But even the new crankshaft showed some allegiance to the practice of the past. The two halves of the crankshaft were drawn into female tapers in the central flywheel by means of a drawbolt through the hollow drive-side mainshaft. Although the central flywheel had been reduced to quite small dimensions in order to improve acceleration, its presence indicated possibilities for a central power take-off at a later date, if required. Because of conventional crankshaft arrangement, provision had to be made to carry outboard main bearings. These were housed in substantial crankcase doors. All bearings were of the ball journal or caged roller type, having their own integral compression and oil seals.

Reprofiled Excelsior Talisman Twin connecting rods were employed initially, until specially-made replacements became available. The Heplex alloy pistons carried a Dykes ring in the top groove, one of two rings positioned very close to the slightly domed crown that had no deflector. There were deep cutaways in the piston skirts to avoid masking the transfer passages. The pistons were the work of Bill Reid, Matt Holder's Design Engineer. The cylinder block was in light alloy, with cast-in Chromidium liners. The cylinder heads were of the squish type. Twin Amal carburettors of the GP type, fitted with 'matchbox' float chambers, looked after the mixture. The five-speed Albion gearbox was of the type normally specified for use with 500 cc models.

The ignition system was based on a modified Ariel Arrow contact breaker assembly, used in conjunction with a coil. It was, however, expected that this set-up would not perform too well at very high rpm and it was

Three Birmingham Scotts at one of the annual Scott Owners' Club Evesham Rallies. The machine in the foreground is owned by Andrew Marfell

anticipated that a change to transistorised ignition would prove essential as development work progressed. The exhaust system, always critical on a two-stroke, comprised short twin pipes, each terminating in a long, tapering expansion chamber.

At this stage of preparation, the machine weighed 242 lb and it was anticipated that a maximum speed in the region of 125 mph was not beyond reality. But like many others before them, the design team were to be faced with innumerable problems, even though the machine did show occasional glimpses of its potential. Things got off to a good start when the new Scott took the class record at the Barbon Hill Climb and then acquired 5th place in the Temple 100. Things even looked good in the Manx Grand Prix, when rider Barry Scully was in 10th place during the Junior race. Alas, the moment of glory was soon over. The battery failed quite unexpectedly and Barry was relegated to the role of spectator. Somehow the new Scott racer never quite made the grade, although it was not for want of dedicated effort or even sheer enthusiasm.

At this time another vintage Scott was very much in the news, a specially-prepared 1926 three-speed Super Squirrel that had been tuned and developed by Clive Waye. With the engine capacity 'stretched' to 625 cc, this vintage racer proved indecently fast and with Chris Williams aboard, shattered the lap records at most of the circuits where vintage events were held. Of the open frame type, the Scott looked so diminutive compared with the rest of the field that its sheer performance took everyone by surprise; surely an old Scott never went like this before! There was more than one occasion when this racer of yesteryear contested the open class, competing on even terms with all the Manx Nortons and Matchless G50's that were no sluggards. On one such epic occasion, this elderly rigid frame model worked through the field into 12th place, much to the chagrin of those who had invested heavily in their modern racer, only to see a disappearing rear view of Chris Williams and the Scott. Racegoers really enjoyed these David and Goliath tussles!

The Clive Waye Scott continued its run of successes, but now another Scott crept into the picture. The machine first came to notice at an event held at the Darley Moor racing circuit on September 1st 1969, when it was electronically timed at 102.3 mph. The rider was George Silk Junior and although his machine was basically of vintage origin, it had been modified in many respects, as may be imagined. The capacity was 620 cc. The rider (and tuner) was not particularly well known at that time, although his father, George Senior, was then Treasurer of the Scott Owners' Club from 1964—67 and a respected member of the Scott community. A great friendship had sprung up between George Silk Senior and Tom Ward, the Scott specialist in Derby, despite the fact that they lived many miles apart. Tom had come to the rescue when George's machine had broken down during one of the early post-war A-CU National Rallies. Although then in his sixties, Tom had worked all through the night to get the Scott back on the road, a typical gesture from the man who had joined Alfred Scott well before the 1914—18 war. It was probably this more than anything else that led to George Silk Junior joining Tom Ward to serve his apprenticeship soon after he had left school. As a reward for his scholastic prowess, his father had given him an old Scott and it was this that sowed the seeds of an intense interest in the two-stroke engine. No one who had an interest in Scotts could possibly serve a better apprenticeship and he learned much during his spell at Wilfred Street, Derby.

When his apprenticeship had been completed, George Junior moved on to a firm that specialised in SAAB cars. Strangely enough, although this move did not work out in the way he had intended, it had unforeseen compensations. When the firm switched over to precision engineering, it became apparent that much of George's love of the Scott had rubbed off on his boss, Alan Cockerill. He permitted George to make use of the company's engineering facilities to develop some of the ideas he held about improving shortcomings in the basic Scott engine designs — shortcomings that had become

Chris Williams on the Clive Waye Scott at Crystal Palace

increasingly more apparent as speeds rose and there was more stress on engine components. The many retirements in both the TT and Manx Grand Prix could frequently be attributed to failure of the crank assembly and it was to the crank design that he first gave attention. Although there was precious little scope for redesign, because the strengthened cranks had to fit the original crankcase casting, he got around the problem by increasing the width of the webs, by making fractional increases in the areas that were most heavily stressed and by having the cranks cold rolled.

   Whilst modifying the cranks, he seized the opportunity to redesign the old crankcase cups so that they would accept an RLS 11 roller bearing that was easy to obtain. He also devised a means of dispensing with the spring-loaded metal to metal compression seals, so that modern counterparts could be substituted.

Attention to other points was also given. Caged roller bearings were specified for the big ends and he even experimented with the shape of the piston deflector, although in the end he had to admit that Alfred Scott had it correct from the start. George has great faith in the retention of piston deflectors in a two-stroke engine, a faith that seems to be upheld by the unquestionably high standard of performance he is able to extract from an engine thus equipped, whilst still retaining good fuel consumption. Other Silk engine modifications included the reduction of crankcase volume by introducing stuffing blocks under the pistons, the use of ported pistons to improve gas flow to the transfer ports, a greatly improved oil pump based on the 1926 Best and Lloyd pump, to replace the Pilgrim pump that has for so long caused Scott owners exasperation, and other detail improvements. All were thoroughly tried and tested, leading to the very high level of performance witnessed at Darley Moor when the much modified engine was fitted into the frame and cycle parts of a vintage racer.

One thing led to another and it was not long before Silk Engineering came into being. George decided it was opportune to start marketing his own special parts, whilst at the same time specialising in the overhaul and repair of Scotts. At that particular time, Tom Ward was in his eighties and was beginning to think about retiring, or at least easing off just a little! And so George occupied premises at the rear of Tom's house in the familiar surroundings of Wilfred Street, leaving Tom to concentrate on his beloved two-speeders.

Aided by Maurice Patey of Derby, another knowledgeable two-stroke enthusiast and a rider of no mean ability, George started to translate into practice a theory he had held for some time. He knew that the greatest handicap of the late pre-war and subsequent Flying Squirrel models was their overall weight, which in the case of the current swinging arm models was now over 400 lbs. He also knew that if he could build a lighter weight version of the same machine that would be roughly equivalent in weight to an early two-speeder, he would be on to a winner. And so plans were laid for the construction of a racer embodying many of his ideas with the objective of securing an entry in the 1970 Manx Grand Prix. Unfortunately the time taken to develop the machine and cure an overheating problem precluded realisation of the objective, but only temporarily. The machine looked right, handled well and had good performance. Above all, it was exceptionally light in weight, scaling only 225 lbs with a 500 cc engine fitted. An entry was made in the 1971 Manx Grand Prix, but hopes were dashed very early on when the Velocette gearbox objected to working correctly on its back. The cause, a lubrication problem, was soon identified and rectified.

Meanwhile, pressure had been exerted by the owner of a badly bent 1949 Flying Squirrel to use whatever parts were salvageable in the construction of a road going version of the Manx Grand Prix racer. Because the original frame was damaged beyond repair, there was every incentive to use the cycle parts that had been specified for the construction of the racer and in due course KVR 235 arose from the wreckage to become the very first Silk Special. As may be imagined, the Silk Special was the centre of attraction wherever it appeared and it was not long before the press caught on. George Silk's objectives were simple. It had always been his intention to market a machine which has its heritage firmly in the roots of the history of motorcycles, using advances in technology bequeathed by spin-off from the aerospace industry. He knew that if advantage was taken of the flow of technical information that was now so freely available, it would be possible to construct a very light machine fitted with a large capacity engine working quite lazily. The outcome was the Silk Special, a true lightweight that would cruise at 70 mph with an engine speed of only 3,200 rpm. The bonus was the extreme smoothness of the engine and the unquestionable standard of reliability.

As far as the general public was concerned, the Silk Special made its debut at the 1971 Sports Machine Show, organised in London by the magazine *Motor Cycle Mechanics*. It was the sensation of the Show, for it was such a splendid piece of engineering that even the hardened Scott 'purist' could not fail to be impressed.

The frame was made by Spondon Engineering of Derby, and is alleged to have been based on a lightweight design originally destined for a Yamaha twin. The forks were also made by Spondon and were similar in appearance to the Ceriani design that was then very much in fashion, although the stanchions were somewhat thicker. A Spondon twin leading shoe front brake was built into the front wheel and a Spondon disc brake into the rear wheel, the latter having the somewhat unusual feature of cable operation. Good brakes were considered to be essential requirements, not only on account of the high speeds anticipated but also because of the noticeable lack of braking effect from a two-stroke engine on the overrun. A somewhat modified 596 cc Flying Squirrel engine was fitted, which had been increased in capacity to 636 cc, giving a power output that could be varied to suit customer requirements. Lubrication was achieved by means of a throttle controlled oil pump of variable setting, which could be regarded as a somewhat updated version of the old Best and Lloyd pump. It had the advantages of the old Scott swash plate pump, but without the disadvantage of complicated construction. Most of the Silk engine modifications were incorporated in the engine, apart from the use of caged big end bearings. These were fitted to the more highly stressed engines only. An LE Velocette radiator formed the key part of the earlier cooling system, but now a chrome plated radiator built on Scott lines is available, with modified connections to the cylinder block and head. Transmission was via a Velocette gearbox fitted with Venom ratios, which was positioned on its back, the whole primary drive being enclosed within a fibreglass case. Both crankcase doors remained detachable, the nearside door carrying a 12 volt alternator and the offside door a car-type contact breaker assembly with the oil pump mounted outboard. Oil was carried separately. A single Amal Concentric carburettor looked after the mixture and the whole

The first Silk Special, based on a 1949 Flying Squirrel

appearance of the machine was greatly enhanced by the slim, graceful black-painted petrol tank mounted above it.

The characteristic Siamese exhaust system, carried on the offside of the machine, was retained, although the point at which the two pipes joined was positioned much further back in the interests of better gas flow. The pipe terminated in a long, slim cylindrical silencer of the absorption type. The most surprising fact was that the fully equipped machine weighed only 266 lbs, despite the use of a swinging arm rear suspension system that will add weight to any machine. Although conventional in general appearance, the swinging arm fork was arranged to have an eccentric pivot, so that movement of the position could be used to effect secondary chain adjustment without disturbing wheel alignment.

The extreme lightness in weight of this fully equipped 636 cc machine gave sparkling performance, with impeccable handling to match. A maximum speed of over 100 mph was available, the exact figure depending on the specification of the engine fitted. Even then, fuel consumption in the region of 70 mpg could be achieved without difficulty, during normal give and take riding. Unlike modern large capacity two-strokes, high performance and a very high rate of fuel consumption were by no means complimentary.

In due course it was necessary to move to larger premises as orders built up. The next move was to Darley Abbey, at the Boars Head Mill address in Derby, still used by Silk Engineering today. An entry was once again made in the Manx Grand Prix, with Stuart Hicken in the now familiar role of rider. Despite the loss of both second and third gears during the early part of the race, 1972 marked the turning point on the path of success. The Silk Special circulated steadily and completed the course at an average speed of over 60 mph. Hicken was awarded a Replica for his performance, which undoubtedly would have been much better had not such a severe handicap occurred. It seems ironic that the new Scott-engined racer should have competed as a two-speeder like so many of its predecessors, even if the ratios were particularly ill-matched on this occasion. Subsequent investigation showed the trouble had been caused by a quite different fault from that which had eliminated the machine in the previous year's event. To the spectators, the unmistakable sound of a Scott engine on full song brought nothing but joy. It must have taken many back to the heyday of the Scott Motor Cycle Company in the twenties.

Following a demolition order as a result of redevelopment in the St Mary's Row area, production of the Scott motorcycle was transferred to Carver Street, Hockley, not very far away. Now it continues at Bromford Lane, Stechford, although comparatively few machines are available during the course of each year since Matt Holder's Aerco Jig and Tool Company is much involved in other engineering work. The general situation is rather like that of the Brough Superior before the war. If you require a new Scott, it may first be necessary to seek audience with Matt and then bide your time until the model that has been allocated to you becomes available. If, on the

A later version of the Silk Special using a Scott-type radiator and drum rear brake

other hand, you require something less traditional which also embodies some of the benefits of modern engineering practice and is very light in weight, then the Silk Special is the alternative. Either category of machine is hand built to special order and can be expected to command a correspondingly high price, for any piece of precision-built machinery made on a small quantity or one-off production basis is never a cheap proposition. But there is joy in owning something that has prestige and is quite different from anything else available on the market. Provided it is kept within reasonable bounds, it is doubtful whether cost then plays such an important role in such pride of ownership.

Thanks to both Matt Holder and George Silk, the tradition of the water-cooled twin cylinder two-stroke lives on, with the prospect of exciting new models appearing whenever the opportunity exists to develop the breed still further. A 500 cc water-cooled twin racer is the latest development from Bromford Lane, although it is yet early days and the new model has yet to show its capabilities. Meanwhile, George Silk continues with the constant development of the Silk Special, the engine of which now incorporates reed valves to improve the induction cycle. He has proved very convincingly that there is a demand for a well-engineered lighter model that represents logical progress of the original Scott theme. His next move is to use an entirely new engine unit designed by David Midgelow, furthering his development programme still more. Even so, there is ample room for both the traditional and the modern approach to the same theme. Long may both continue.

Riding Impressions

THIS BOOK portrays the romance of the Scott motorcycle through its history — its successes and failures. These apart, there is something more to this marque of motorcycle, something which can only be really felt by sitting on the saddle and riding one. Here, Jeff Clew, at the publisher's request, describes what it is like to ride his machine — a 1946/47 prototype

IT HAS been said that one of two things is sure to happen to the purchaser of a Scott. Either he will like it immensely, to the extent that any other machines he may own will soon take second place and eventually disappear, or he will loathe it and quickly dispose of it, never to own a Scott again. To an extent, this would seem to be true, for I have yet to encounter anyone who has taken the middle road and tolerated a Scott as a second string.

To my mind, ownership of a Scott is a test of enthusiasm, especially if the machine has to be reclaimed from the inevitable heap of rusty and badly worn parts. No machine suffers more from neglect; a most peculiar love/hate relationship can develop between owner and machine until the latter is eventually restored to good running order. Even then this relationship can still exist. A Scott is a temperamental machine and somehow manages to retain an aura of perverseness that will at times vex even the most hardened enthusiast. But this is part of the make-up of any true thoroughbred, which is highly strung and has to be treated with special care. It is more than outweighed by the sheer joy of owning something a cut above average.

Sadly, there are many who may never own a Scott, for these machines are becoming increasingly rare, with an ever appreciating value. Whilst it is virtually impossible to describe the sheer pleasure of owning and riding a Scott (it is a sensation that has to be experienced — there is no other way) I nonetheless hope I can convey just a little of what can be expected.

Firstly, there is something very special in owning a machine that is not only a thoroughbred but is also highly unorthodox too, when compared with existing designs. The Scott has been compared with that most exciting of French cars, the Bugatti, on occasions, and I believe this to be a very fitting comparison. Although my own machine is an early post-war model and is not one of the more desirable open frame two-speeders, I find it impossible to make a hurried journey on any occasion. A pause for petrol or a stop for refreshment invariably provokes comment from someone close by. Some have owned a Scott during their youth and are keen to reminisce, whilst others have always had a sneaking regard for the Scott yet never the money to purchase one of their own. A few are taken aback by the unconventional appearance of the machine and ask innumerable questions. It is frequently necessary to explain the nearside crankcase door strap is not an exposed connecting rod!

On the road, it is the turbine-like smoothness of the engine that really appeals and the zest for smart acceleration when the throttle is tweaked. The exhaust note is a mellow, gentle purr, which changes in a most satisfactory manner whenever the gearchange lever is depressed. Acceleration at high speed produces the familiar Scott yowl, albeit muted by the silencer. Hills are climbed virtually unnoticed, apart from an overtone in the form of a buzzing noise that originates from the vicinity of the induction when the engine is pulling hard. Whilst waiting at traffic lights and road junctions, the engine hunts in a very distinctive manner, accompanied by a peculiar jangling of the clutch plates when the clutch is withdrawn. This will identify the presence of a Scott, even if it cannot be seen.

The gearchange itself is both clean and positive. Those who have an earlier model fitted with hand change can indulge in the art of snicking, whereby the change is without using the clutch. This necessitates a deft movement of the left hand across the tank to the hand change lever, whilst the right hand manipulates the throttle to give the correct rpm. Some experience is necessary to perfect this technique, which was used by riders in the Isle of Man and other speed venues. If the machine is of the even earlier two-speed type, gear changing is even more fun! Movement of the rocking pedal from Low to High (or Soft to Loud, as some prefer!) produces the most delightful change in exhaust note without a break in continuity.

As may be expected, the triangulated frame structure gives a high standard of road holding, backed up by the Webb girder forks. By modern standards, the brakes leave something to be desired; the twin front brake of the early post-war models is something of a misnomer and needs the so-called 'Black Pudden' brake linings for reasonable efficiency. The rear brake suffers because the brake plate was not stiffened internally by ribbing. The first heavy application of the brake distorts the brake plate permanently and thereafter much efficiency is lost.

Starting is easy. The Lucas Magdyno is driven at engine speed and in consequence a remarkably good spark occurs at low rpm. A special reduction gear is used to slow down the dynamo, which would otherwise overtax the avc unit. A 'T' battery is fitted so that the internal plates are isolated from the hammering of the rigid frame and the life of this vital component is prolonged. As may be expected, the performance of the lighting equipment is not really up to scratch, although speeds of up to 50 mph in darkness can be achieved with safety. The beam from the separate bulb and reflector headlamp provides a poor defence against today's quartz iodide lamps, dazzle from oncoming vehicles being the main problem.

The Achilles heel is unquestionably the Pilgrim oil pump, mounted on the offside crankcase door. The setting is critical and seems to be prone to unsuspected variation, so that one has to check the 'two spits and a drip' from each feed at regular intervals. A curious feature of the Scott is the manner in which the engine temporarily over oils after hitting a pothole. This would seem to be caused by rapid agitation of the oil content in the well within the base of each crank chamber. The well serves an important function, since it contains a reserve of oil that will enable the machine to be driven for about eight miles at moderate speeds if the oil supply fails or runs dry. The choice of oil is important and multi-grade or self-mixing oils should be avoided except in dire emergency. I have found an SAE 40 oil to be the answer, especially Silkolene Super Two which was formulated with the Scott owner in mind.

Maintenance presents no real problems, but if it is necessary to remove either the primary drive chain or the magneto chain, a major operation becomes necessary! The main difficulty arises when attempting to refit the chains by feeding them around their respective sprockets each side of the central flywheel. Even with guide strips mounted permanently inside the crankcase casting this is no easy task. The knowledgeable owner keeps his old chains and links them to the chains requiring attention, so that one pulls the other into position.

I cannot quote a maximum speed since I have yet to find the opportunity to exceed 70 mph, but I suspect the post-war Flying Squirrel to be capable of just over 80 mph. Average give and take riding results in a petrol consumption figure of about 60 mpg; the rate of oil consumption is quite high, partly because some is used to lubricate the chains by means of a controlled drip feed. Sparking plugs of all makes and varieties have been tried; in my own case NGK B5ES plugs have defied even the worst build-up of oil in the crank chambers.

These observations are based on my experiences with my rebuilt 1946 596 cc model, in which the original pistons have been retained and the cylinder bores untouched. Some over-zealous cutaways made in the base of the cylinder spigots by a previous owner may account for some variation from what is to be expected, although I have yet to discover the significance of these modifications or how, if at all, they have affected engine performance. In all other respects the machine is quite standard and seems to perform like similar models of that period. The fact remains that I have joined the ranks of those proud to be the owner of a Scott that originated from the traditional home in Shipley, even if my machine is a shade too modern for my liking and a little overweight. It resides in harmony with the other thoroughbred machines that share the same garage and is definitely **not** for sale.

The Scott Owners' Club

DURING the vintage years, the Scott motorcycle enjoyed a sufficiently large following to encourage the formation of a number of Scott owners' clubs, each of which covered a certain territorial area. After all had become extinct, a group of Scott enthusiasts formed the Scott Owners' Club in July 1958. The basic objective was to preserve and run whatever examples of the marque still existed and to bring together Scott enthusiasts for their mutual benefit. As a result, the Club now has 650 members and active sections in each of the following locations: East Midlands, North West, Northern, London area, South West, Scottish and West Midlands. Overseas members can be found in Canada, Denmark, Holland, South Africa and the USA. The highlight of the year is the Scott Owners' Club National Rally, held on the first Sunday in September at Stanford Hall, near Rugby.

In 1960, the Club was co-supporter of an exhibition stand at the Earls Court Motor Cycle Show with the late Matt Holder, who had saved the company from oblivion in 1950. The first President was the late Harold Scott, nephew of the inventor. Many members have been life-long Scott owners; some have consistently ridden Scotts since the vintage era, thus preserving the enthusiasm for the marque and its unique qualities. 'Scotting' provides many enthusiasts with an enduring hobby, rather than just a passing phase.

The Club operates a spares scheme, with parts usually available which include 'consumables' not available elsewhere such as gaskets and bearings. Unfortunately very few 'cycle' parts are currently in stock. It also has a number of members who trade on their own account, offering highly specialised services such as radiator manufacture, pattern parts, overhauls, restorations and repairs. Within the SOC, technical advice is given, and there is also a library, photographic archives, a machine register and motorcycle dating service, and there is club regalia.

A quality magazine, *Yowl*, is published bi-monthly and sent to all members. As well as keeping them up to date with events, the magazine has useful technical articles and photographs, and offers readers the opportunity to exchange views. In addition to the magazine there is a website to be found at www.scottownersclub.org, with all the usual on-line features. Membership expands yearly and the Registrar, John Underhill, keeps an accurate register with nearly 2,500 machines recorded, while many more are known to be in existence.

The Club caters for the owners of all Shipley-built Scotts (1908/09 to 1950), Birmingham-built Aerco Jig & Tool Company machines (1954-1972), and the Derby-built Silk motorcycle (although Silk spares are not generally available from the Club.) Ownership of a Scott motorcycle is not a qualifying requirement if an enthusiast wishes to join the SOC. The annual subscription is currently £16, and the Membership Secretary is Richard Tann, 88 Deacons Hill Road, Elstree, Hertfordshire WD6 3JQ, tel: 020 8427 0945. Press Officer is Roger Moss, 33 Kings Lane, South Croxton, Leicestershire LE7 3RE, tel: 01664 840215.

Dating guide to Scott motorcycles

IT IS difficult to provide any infallible guide to the dating of Scott motorcycles from serial numbers of engines and frames because only the former were stamped concurrently in order of machine production and irrespective of model. It should also be remembered that in common with many other motorcycle manufacturers, the factory brought out new production models towards the close of the year, even though they were regarded as being of the following season. In other words, the 1927 Flying Squirrels were available late in 1926, following their introduction at that year's TT races. In consequence, any Scott given a catalogue date could have been available at the end of the previous year, if it was one of the earlier production models.

Engine numbers only were used up until 1924, when alphabetical prefixes were introduced late that year. The only exception occurred with some earlier engines that had SC stamped with the engine number. This signified the cylinder block had been bored out for sidecar work.

Some further confusion occurred during 1927 as numbers approached the 10,000 mark. At this stage the suffix M was added for a short while. Later that year, the numbers were restarted from a low number, when the suffix A replaced the M. This arrangement continued until mid-1931, but was never applied to Replica models.

The numerical sequence went as follows:

Year	Number	Year	Number	Year	Number
1909	508 - 544	1922	5463 - 6229	1934	3906 - 4059
1910	545 - 731	1923	6230 - 6781	1935	4060 - 4165
1911	736 - 1040	1924	6782 - 7525	1936	4166 - 4303
1912	1041 - 1585	1925	7526 - 8417	1937	4304 - 4479
1913	1586 - 2172	1926	8418 - 9655	1938	4480 - 4697
1914	2173 - 3832	1927	9656 - 10096	1939	4698 - 4800
1915	2894 - 3398		then to 601	1940	4801 - 4817
1916	3399 - 3419	1928	602 - 1196	1946	4818 - 4915
1917	3420 - 3500	1929	1197 - 2595	1947	4916 - 5174
1918	Nil	1930	2596 - 3460	1948	5175 - 5426
1919	3501 - 3963	1931	3461 - 3682	1949	5175 - 5426
1920	3964 - 4886	1932	3683 - 3841	1950	5175 - 5426
1921	4887 - 5462	1933	3842 - 3905		

The Birmingham Scotts followed on from 5427 onwards, using Shipley-made engines. The Aerco Jig and Tool engines commenced production during 1956 but unfortunately were not numbered in sequence.

The alphabetical prefixes introduced during late 1924 provide additional information, as follows:

S	Squirrel	70 x 63.5 mm	486 cc
T	Standard Touring	73 x 63.5 mm	532 cc
Y	Super Squirrel and Standard 596 cc models	74.6 x 68.25 mm	
Z	Super Squirrel	68.25 x 68.25 mm	498 cc
FZ	Used on first Flying Squirrel models	68.25 x 68.25 mm	498 cc
FY	Used on first Flying Squirrel models	74.6 x 68.25 mm	596 cc
TY	1926 - 1928 Touring models	74.6 x 68.25 mm	596 cc
FZ - M		68.25 x 68.25 mm	498 cc
FY - M		74.6 x 68.25 mm	596 cc
FZ - A		68.25 x 68.25 mm	498 cc
FY - A		74.6 x 68.25 mm	596 cc
RZ	TT Replica models only, 1929	66.6 x 71.4 mm	498 cc
RY	TT Replica models only, 1929	73.02 x 71.4 mm	596 cc
PZ	Power Plus Replicas, 1930 - 32	66.6 x 71.4 mm	498 cc
PY	Power Plus Replicas, 1930 - 32	73.02 x 71.4 mm	596 cc
FZ or FY	(no suffix) Late short stroke engines		
LFZ	Longstroke Flyers, non-detachable heads	66.6 x 71.4 mm	498 cc
LFY	Longstroke Flyers, non-detachable heads	73.02 x 71.4 mm	596 cc
DPZ	Detachable head Replica engines	66.6 x 71.4 mm	498 cc
DPY	Detachable head Replica engines	73.02 x 71.4 mm	596 cc
GPZ	Grand Prix engines (very rare)	66.6 x 71.4 mm	498 cc
GPY	Grand Prix engines (very rare)	73.02 x 71.4 mm	596 cc
X	Single cylinder engine		300 cc
CS	Suffix for Clubman's Special models		
3S	Three cylinder engines		
SP, M.EXP, TT etc	Works engines		
DMS	Engines built by Aerco Jig and Tool Company, 1956 onwards		
MDH	Engines built by Aerco Jig and Tool Company, 1956 onwards		

No record of frame numbers appears to exist. However, it is questionable whether this would be of value since so many machines have been rebuilt or modified that it is doubtful in many cases whether the original frame number is still in use.

John Underhill of 82 Deansway, Ash Green, Exhall, Coventry is the best source for dating enquiries, in his capacity as Registrar of the Scott Owners' Club and Scott marque specialist of the Vintage Motor Cycle Club.

British Patent applications for the Scott Motorcycle

Inventor	Patent and/or application number	Date	Title	Brief synopsis
A.A. Scott	1626	21 January 1897	Bicycle brakes	Rod operated caliper brakes
A.A. Scott	9908	30 April 1898	Cycle and brakes etc	Application abandoned
A.A. Scott	12,369	14 June 1899	Rotary engines, pumps or motors	Application abandoned
A.A. Scott	20,270	10 October 1899	Cycle etc brakes	Brakes actuated by a flexible cord passing through a tube
A.F. Scott	14,969	21 August 1900	Engines etc	Lubrication of bearings
A.A. Scott	16,233	22 July 1902	Internal combustion engines	Application abandoned
A.F. Scott	5798	8 March 1902	Gas etc engines	Design of gas and explosive vapour engines
A.A. Scott	23,484	29 October 1903	Printing and cloth etc	Stencilling apparatus for printing designs
A.A. Scott and H.S. Smith	244	5 January 1904	Stamping and textile goods	Hand stamp for marking textile fabrics
A.A. Scott	3367	11 February 1904	Internal combustion engines	Design of the original twin cylinder engine
A.A. Scott	25,068	18 November 1904	Motorcycles	Application abandoned
A.F. Scott	29,214	31 December 1904	Internal combustion engines	Charge of air used to sweep out exhaust before inlet charge
A.A. Scott	1033	16 January 1908	Internal combustion engines	Application abandoned
A.A. Scott	16,564	6 August 1908	Motorcycles	Design of original open frame
A.A. Scott	18,876	8 September 1908	Motor vehicle speed gears	Design of original two-speed gear
A.A. Scott	27,667	19 December 1908	Starting internal combustion engines	Pawl and ratchet starter, using a cord

Inventor	Patent and/or application number	Date	Title	Brief synopsis
A.A. Scott	7845	1 April 1909	Motorcycle forks	Design of original 'telescopic' forks
A.A. Scott	25,517	5 November 1909	Acetylene generator and number plate	Application abandoned
A.A. Scott	25,755	5 November 1910	Lubricating internal combustion engines	Design of original metal to metal crankcase seals
A.A. Scott	5721	7 March 1911	Fly cutters etc	Application abandoned
A.A. Scott	5895	9 March 1911	Internal combustion engines	Chain driven rotary inlet valve
A.A. Scott	19,249	28 August 1911	Grinding machines	Design for grinder and polisher
A.A. Scott	22,695	14 October 1911	Number plate and mudguard	Detachable front number plate and mudguard extension
A.A. Scott	23,709	26 October 1911	Milling machines, fly cutters etc	Tool holders for machine tools
A.A. Scott	24,366	2 November 1911	Reversing gear	Application abandoned
A.F. Scott	28,883	22 December 1911	Internal combustion engines etc	Application abandoned
A.A. Scott	1387	17 January 1912	Motorcycle sidecars	Design of straight tube chassis
A.A. Scott	27,418	28 November 1912	Bowden wire controlling devices	Means of anchoring cables in handlebar levers
A.C. Scott	2418	30 January 1913	Internal combustion engines	Application abandoned
A.A. Scott	26,924	22 November 1913	Windscreens	Application abandoned
A.A. Scott	9877	21 April 1914	Motorcycles	Open frame design where single seat tube is replaced by duplex arrangement

Applicant	Number	Date	Subject	Description
A.A. Scott	9878	21 April 1914	*Cycle saddles*	Design of cantilever sprung saddle
A.A. Scott	9879	21 April 1914	*Internal combustion engines*	Application abandoned
A.A. Scott	9880	21 April 1914	*Valves*	Oscillating inlet valve connected to connecting rod
A.A. Scott, Sir A.T. Dawson and G.T. Buckingham	19,175	28 August 1914	*Sidecars*	Design of sidecar-mounted machine gun with gun at apex of triangulated structure
A.A. Scott	19,176	28 August 1914	*Sidecars*	Luggage carrier for sidecar
A.A. Scott, Sir A.T. Dawson and G.T. Buckingham	20,874	12 October 1914	*Sidecars*	Design of sidecar mounted machine gun where gun is operated by person other than rider
A.A. Scott, Sir A.T. Dawson and G.T. Buckingham	21,195	19 October 1914	*Sidecars*	Ammunition-carrying sidecar
A.A. Scott	24,045	14 December 1914	*Motor vehicles*	Design of gun car/Sociable
A.A. Scott	1019	21 January 1915	*Motor starters*	Application abandoned
A.A. Scott	1290	26 January 1915	*Valves*	Cylindrical valve on crank chamber
A.A. Scott	1291	26 January 1915	*Clutches*	Design of friction band clutch
A.A. Scott	1292	26 January 1915	*Internal combustion engines*	Quickly detachable cylinder barrel
A.A. Scott	1293	26 January 1915	*Variable speed gears*	Design of countershaft gearbox
A.A. Scott	1294	26 January 1915	*Motor vehicles*	Mounting of engine in line with wheels
A.A. Scott	4146	16 March 1915	*Flexible material*	Chain mail seating using interlaced leather or fabric rings
A.A. Scott	11,707	13 August 1915	*Motor vehicles*	Steering arrangement for Sociable type vehicle

Inventor	Patent and/or application number	Date	Title	Brief synopsis
L.S. Parker	118,441	27 August 1917	*Motorcycles*	Sprung saddle support controlled by tension springs
L.S. Parker	118,453	28 August 1917	*Motorcycles etc*	Construction of frame with flexible saddle support
A.A. Scott	102,037	29 August 1916	*Lifting jacks etc*	Bar-type jack design
A.A. Scott	16,693	26 November 1915	*Motorcycles*	Steering arrangement for Sociable
A.A. Scott	103,098	26 November 1915	*Vehicles*	Construction of frame with interchangeable struts
A.A. Scott	109,276	28 July 1916	*Vehicle wheels*	Detachable disc wheels
A.A. Scott	114,368	13 June 1917	*Sparking plugs*	Twin electrode plugs
A.A. Scott	126,591	29 January 1919	*Engine turning gear Internal combustion engines etc*	Design of segment starter
A.A. Scott	129,926	7 January 1919	*Struts or ties*	Design of aircraft struts
A.A. Scott	153,671	12 August 1919	*Bodies of automobiles*	Arm rest design
H.O. Wood and Scott Motor Cycle Co	150,944	14 February 1919	*Steering wheel forks for vehicles*	Swivel bearing fork ends
H.O. Wood and Scott Motor Cycle Co	151,552	23 March 1919	*Frames etc for motorcycles*	Duplex tube frame
A.A. Scott	162,464	25 February 1920	*Internal combustion engines*	Detachable cover for rotary inlet valve
A.A. Scott	162,968	2 July 1920	*Internal combustion engines*	Shape of piston deflector
A.A. Scott	163,344	24 April 1919	*Springs etc*	Tension springs for saddle

A.A. Scott	174,457	30 October 1920	*Brakes for road vehicles*	Design of band brakes
A.A. Scott	174,724	30 October 1920	*Nut locks*	Method of securing quickly detachable wheels
S.G. Barnett	373,635	26 February 1931	*Improvements in or relating to rear wheel spring suspension device for road vehicles or the like*	Master plunger-type rear suspension system

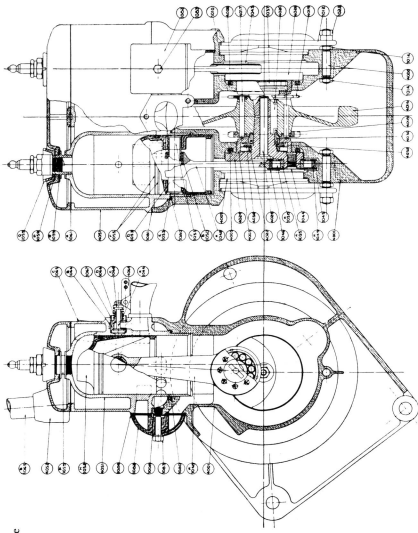

The 596 cc Flying Squirrel engine

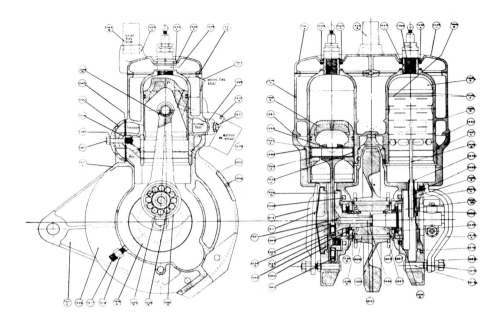

The 1926 and later Super Squirrel engine

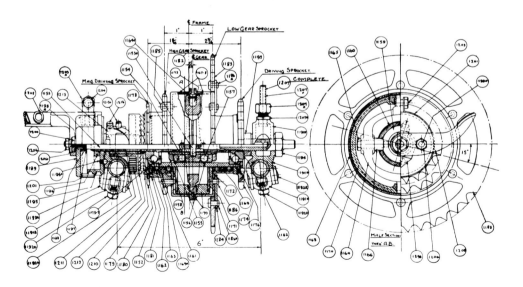

The two-speed gear

231

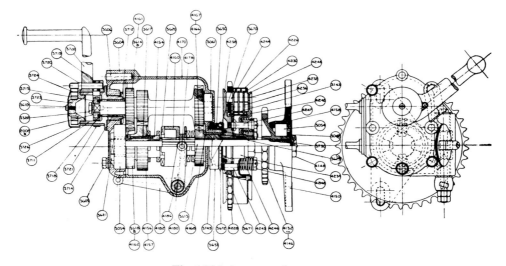

The 1930 three-speed gear

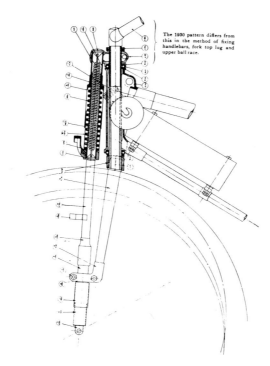

The 1930 pattern differs from this in the method of fixing handlebars, fork top lug and upper ball race.

Super Squirrel type front forks

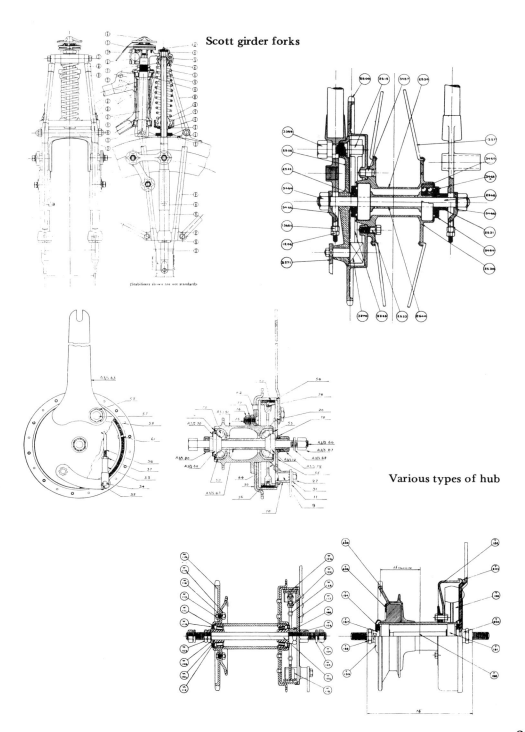

Scott girder forks

(Stabilizers shown are not standard).

Various types of hub

233

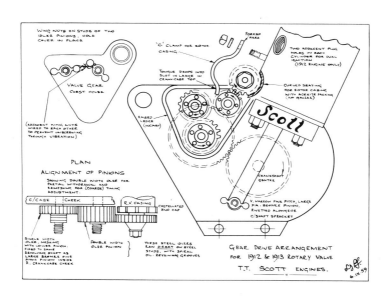

WING NUTS ON STUDS OF TWO IDLER PINIONS, HOLD COVER IN PLACE.

'C' CLAMP FOR ROTOR CASING.

FORCED FEED

TWO ADJACENT PLUG HOLES IN EACH CYLINDER FOR DUAL IGNITION (1912 ENGINE ONLY)

TONGUE DROPS INTO SLOT IN LEDGE IN CRANK-CASE TOP.

CURVED SEATING FOR ROTOR CASING WITH ACEITE PACKING (NO GAUZE)

VALVE GEAR CHEST COVER

(ADJACENT WING NUTS WIRED TO EACH OTHER TO PREVENT UN-SCREWING THROUGH VIBRATION.)

RAISED LEDGE (IN-CAST)

Scott

CRANKSHAFT CENTRE

V. NARROW FINE PITCH, LARGE DIA. BRONZE PINION, RIVETTED ALONGSIDE C/SHAFT SPROCKET.

PLAN
ALIGNMENT OF PINIONS

SHOWING DOUBLE WIDTH IDLER FOR PARTIAL WITHDRAWAL AND REMESHING FOR (COARSE) TIMING ADJUSTMENT.

C/CASE   CHEEK

R.V. CASING

CASTELLATED END CAP

SINGLE WIDTH IDLER, MESHING WITH LOWER PINION, FIXED TO SAME REVOLVING SHAFT AS LARGE BRONZE FINE PITCH PINION INSIDE R. CRANKCASE CHEEK

DOUBLE WIDTH IDLER PINION

THESE STEEL IDLERS RAN DIRECT ON STEEL STUDS, WITH SPIRAL OIL-RETAINING GROOVES

GEAR DRIVE ARRANGEMENT
FOR 1912 & 1913 ROTARY VALVE
T.T. SCOTT ENGINES.

6.IX.'59

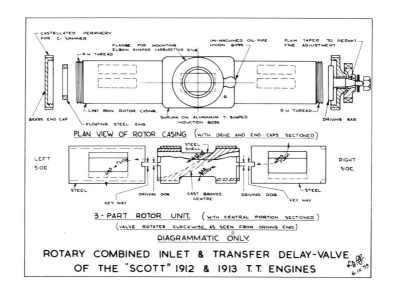

CASTELLATED PERIPHERY FOR C- SPANNER

FLANGE FOR MOUNTING ELBOW SHAPED CARBURETTOR STUB

UN-MACHINED OIL-PIPE UNION BOSS

PLAIN TAPER TO PERMIT FINE ADJUSTMENT

R.H. THREAD

BRASS END CAP

CAST IRON ROTOR CASING.

FLOATING STEEL RING

SHRUNK ON ALUMINIUM T- SHAPED INDUCTION BOSS.

R.H. THREAD

DRIVING BAR.

PLAN VIEW OF ROTOR CASING (WITH DRIVE AND END-CAPS SECTIONED.)

LEFT SIDE

STEEL SHELL

RIGHT SIDE

FLOW

STEEL

KEY WAY

DRIVING DOG

CAST BRONZE CENTRE

DRIVING DOG

STEEL

KEY WAY

3 - PART ROTOR UNIT. (WITH CENTRAL PORTION SECTIONED.)
(VALVE ROTATES CLOCKWISE, AS SEEN FROM DRIVING END.)

DIAGRAMMATIC ONLY.

ROTARY COMBINED INLET & TRANSFER DELAY-VALVE
OF THE "SCOTT" 1912 & 1913 T.T. ENGINES

6.IX.'59

INDEX

235

Photographic acknowledgement

Grateful thanks is given to all those who gave permission to reproduce their photographs and illustrations. They are as follows

Les Brazier   page 193
Controller of Her Majesty's Stationery Office (Patent specifications)   page 22
Derek Cox   page 91
K. G. Draper   page 178 (left)
H. W. Henderson   pages 89 and 90
Dennis Howard   page 42, 45 and 149
Andrew Marfell   pages 55 (middle), 67, 106, 111, 150, 156 (top), 165, 189, 197, 205 (lower), 209 and 216
Noel Mavrogordato   pages 130 and 199
Mrs N. Milnes   pages 37, 87 (top two), 88, 94, and 101
Motor Cycle   pages 133, 144, 147 (top), 159, 162 and 170
Newark Air Museum   page 180
Old Motor   page 63
Mrs E. Oliver   pages 61 and 82
RAC Tank Museum   pages 71 (lower), 72 and 78
Sir Hilary Scott   page 33, 68
Silk Engineering   page 214
R. G. Sinclair   page 185 (top)
C. H. Wood   pages 65 (lower), 85, 87 (lower), 93, 116, 119, 123, 125, 156 (lower), 161, 172, 175, 179, 181 (top), 185 (lower), 186 and 188

Editor   Tim Parker
Jacket Design   Edward Piper
Typesetting and Printing   J. H. Haynes and Company Limited, Sparkford, Yeovil, Somerset